A BOY MINER

Brett J Jenkins is a Western Australian writer. He has worked as an underground miner, before gaining his PhD in English and Comparative Literature, and is now a proud stay-at-home dad—the greatest challenge of them of all.

A BOY MINER

TALES FROM THE AUSTRALIAN UNDERGROUND

Brett J Jenkins

Copyright © Brett J Jenkins 2019
The rights of Brett J Jenkins to be identified as the moral rights owner of the Text of this Work have been asserted by him in accordance with the Copyright Amendment
(Moral Rights) Act 2000 (Cth).
This book is copyright.
Apart from any fair dealing for the purposes of private study, research, criticism or review, as permitted under the Copyright Act, no part may be reproduced by any process without written permission.
Book Design and Typography by Logorythm

A CIP catalogue record for this book is available from the
National Library of Australia.
ISBN: 978-0-9954086-5-4

LOGORYTHM INDEPENDENT
This book is published by the author using Logorythm Independent publishing services.
Direct enquiries to logo@logorythm.com.au

I must obey the rules
I must be tame and cool
No staring at the clouds
I must stay on the ground
In clusters of the mice
The smoke is in our eyes
Like babies on display
Like angels in a cage
I must be pure and true
I must contain my views
There must be something else
There must be something good
Far away
Far away from here
Far away, far away from here
Far away, far away from here
Far away, I'm far away from here
And I'll be here for good
For good

Boot Camp, Soundgarden (1996)

Preface

The boy—who will be known as the boy, and then Neph, again the boy, and finally Shaggy—is me, the author of this true story; and he is not me. I do recognise him: we share the same proper name, similar facial features, height, eye colour, the same voice, the same limp. But then I don't recognise him, the boy who spent four-and-a-half years, from July 1996 to December 2001, working in underground mines deep beneath the red dirt of the Western Australian goldfields, and then the flat red wastelands of the Northern Territory's Tanami desert. I remember him, imagine him, but I don't know him. I don't know this past self almost as much as I don't know my future self. I can imagine who I will be but I do not know why he will be that way, different from what I am now, and different to what I would imagine. Even now my present self astounds me by his ignorance, strengths, desires, anxieties, and pretence. The boy from the underground is not me, a stranger, but he was part of my becoming. And, would if I could, I would thank him, shake his unfamiliar hand, for what he did.

PART 1
Bronzewing

A Mistake
July 1996

It was his step-uncle Peter who got him the job, working in an underground mine as a diamond drill offsider, so called not because the rig drilled for diamonds, although it could, but because of the diamond-impregnated drill bits needed to cut through the rock. Rock so hard they needed the hardest rock to cut it. The diamond drillers drilled for core samples, from the underground, holes up to 500 metres deep, mapping the course of the ore body.

Fly-in, fly-out. FIFO. Two weeks on, one week off. Peter sold it to the boy with the promise of big money, silly money, more than he could have imagined. It wasn't too hard, convincing the boy, given that he still lived at home with his parents, had a second-rate education, didn't have a car, qualifications, or any clear, long-term aspirations in his jobless town. Which is to say he really had no choice.

'Come to the mines. Come up north,' his uncle said, where north mostly meant east and away from the coastline. 'Come to the outback. Come to the deserts' was what he meant. This was the familiar call for many generations of willing, strong-backed young men not only from Western Australia, the great mining state, but for young men from Australia's eastern states, New Zealand, and beyond. There were few who didn't know someone working FIFO. Gold, iron ore, nickel, alumina, copper. Plenty of ways to make a buck if you're willing to dig.

His uncle's heart was in the right place, taking a gamble

on a scrawny eighteen-year old boy, even if the gesture wasn't appreciated at first. This is because the boy, ignorant of his ordinariness, had it in his head that he was destined for something more important, more fulfilling and intellectually stimulating than the brute labour of mining, even if at the same time he was utterly lost as to what that destiny was, or the steps he would need to take to make it happen. Lost on the boy also that work was hard to come by, let alone paid this well, or that it was an opportunity that would be prized by many. Even so, Peter was rubbing the boy against his urban nap, the harsh lonely outback never the place for making his mark.

It was July 1996 when the boy made his start, two months after his eighteenth birthday. He was at a small satellite terminal near Perth's domestic airport, mid afternoon, readying to board a Dash 8, a small propeller plane, with seating for about forty, for the hour-and-a-half direct flight to Bronzewing, a gold mine about eighty kilometres north-west of Leinster, itself almost one-thousand kilometres east north-east of Perth.

He handed his bag over to the boarding staff, was handed a ticket, before taking a seat amongst twenty or so men to wait. Men of all kinds: mostly tall, some short, cologned and malodourous with cigarettes, wide and thinnish, bearded and clean-shaven, casual, plain-clothed in blue jeans, thongs and flannos (hi-vis not yet part of the FIFO zeitgeist). The boy was the youngest there by some seven or eight years; young enough to be someone's son to at least half of them.

He was rightly ignored, the men looking past him as you

A Boy Miner

would an outsider, not wanting to make accidental eye-contact, worried the boy might latch on, imprint on them the role of father. As if in war, he was the brand-new recruit about to be thrown into the jungle and sure to get his fool head blown off within days. A liability. Best to keep a distance, leave him anonymous until he proved himself. Freeze him out, cold shoulder; mumble an insincere greeting, but only if they have to. He did the same, not meeting their eye, not avoiding it either, as if to say that he had a right to be there. Cagey, trying to look tough amongst the even-cagier men, trying his best to fit in and hide. Some were talkative, chatting to each other, but most were taciturn after the exchange of a few g'days. Not a word his way. Peter was meeting him at Bronzewing. A stranger amongst strangers till then.

There wasn't the excited push and shove he expected when they got the boarding call, more a languid reluctance. No rush, no prize for being first. On take-off, most fell asleep immediately, folding the meal tray down in front of them and resting on it, their heads nestled in their folded arms, quickly filling the plane with chainsaw snoring and noxious suffocating farts. The men were taking the opportunity to steal some sleep given that this crew—what would become his crew—were heading straight for a twelve-hour night shift, which, for most of them, meant they would be up for more than twenty-four hours before they slept again. The boy was wide awake, not because it was his first time in a plane (he, like almost every Western Australian, had been to Bali at least once) but because he was still unsure of the procedure, whether they would eat or drink, be entertained. Those still awake were served refreshments (a bottle of water and pre-packed cheese and crackers) by the hostess, a beautiful, tall, nameless woman.

The rest she snuck by as if stepping amongst coiled rattlesnakes.

They flew turbulently across the tree-green Darling Range, before the ground beneath flattened and became divided into the yellow, brown, and green rectangular patchworked shapes of the Wheatbelt farmland—other generations, ancestors, passing down an old quilt, to be tilled and sown and reaped. Finally, it became the red dirt and sparse trees of the Goldfields, leaving his understanding of civilisation well behind.

Much of the journey was spent contemplating exactly what he was in for—the nature of the job and what the underground would be like. Peter hadn't told him much, and what he did tell hadn't make much sense, abstract and incomprehensible. His own understanding seemed to be comprised of flitting images from TV or photos, but nothing vivid or solid in outline. He also didn't know much about the camp. He thought of his school camps, all of which were located in or near towns, and had been down south where it was green and cool. That the camp resembled any of this became increasingly unlikely with each minute as they made their way deeper into the red outback. All he could be sure of was that he was working for Eltin mining contractors—his new company and employer—and that Bronzewing was his mine.

The drone of the plane and his thoughts were finally broken by the pilot announcing that they were about to begin their descent. The boy looked out the window to see the abyss of an open pit mine disrupting the red flatness, and then in the distance the angular shapes of what was the mining camp. He was wrong about the camp, and was equally disheartened and amazed that a place such as this, here, could even exist, smack-bang in the middle of nowhere, looking more like a makeshift colonisation on Mars, with clustered transportable buildings organised in futuristic hexagonal patterns, red dirt all around except for a contrary patch of green grass in the centre of each hexagon, and a larger patch of green for an inexplicable half-size footy oval, goalposts at each end. It seemed that the frontier of the alien Red Planet, the setting of so much science fiction and, now, his new home, was merely a short flight from Perth. He wasn't there to mine gold: he was there to take soil samples and test the breathability of the atmosphere, terraforming it to establish the colony, before sending word to bring others—women—to populate it. A Brave New World indeed.

A short red-dirt airstrip magically opened up out of the scrub, and they made a bumpy landing onto corrugations. The sky was mostly clear but there had been heavy rains a few days earlier, and everywhere the ground had broken out into slippery wet mud. And when he stepped off the plane it was into a red-dirt puddle, the white of his shoes splashed red, forever stained, sealing his fate like a blood oath.

A crowd of men were waiting for them: twenty-odd stern, impatient faces—the returning crew, their cross-shift and doubles. They came together, with some shaking hands, a few words exchanged, but only briefly: those flying home were eager to leave, and those flying in were eager not to be reminded that they weren't. His uncle retrieved him, the boy looking lost, but also thankful that someone familiar to him could be found so far from both their homes. Peter had been a tall man, but was now slightly stooped—too much mining and football. And for the most part he had a big and wide smile. As he did now, happy, but also somewhat amazed that the boy had actually turned up and was here in the outback. Both out of context: Peter his uncle, now also his boss.

'You finally made it, eh? What do you think? How you been?' Peter said, shaking the boy's hand, engulfing it in his giant mitt, still smiling, seeing a kind of jet-lag stupor about the kid.

'I'm good, glad I'm here,' the boy replied, trying unconvincingly to look enthusiastic.

'Grab your bag and jump on the bus, get yourself inducted at the camp, and I will see you at dinner, about six-fifteen, okay?' And with that Peter jumped in his own ute, and was off. This was because he was not part of the Bronzewing crew: Peter was the drill supervisor, no longer drilling himself, based in Perth, and only came to site occasionally. And, anyway, he didn't want to show any partiality to his nephew, even if the boy would have been happy for Peter to hold his hand for a bit, get him settled in.

So the boy joined the rest of the incoming crew who loaded themselves into the two empty waiting minivans and drove to the camp—a five-minute drive from the airstrip, on red-dirt roads, more corrugations vibrating through spines and the loose panels of the bus. It was quieter on the bus, conversations about their break exhausted on the plane, if not already at the terminal; those who spoke spoke in jargon about the work ahead of them, the state of their machines, and where they could find them. And when they arrived at the camp, the regular crew drifted off in silence to their dongas—their rooms—to ready themselves for their first night shift which started at 6pm, enough time to drop off their bags, grab some dinner and pack what was to be their midnight lunch.

A Boy Miner

The boy and two other newcomers remained, looking stranded like hitchhikers on the side of the road. The two men lit cigarettes, separately, aloof, dragging deep and comfortably, before drifting over to the boy, as if only just noticing him. He shook their hands, which felt cold on his, the thick calloused skin of theirs like a leather glove.

The first, Mick, was a foot taller than the boy, well-built, shaved head, in his mid-thirties, wore a dark Ned Kelly beard, black Harley Davidson t-shirt, black stovepipe jeans, black desert boots. A bikie in his spare time, maybe. Mostly silent, guarded. His occasional laugh was also silent, evidenced only in the slight bouncing of his shoulders. He was starting on the trucks.

The other introduced himself as 'Horse'—a not-so-tall, but very wide Irishman, also in his mid-thirties. A rugby union player in his hey-day, front rower, immovable, ears showing signs of cauliflowering. He walked and spoke as if he had always been there, at Bronzewing, seemingly halfway through a conversation with the crew as he exited the plane, greeting everyone at the mine like old friends.

'Another day in paradise, eh boys?' Horse making conversation in a strained voice, like an old bear growling in a whisper, made almost uninterpretable for his thick Gaelic accent, the boy wondering if he meant 'Hoarse' when he gave his name. Making conversation but looking for no answer, and not getting one: Mick laughed his silent laugh, and the boy smiled, disarmed. Horse was also starting on the drills.

The ensuing quiet was only broken by a spritely and jarring voice coming from nowhere: 'You must be the new blokes for Eltin.' The voice of the camp manager. 'Let's get you inducted, and then find you your dongas. Induction for the mine is tomorrow. But that's not my business.'

They signed some papers, had photos taken for their name tags, and were shown to their dongas, down concrete pathways past the transportables, the manager pointing out the mess, the wet mess, the phone boxes, toilet and shower blocks, and the laundries. It was a longer walk than the boy had anticipated, the camp looking far smaller from the air. And it was quieter than he expected: the camp was home for hundreds of people and yet at this time of day it seemed a ghost town, hushed, except for the scraps of talk between the manager and Horse who were leading, then Mick, and finally the boy, trailing in Mick's shadow.

'All the newcomers are sent to the Bronx,' said the manager, still enthusiastic and increasingly irksome.

Horse replied, similarly upbeat and without a hint of pretence: 'The Bronx, you say. Well, it is all the same to me. Any bed anywhere will do.'

'I'm flying out tomorrow,' the manager blurted out, telling everyone, as if a secret he'd been itching to tell, which also explained his cheerful demeanour.

'Very good,' said Horse, still upbeat and polite. The boy and Mick were quiet, keeping less than courteous opinions to themselves.

The manager pointed Mick and Horse in opposite directions down forking pathways, confident they knew what they were doing, but walked the boy to his. Maybe a word from Peter to keep him close. The manager speaking now for them both, the boy having no questions, and nothing to say other than he was going to be a diamond driller. Underground, he added, which impressed far less than he had hoped.

When the manager opened the door of the donga, the boy's first impressions were that it was small and lonely and old and cheap and quiet and dry and hot. He entered reluctantly. It was barely wider than his outstretched arms, no bigger than a walk-in-robe, and could easily be taken in with a single glance. In the left corner there was a single bed with a metal frame and tired springs across, a thin mattress and thin pillow, which complemented the thin carpet, thin walls, and his thin body. Next to the bed was a bar fridge, and then a small school desk and plastic school chair. In another corner, at the foot of his bed, stood a wardrobe. To the right, above the desk, was a small curtained window, attempting to open up the little room.

'You might want to get that air-con started,' the manager suggested, frowning slightly, as if also seeing the inside of a donga for the first time. It was a mild day but the sun was biting as it glared hard from the mostly cloud-free sky, and the humidity was boiling off the wetness that persisted in the clay soil. And the little room, and the boy, needed to breathe.

He flicked the switch on the dated, imitation-woodgrain air conditioner, which buzzed and sputtered to life, before settling to a steady vibrating hum, like white noise recorded at an airport. Over time he would find the racket soothing, essential even; more importantly it was cold when he needed it to be in the heat of summer, which could reach the mid forties, and never looked like quitting, despite being kept running twenty-four-seven, even when he was on break, and even when the nights dropped to zero.

With that the manager took his leave and the boy was left to himself to unpack his meagre possessions: socks, jocks, his clock-radio-alarm, borrowed last-minute from a mate back home. He then looked in the fridge, like he would the minibar of a hotel, and in the wardrobe where he found haphazard and unnecessary coat hangers. Someone else had been here. But now it was his. Certainly the footprints of caked mud that he had tracked in were his.

All of a sudden it became very real. The long journey—from his uncle's initial proposition from a few months ago to standing in his donga—had come to an end. He had been picked up and plonked in the middle of the desert, the horizons of the outback to nowhere, with this little room, a life-raft anchored in a desert ocean, his home for the next two weeks, and, if he stayed, where he would spend two thirds of his life. It could have been claustrophobic, the donga, but he guessed it was big enough for the spare furniture and the very little time he would spend there other than sleeping and the few hours to himself between the end and beginning of the shift. Convincing himself of this, coaxing himself from his growing apprehension, wondering whether it was the first signs of a panic attack.

He was overwhelmed by the solitude, but he had also been intimidated by Mick and Horse. They were men. He was a boy. It was obvious that he was too weak. They weren't here because of an uncle. They were here because they were men suited to this job. It began to play on his mind: trapped at the camp and tomorrow he would begin a job that for all he knew would crush him under its weight.

And with an hour before dinner, he had plenty of time to let these thoughts spiral, especially after catching an unfortunate glimpse of his wiry self in the mirror attached to the door of the wardrobe. He pushed up his sleeve and flexed an underwhelming bicep, straining so hard he almost shit himself. His was not the body of a miner; his was not the body of a man. He wanted to laugh, hysterical, like a madman, at the absurdity of it all. But, instead, he steeled himself, and, with nothing else to do, got down on his belly and did two sets of twenty push-ups. There was just enough room in the donga to do the push-ups: laying flat on the hard threadbare carpet, his head just missing scrubbing against the door. It too was absurd—doing push-ups. Like training for an Olympic marathon by walking to the letterbox to fish out the junk mail. Like taking a warm, essential-oiled bubble bath as preparation for a frigid swim across the English Channel. And yet, regardless of the negligible physical benefits, it was a psychological victory over, and despite, himself. A show of mental strength in the face of his self-imposed adversity. Time to get strong. And impossible to think of life's larger problems under the strain of the exercise.

With his heart still beating from the push-ups, he lay on the bed, which squeaked as if frightened, and sagged as if defeated, and stared at the ceiling and waited, alone, marooned in the outback.

But it would be untrue to say that he was a stranger to these parts—that this was not his place, if ever a white person can make such a claim. Indeed, if it were possible, the red dirt of the outback would have run in the boy's veins. Having been born in Kalgoorlie, it could have only been red dirt—Western Australian Goldfields dirt. Born in Kalgoorlie, but from the age of six he had lived in the beachside town of Mandurah, an hour's drive south of Perth where the WA coast met the Indian Ocean. Living on the coast where blue saltwater has run in the veins of centuries of sailors leaving and returning to the port of Fremantle; and in the veins of fishermen from the north; and, in a distant past, whalers to the south-west, near Albany, the lolling deck of a ship more familiar than any firmness of land. Men of the sea begetting men of the sea. Implying that a particular kind of blood runs in their veins, determining their line of work as a mariner and the life that it brings.

But for the boy at least, the metaphor of blood was a falsehood. Goldfields-born but hardly Goldfields raised. Blood can flow in your veins. Seawater can too, theoretically. Red dirt can't. Not red dirt, not even red mud, clotting and viscous as it is. But the red dust will cling to you, get into your hair, the folds and threads of your clothing, and in the creases of your skin, which was almost as good as the essence of your DNA, taking it with you wherever you go.

It had clung to his father who was also born in Kalgoorlie and who had also left the Goldfields as a boy, his parents leaving for Manjimup in the southwest of Western Australia. And like the boy, the red dirt had called him back, lured like many by the chance of making a meagre fortune. This happened about the time he got married to the boy's mother—a Fremantle girl, nineteen-and-a-half-years old, who bravely followed his father, twenty-five-and-a-half, into the desert, whisking his new bride off on an adventure to Menzies, which lay a bit over one hundred kilometres north of Kal. Menzies: founded in 1895 following a rich gold find, a thriving population of 10000 people in 1900, thirteen hotels and two breweries. Eighty years on, in the seventies, as the boy's parents found it, there was not much left other than a road with

A Boy Miner

trees running in a line in the middle of it—more trees than any that stood lonely on the red plains that flanked it—a general store, a few houses, Town Hall, hotel and service station. Blink and miss it. Together they ran the Menzies general store, living in a small house next to it, with a thunderbox for a toilet, emptied weekly on a Friday. They ran the store but also acted as telephone exchange, postmaster, community welfare officer, BP fuel agent, agent for two banks, and took the weather reports for the Bureau. The boy was born in Kalgoorlie Hospital, 1978, but lived his first three years in Menzies where he was supposedly adored by the mainly aboriginal population, especially his baby-blonde hair. One of the aboriginal women, a single mum, lived in a corrugated home attached to the store. A mob of kids—too many for the space. Hard living for all, white and black, but too young for the child to remember. For the new family, they worked their way up and eventually moved to the big city—Kalgoorlie. His brother was born there too, three years younger than the boy, completing their family in the bush.

He also had relatives from both sides that had been born and raised in these parts. Landlubbers, living and working remotely in outback WA mining towns: Cue, Roebourne, Norseman, and Southern Cross. Peter, his step-uncle, was not a blood relative, married to his mother's sister, but he shared a red-dirt lineage all the same.

From his cradle, the dust of red dirt towns had settled on the boy, as if his baby-cot were sat on the side of an unsealed, outback road, a steady parade of haul-pack road trains thundering past, stirring up clouds of the fine, rusted powder. And it had stuck, albeit hidden, even after his family had packed up for Mandurah.

For good. But not for good. Not for the boy, anyway. Having long said that he would never mine, never do hard labour in the outback, it was inevitable that his blood would contradict him.

○

From his father he had not only inherited the clinginess of red dirt, but also an excellent metabolism, which meant that he was very good at eating. Where others are gifted in the ways of painting, math, guitar, cryptic crosswords, tennis, flirting with women, the boy's talent was putting food away without adding any weight. This was despite his size: at five-foot eight, he weighed a puny sixty-five kilograms before breakfast. Hardly a muscle on him, and also no fat. His spine stuck out like cats eyes on a bitumen road. So when he eventually raised himself from the sunken embrace of his mattress, made his way up to the mess for dinner and opened the doors to see the polished silver of a long bain-marie and its numerous deep troughs of warm, comforting victuals, a sense of homeliness returned. His fears and worries could be temporarily allayed by the simple act of eating, just him and his food.

He waited in line, his plate like a steering wheel in his hands, cutlery in his pocket, sharp ends poking out, like he had seen others doing. Standing there, amongst the men, his lesser size was once again thrown into relief. Broad men, with big hands and feet, taking up space, their existence undeniable. He looked as if he were merely filling in the cracks between their respective bulks—loose mortar between gnarled shithouse bricks. This was something he would need to change if he were ever to pass as a man, especially a mining man. Growing taller was wishful thinking, as was enlarging his Cabbage-Patch doll hands and feet; but he could set his mind to adding some flesh to his frame and do more push-ups, stake a claim for his own existence. 'I eat, therefore I am.' His only claim to being one of them was his facial hair, having had an enviable moustache from the age of twelve.

It was his turn, soon enough, and set about his fattening, serving himself generously with silverside, a square of lasagne, curry and rice, roasted vegetables, and a good ladleful of béchamel sauce. The conventions of what traditionally constituted a main meal were forgotten as he piled the less than complementary foods onto his plate. He wasn't a prejudiced eater, open to the new and unknown. His was a gluttonous egalitarianism, a culinary multiculturalism, where all the foods of the world were equal in his eyes. He took his time, savouring the moment, heaping his plate high, as if serving for two or three proper-sized men.

At the end of the trays, he put the last serving spoon down, and turned to survey the room. The mess was large enough to seat one hundred, and looked like a cafeteria at a school camp, or maybe a prison, with rows of tables and plastic chairs. He found fifty or so unknown faces, all seated and eating, ensconced in conversation, with well-established friendships. A cacophony of voices and the cutlery scraping of hurried eating. Voracious appetites, none eating like birds; eating how they would eat if unwatched by civil society. If the way to a man's heart was through his stomach, then each man was in love with the cook; not the electrified passion of new romantic love—the food not dressed or made up to impress—but the enduring unadorned love of a satisfactory marriage, each capable of weathering their beloved's deepening wrinkles and frustrating idiosyncrasies.

Having somewhat taken him under his wing, Horse had now abandoned him, already accepted. And he wanted to avoid Mick the bikie. Instead he spotted his uncle Peter and bee-lined to his table, in slow motion, as if hungover, concentrating only on his plate, which was not only piled high, but flooded with the white sauce, surrounding the meal like a food moat.

He hardly cared that his uncle's company consisted only of shift bosses and mine managers, distinguishable by them still wearing their company-logoed shirts and trousers, not a lick of dirt on them. Men in charge. Men who had mined their whole lives and in that time accumulated many harrowing stories of the good ol' mining days that would send shivers down the spines of any eavesdropping Occupational Health and Safety officers.

The polite boy asked if he could sit, and was responded to in the affirmative with a combination of confused and amused nods. Peter offered the spare seat next to him and made a good-natured but pointless introduction to the bosses and managers—men the boy would have very little, if any, contact with in both the immediate and distant future. An absurd scene, like a new convict casually sitting down to dine with the prison guards, before boldly dipping a slice of bread in the warden's pumpkin soup.

Smalltalk out of the way, the boy was ready to eat, eyes only for the plate in front of him, mouth only for the fork in his hand. Finding peace amongst the din, banishing unwanted thoughts and letting the pleasure endorphins do their work. But his inner-sanctum was quickly disturbed, as only a few mouthfuls in a sickly sweet taste unexpectedly hit his tongue—something foreign and offensive, out of place and contrary to his sensibilities. Another bite to be sure, attempting to solve the mystery, until the terrible truth dawned on him: far from what he assumed to be a hearty béchamel sauce was instead dessert custard. Only now did he notice the bile-yellow tinge of the sauce, which had meandered in and around the other various food groups, tainting them all, creating an unholy marriage of sweet and savoury. If food was his fetish, then he had unwittingly stumbled into the sadomasochistic. Worse, the honeymoon between him and the cook it seemed was already over; as if the cook had cheated on him by placing the custard too close to the roasted vegies.

Embarrassment and the assault on his tastebuds caused a cold tingling flush from head to gut, his heart rattling against his insides, a tremble running through his body; yet his countenance remained measured and unchanged. In that same instant of recognition he had decided that it was just palatable enough for him to struggle through and maybe even keep down.

This was a test. A cruel and strange test.

Poker-faced, he ploughed on, stalwart, stoic, like the proud, hard-working miner he envisioned he was going to be, hardly taking a breath between shovelling, anxiously consuming the evidence. Angst comes from the word angina—heartburn—of which he now had both. But he made sure it didn't show. Instead, he was steadfast, unshakeable from his goal, finishing it all, leaving only minimal accusatorial traces of the wrong sauce on his empty plate. Besides, he was not one to waste food, going out of his way to eat the burnt chip, the staling bread-crust, the bruised apple— biting purposefully into the floury-textured darkness.

He had made a huge mistake. At worst, he thought, if his faux pas was noticed by the bosses, he would be forever known as the camp simpleton, with the somewhat uninspired nickname of 'Custard boy', or something like it. At best, the other miners would be jealous, not only of the skinny kid's metabolism and unfathomable hollow legs, but of the béchamel sauce they had overlooked. The latter was less likely, considering the bosses, and seemingly everyone else in the mess, had successfully negotiated the service procedure, bringing to the table a separate bowl for their pudding and custard. Show offs the lot of 'em.

Nothing was said. The bosses finished their meals and announced they were heading to the wet mess. An earnest invitation was extended to him by his uncle, the boy looking as if he needed something to take the edge off. But he declined—the last thing he needed was to have beer thrown into the mix. What he needed was the solemnity of his donga to regroup and recuperate. Or to vomit both food and humiliation and bring the day to a close.

And it should have ended there, the story of his first day, if there was any justice in the world. But the solace of his donga would be delayed by an interlude: he returned to his room to find the door locked, the key missing from his pocket and not in his crib bag. Locked out of home, the only space that was his in this unhomely outback. His stomach lurched again, angst and angina battling for primacy. The only thing that stopped him from swooning in a panic was knowing where the camp office was and that it would be open for another hour, so he fretfully walked to the camp office area, in the dark except for a few fluorescent lights marking the pathway, to get a second key, all the while murmuring hateful castigations to himself, frightening other users of the path. The office was open and manned, and key in hand, he returned to his room. Door unlocked, finding his original key on his fridge, he walked back to return the second key, before again returning to his room.

It had been almost half an hour since coming from the mess, and now, back in his room, he promptly sat down on his bed and gently wept. Finally he could release. It had been too much, too much change, too much of the unknown. The push-ups meant nothing. Overwhelmed and weeping, just as he had when he started each year of primary school; just as he had when he began high school. He was still a child. The sook child, or, more charitably, the sensitive child, the anxious child, had followed him into the desert.

He had made a huge mistake.

But that wasn't entirely true: clearly he *was* and had always been a sook child, a sensitive child, a kid, clearly incapable of looking after himself: combining dessert with his main meal; locking himself out of his room; crying like a motherless child. He could therefore be excused from blame. A pardoning for Custard Boy, the camp simpleton. His uncle, however, was not so lucky. Uncle Pete had made a huge mistake.

Day Two

Tomorrow was another day, even if it was hard to tell given that the sun wasn't up, and at 430am, the July-height of winter, it wouldn't for a few hours still. A good time for burglarising houses, or at least for making a hasty, loot-laden exit. And also apparently a good time to get dressed, pack his crib bag, and get to the mess for 5am to scoff some breakfast, piling more on the heartburn, pack his crib—his lunch—get on the bus by 530am, and arrive at the mine site at 540am to start at 6am.

He was already tired—could have comfortably slept on a red gravel road, using a roadkill-kangaroo's ribcage for a pillow. Tired from the previous night's stress, from flying, from over-thinking what trials the day would bring, what the underground was really like. Above all he was tired from the anxiety of the alarm not waking him. Throughout the night it had played on his mind, drifting from the foreground of his thoughts, then somewhere to the back, before returning to disturb his sleep, redoubled. And there was so much hinging on the alarm. Here, he wouldn't just be late for work, he would also miss breakfast, miss making his lunch, and hold up the whole crew as they waited for him in the minibuses to go to the mine. All eyes would be on him, which he hated.

The alarm worked perfectly, his mate said. If there was a problem, then it was him that caused it, not the alarm. Human error, like forgetting to turn the alarm switch to 'on'; or mistakenly reversing the am/pm setting of the clock or the alarm time, resulting in the set time being out by half a day. If he set the alarm to play the radio when it came on, he could make the mistake of leaving the volume down, or of not having it tuned to one of the few outback AM stations. To avoid this last possibility he would need to set the alarm to BUZZ instead of RADIO. The onomatopoeia of 'buzz', though, was misleading, as in no way did it resemble a steady rhythmic hum, like that of a lazy carefree bee in a flowery spring meadow. The buzz of this alarm sounded more like the violins and cellos played over the shower scene from Alfred Hitchcock's 1960 film Psycho, where Norman Bates (dressed elegantly as his mother) violently and repeatedly

A Boy Miner

stabs a screaming Marion Crane, her blood left to drain down the plughole. BUZZ...BUZZ...BUZZ. It is a chilling sound—befitting of a stabbing sound—and a cruel way to be woken, the tip of the blade finding his ear, the shock causing him to lurch across to swat at the off-button.

For these reasons (and a touch of restless-leg syndrome inherited from his grandmother, and undiagnosed sleep apnoea from a broken nose at thirteen) he would find it hard to sleep soundly, forever anticipating the alarm, at best stringing six hours of disturbed sleep together, with this same uncomfortable start, before the twelve-hour shift, for six days before the shift change. Every time the same: every time too early, and too loud.

However, his first night's sleep, as it turned out, was to be one of the worst, not only because of the alarm, but also because of something out of his control. Just as he lay his head down on his wretched pillow, trying to debrief and compartmentalise the day's trials—the custard, the lost key—his neighbour returned from the wet mess, stumps being called, accompanied by a few mates and a block of beer, ready to continue the party. The boy's donga was one of four in the transportable building, which seemed only slightly bigger than a sea container. He had a neighbour on both sides, although he never once heard or saw the neighbour to his left. It was the neighbour to his right, and his mates, it being their shift change and not having work in the morning. There would have been very little space in the donga for the three of them (which he gathered from their three distinct voices and laughs), and the wafer of wall between them would bend and creak under the pressure as they leaned against it. Judging by the bowing in the wall, they were big men, not to be reckoned with. A quiet word later in the week, maybe, if he had the stomach for it. He could introduce himself before dropping hints of his recent occupation of the room next door. A wink and a nudge and maybe keep it down next time, eh? Maybe he will say this. Maybe, but unlikely.

The red glowing digits of his alarm told him that his neighbour and his guests' revelry ended just after midnight—the last time he remembered before finally drifting into sleep. Four short, fitful hours later, this same alarm, bewigged, gleaming kitchen knife in hand, crept up silently to his sleeping body, drew in a breath, before cruelly drawing the shower curtain.

Bad news, evils, celebrity deaths, come in threes and no more, so they say. Which should have given him some comfort today, his first proper working day, knowing that three evils had befallen him. But he was not superstitious. Anything could still happen, consigned to a roll of the dice.

He would be left in the hands of his driller to perform the job of driller's offsider—the driller's labourer—whether he was physically capable or not. But before that, he would be spending a good part of the day in offices undergoing safety inductions, joined by Mick and Horse, the three of them together again. The inductions consisted mostly of disconcerting instructions on how to use a self-rescuer (a personal breathing apparatus) in case of smoke or gas in the underground, and on how to escape the mine from fires, rockfalls, blocked declines, floods—all so that they each didn't die. They dressed him in *brand new* full overalls, which were sharply creased from having sat in the storeroom for too long, and came sealed fresh in plastic, as if just collected from the dry-cleaners. They were dark green, which did well to both literally and figuratively betray his newness. The green of the new was a stark contrast to the overalls of the seasoned miner, which were stripped of their dye, faded almost to a dull grey, hardened and torn with wear, the long sleeves removed at the shoulder to keep cool. Some miners coming from other mines brought with them their already worn-in overalls, and even if they were the wrong colour or had a different company's name stitched into them, they blended in seamlessly, as if they had always been there. The boy's overalls were several sizes too big—the larger size selected for him under the proviso that they would shrink after a few washes (which they would, but not nearly enough). Or, that he would someday grow into them, maybe a chest, waist, thighs, shoulders. Until then, he looked like a destrawed scarecrow; or a coat rack, truncated at the base, draped in a much larger man's clothes.

Cinching the billowing overalls was a *brand new* belt, which carried his self-rescuer and a cap lamp battery, the cord of which ran up to the cap lamp (attached to his *brand new* hardhat which sat askew on his small head) so that he could see in the dark. Finally, they gave him *brand new* knee-high gumboots, which exaggerated the limp of his left leg, the result of a seemingly innocuous break from the equally innocuous act of running down a sand dune at fifteen years old, his leg bending the wrong way at the knee. It was a botched recovery—three months in hospital, six operations, compartment syndrome, infections, dead tendon. Almost lost the leg altogether. He was left with a messy scar the size of a shark bite, and drop foot which caused him to repeatedly stub his toe, tripping over little nothings.

Outfitting complete, he looked like a newly-minted coin

about to be thrown into a beggar's cup.

Horse's overalls were similarly ill fitted but for very different reasons, with the strong fabric barely containing his bulk. Standing next to him, the boy was a runt-mule—bones and skin, wobbly on its legs, nothing behind the eyes—the two of them looking less like miners and more like a comedy team: Abbot and Costello, John Candy and Steve Martin, Chris Farley and David Spade. They were the premise of a joke, a nursery rhyme: *Fat and Skinny went to war, Fat got shot with an apple core.*

Mick the truck driver's overalls fit perfectly.

Before being dropped off at the drills, he and Horse were taken for their first trip underground by Peter. Mick went with the shift boss, truckies apparently being different to drillers. They were shown the escape ladders and the underground Fresh Air Bases, which were important for when they couldn't easily escape the mine; they were important so that they didn't die. There was also a tagging system where each miner placed a metal tag on one side of a peg board situated at the entrance of the portal, the opening of the underground, when they entered the mine—they placed their name tags on the other side when they exited. This was so the rescue crew knew who they were looking for in an emergency; to ensure those trapped underground weren't left to die. Or if they were too late, whose body they needed to find.

They went in a single cab Landcruiser ute, with a bench seat for three. As he sat next to Horse on that first trip into the tunnel of the underground, entering the dark of the portal, looking like a giant mousehole in a skirting board, barrelling down the decline—

the highway corkscrewing its way underground from the surface, passing the drives—the levels or streets extending perpendicularly from the decline, surrounded by unforgiving immovable rock walls, pitted and scalloped like a reef, he was consoled by how Horse had appeared to have swelled up and consumed any available space in the cab, like a human airbag. The boy also wore his seatbelt which neither Horse nor Peter seemed to bother with; a struggle to find under Horse's massive gluteus maximus, and when he did, the muffled click of the fastener sounded as peculiar as pouring custard on silverside.

Feeling safe as they made their way deeper underground didn't mean he was comfortable due to what he understood to be a design flaw in the layout of the ute's interior. Older early-model cars with front and rear bench seats, like his mate's 1970 Holden HG back home, had a '3-on-the-tree' gearstick extending out from the steering column. It was hard to use for the uninitiated—an anachronism for kids of the 1990s—but was a pragmatic solution to the seating-shifting problem. The gearstick in the underground ute was instead in the middle, protruding from the floor, as it would for an ordinary two-seater vehicle, ostensibly positioned between the middle passenger's legs. It was understatedly impractical, dangerous even, as the middle passenger's right leg would need to dangle near the clutch pedal in the driver's foot well. And it would have been awkward, with the gear-shifts taking place amidst the passenger's groin. Therefore, for the boy to avoid accidentally shifting gears or being intermittently felt up by the driver as they fumbled for a stick, it was necessary for him to squeeze his legs together and wrap them around the left-hand side of the gear stick, as if riding side-saddle, facing the passenger at a forty-five degree angle. His legs would be pressed up against the other passenger's legs—also an unwanted intimacy, but preferable to the casual sexual assault of sitting the other way. To complete the emasculation, there was nothing for him to grip on to, no armrest or 'Oh Jesus-bar,' such that his hands would need to rest in his lap, like a genteel young lady tentatively waiting for her dance card to be filled at a debutante ball. It was an uncomfortable and effeminate way to sit, and implied that the middle passenger had no male genitalia at all. There was no question as to whether Horse or the boy would be in the middle. Indeed, from that first trip to the very last, he would never find someone skinnier or younger or more effeminate than himself, ensuring that the position was forever his. No question or quarrel was ever made. Even as he begrudgingly retrieved his balls from wherever they had gone each time their destination was reached.

The Onram

When the underground tour was complete, they were returned to the surface for a final briefing, and then his uncle dropped him off at the drill site, pushing him out of the nest, to fly or fall on his own. His rig to offside was the smaller Onram 100. It wasn't in the underground; instead it was set up half way down the open pit that lead to the underground portal, in a cuddy, a specially cut cave in the pit wall away from the trucks that ground their way up and down the pit. Outside of the cuddy, the walls of the pit looked almost vertical, fifty or more metres high, opening to an oval of blue sky. They worked during the day, the light being better, and for the time being they had no cross-shift. The normal roster was going straight onto night shift for seven nights, have a shift change, begin seven day shifts, before flying out. Instead, after flying in, they went to work on the following day, with thirteen more shifts after that.

His driller was Lee—a Maori, in his late twenties, shorter than the boy, but with a solid frame. His eyes bulged slightly from his face, as did his jaw and teeth, like some pressure from within his skull was pushing his features outwards. Lee spoke plainly and moved quickly, had high expectations of his offsider, and didn't hide that he was crestfallen when he saw that the boy had been assigned to his rig instead of Horse. He already knew the boy was his offsider but the reality still hit hard seeing Horse in the ute waiting to head underground. Though, as the boy had seen on the plane, not everyone there looked like Horse. There were a few shorter, thinner men there. Frank, one of the drillers, in his early forties, was only about five-foot-two, with big ears and not much of a body to him. They sometimes called him Papa Smurf, Smurf for short. The boy had also been worried about how his gammy leg would go. But Pete had assured him that there were plenty of deformed and messed up blokes at Bronzewing, which wasn't at all true.

Lee also had a quick wit, cutting and sarcastic. And it was Lee who almost immediately pinned the nickname 'Neph' on the boy, having let it slip that Peter was his uncle. 'Neph', which was half-playful, half-contemptible, because of the too-easy way the boy had got the job, which for Lee was the wrong way. Neph had cheated the system, whereas Lee had gotten his job meritoriously, through persistence, pushiness, and stubbornness—the only way he deemed appropriate and necessary for any Kiwi finding work in Australia. What really got to Lee was how Neph acted like he didn't want the job; he wasn't thankful enough for the opportunity given him. Which was true.

Lee already had an offsider—Dave, the fitter for the rigs when they were down, and an offsider for when they were up. Where Lee was younger, somewhat manic and uncompromising, Dave was in his late thirties, had kids, was softly spoken, calm, and unassuming. He walked and talked slower, wanting to get the job done and to do it well, but wasn't going to kill himself doing it. The wisdom of age, lost on strong, juvenile backs. It was Dave who advised Neph to cover over his window in the donga for when he needed to sleep during the day for night shift. He found the boy black plastic sheeting and electrical tape to hold it up, sealing the room permanently from the hateful intrusion of natural light. Dave, a beacon in the darkness.

The driller's job was to control how the drill drilled, including its speed and the weight pushing it, the water pressure, and the movement of the head when pulling rods. His place was almost exclusively behind the levers and dials of the control panel. The offsider was expected to be everywhere else.

The drilling process was simple enough, even if it resembled nothing comparable from back home except maybe the coring of an apple: they drilled into a rock wall—the apple—and pulled out the core—the apple core. The difference being that instead of tossing away the apple core, the rock core was kept, washed, measured and studied.

But an apple analogy defies the mechanical complexity of the process, which is what he needed to learn: a drill bit and a reamer were attached to one end of the outer core barrel, and an end cap attached with a water line to the other. The barrel was fed through the jaws inside the head of the rig, which clamp onto the barrel, with the inner core tube inside. The driller then turns on the water, begins the rotation, and slowly makes the opening cut. Once the barrel cannot go any further, drilling is stopped, and the barrel is pulled out, removed from the head by the offsider, before the inner core barrel is removed and an empty inner tube inserted. The barrel is loaded again, moved down by the head, and the next rod attached by screwing it onto the thread of the next. Drilling would recommence, and the offsider would remove the core from the inner tube, place it in trays, clean it, measure it, and prepare the first inner barrel for the next run. Once that run was finished, the barrel and the rod were removed, full inner tube replaced with an empty tube, before being run in the hole with another rod added to the rod string. Each run drilled three metres of core. This was unless poor ground lead to the drill bit becoming blocked, which could happen at any time, even after only a few centimetres of drilling. A blockage meant no water was making its way between the drill bit and the rock to cool it down. If drilling wasn't stopped when it blocked, the not-cheap bit would heat up and melt, cooking it. The other possibility is that it could weld to the rock, which meant losing the bit, the core, and possibly part or all of the rod string, all of which would need to be fished out or drilled out, taking time and a good deal of money.

For the two bigger LM75 drill rigs, the rods were NQ size, three metres long and weighing just over twenty-three kilograms. This meant a rod pull for a hole about 300 metres deep involved moving 2300kg from the rig to the rod rack and then moving another 2300kg to put them back down again. This was only needed when the hole was completed or they needed to change a worn-out bit. For pulling the core out, the rods were left in the hole and a wire system was pumped down to retrieve it.

On his rig—the Onram—the BQ rods were also three metres long but weighed only eighteen kilograms. The rub was that there was no wire retrieval to pull the core out; instead, the whole rodstring was pulled for every run. It was called 'conventional,' which he took to mean standard, rudimentary, outdated. The holes were sometimes 150 metres deep, which meant moving some 900kg worth of rods back and forth, six or seven times over a twelve-hour shift. On some days, he lifted over ten tonne of rods.

When the hole was completed, a survey was taken to see where the hole had gone, versus where it was intended. If the geologists okayed it, they repositioned the rig, often by only moving the angle of the rig up or down a few degrees, a fan of holes, and drilling would begin again.

Simple enough. Repetitive. But for a boy who knew next to nothing about engines, cars, machinery, power tools—those things that might give him some insight into mechanical processes—it was confounding. Because of this, his first day offsiding mostly involved being shouted at, and fingers being pointed; learning the procedure, but forgetting crucial steps, which negated the headway made by the steps he got right. He did pay attention, looked into Lee and Dave's eyes, nodded at the appropriate times, but listened without comprehending, as if the individual words spoken were absorbed but not reconstructed in his mind as a meaningful actionable sentence. He worked too hard on the *act* of paying attention, not the substance of what was being communicated. Like when he met a stranger, concentrating more on a firm handshake than remembering the name they gave him. And his ear-plugs, necessary to dull the cacophonic sounds from the rig and the drilling and the trucks, also dulled the voices speaking to him. Adding to the sensory overload were the movements of the machinery, the feel of grease, water, and mud, the assaulting fumes of diesel and hot hydraulic oil, the uneven ground, the rubble caught in the mesh of the cuddy above him, the threatening cracks in the walls, and the uncomfortable baggy overalls and clumsy boots, all of which conspired to distract him from attending the job at hand.

He was worn out within the first few hours, his wrists and forearms especially, where the weight of the rods was mostly concentrated. Was trudging around the site like a shipwrecked sailor having just dragged himself from the cloying ocean. He tried to work quickly, to show enthusiasm, but the body and mind wouldn't synchronise—were at cross-purposes, cross-threaded. Enthusiasm meant nothing when the flesh gave way. There was no smoko and they didn't stop for lunch, instead eating between runs, hungry only for metres. Which was probably for the best as if he paused for more than ten minutes, was given any sense of respite, his body could take it as a cue to give up the ghost; a ghost that then might seize the opportunity to fly its own way home.

It was just after 1130am when he dropped a rod, denting the thread. He had pulled the rods six times already, 100m deep, and was getting clumsier and slower with each run. Not a big deal, a dented thread, but Lee, by now exasperated, did tell him to take a break, eat his lunch, and Dave took over. The boy walked away from the machine into the open to sit on a nearby rock, and could think of nothing else but quitting, already unable to cope with the job given him. They wanted him to quit too; because of his size, his age, the nepotism that got him there. But his start in mining had been built up for so many months, telling everyone what he was going to do. Instead of bullshitting on his dole form about jobs he had applied for, or avoiding the question of what he was going to do with himself after finishing high school, he could respond vaguely, if not smugly, by saying that he was going up north—his uncle was getting him the job. It was a done deal—he was going to be a driller's offsider, whatever that meant. If he threw it in now, *snatched* it, he would be a failure to his uncle, and to his parents who needed him to be directed towards something. Better for them that he stayed there: underground, safe and sound.

 He wanted to sob again. Like he had last night. And when Dave came to check on him, the boy kept his head down so as not to be betrayed by the welling tears and his ugly quivering chin. Dave sat down next to him and kindly let the boy tell him how he wasn't up to it, he should go home, listening to the boy's quiet, tremoring bursts of dialogue. When he was done, Dave replied with a pragmatic list of cons if the boy were to consider leaving, including that he would have to wait another five days before an Eltin plane arrived to take him home, and that he wouldn't be getting paid while he waited. Or he could catch one of the planes flying in with the workers from the other company, but he would have to pay for it himself.

 He ended his pitch and waited, letting it soak in, watching

Neph's mournful face to see if it was registering, before asking Neph if he wanted to get this next run. He did, he would, steeling himself again, just as he had with his push-ups, just as he had with his custard.

But this was more, a decisive moment, a fork in his road, and certainly some shift inside him took place; not that he suddenly showed promise, was a natural at offsiding, or that maybe he would start to enjoy the job and embrace it, dancing a jig between rod pulls. It was decisive in that it would be the last time he would cry for being out of his depth, his perceived fears of newness and the unknown, or homesickness. It was decisive because he kept going and it was the last time he would think of giving up, at least for any of the reasons he had told himself in those first two days. Quitting was no longer a possibility—at least not until he finished the swing. This was less an affirmation of the path he had chosen—that he will be a driller's offsider—and more a stoic denial of the path he hadn't—he will not not be a driller's offsider.

Shower

With Dave's help and soft words, he completed his first shift, having neither died, nor his ghost absconded. Lee told him to pack the tools away and when the ute arrived with the underground drillers he helped load the full core trays, ready to head out of the pit and up to the surface.

There was time enough for a shower, to change into his 'civvies' (his trackies and flanno), before the bus headed back to camp for dinner. Never having belonged to a footy team or fraternity or the like where it was commonplace for men to shower and be naked with each other, walking the repressed tightrope of latent homoeroticism, meant he was unprepared for this new experience. Not that there were any gay men there, or at any mine he would come to work at, either because there weren't any or, more likely, because a 'don't ask, don't tell' mentality was strictly enforced.

His angst of exposure was soon allayed when he found that the change rooms had cubicles with shower curtains. Although not wholly ashamed of his body, he showered and changed in the cubicle, all with the curtain drawn, to save anyone getting a glance, particularly his hairy arse, which he had always tried to conceal as much as possible. He took his time getting dressed in the cubicle, careful not to drop his clothes on the wet floor, as he threaded sore legs and arms though the holes.

It was uncommon behaviour, him hiding in the cubicle, and soon piqued the interest of the crew. From somewhere behind the curtain he heard the voice of his driller, Lee: 'You alright Neph? What's going on in there? Got something to hide, have ya?'

'No!' he called back, too urgently, but also too long after a pause, struck dumb by the sudden and unwanted attention. His reply hung momentarily, before being drowned out by the hearty guffaws of the crew. Although he probably should have, Lee had no such hang-ups, strutting around with nothing but thongs on his feet to battle the scourge of tinea, proudly displaying a rotund and enviable hairless body. Like a newborn rat.

For the life of his mining career he would see many, many naked male bodies and just as many penises. It was impossible not to catch a glimpse of the latter, no matter how unwanted or even unwarranted. The variety of ugly and weird shapes, colours, and sizes made him feel very sorry for women, particularly those of more conservative times where their first real-life penis sighting was when their dashing bridegroom unveiled it on their wedding night. Like a wound up jack-in-the box, the inaugural reveal may have been long-anticipated but would nevertheless come as a surprise when finally unsprung.

Several years later, when he was sent to The Granites gold mine, the anxiety of exposure was moot as there were no cubicles or shower curtains, just a wall of shower-heads. No curtain to be drawn. Nowhere to hide. The only thing for it was to keep his chin and eyes up as he made the long walk back to his towel, embracing his nakedness, and act as if he had nothing to be ashamed of. His was not the worst body after all, with so many beer-guts on display, tanless pink-white mottled flesh, and hair that colonised almost every inch of skin. And, objectively, be believed his not to be the worst penis. Unfortunately, he would see far too many to be more than confident in this evaluation.

That night, within the space of twenty-four hours, he had earned a rightful place in the queue for the lovely bain-maries, his hunger making him forgetful of the previous night's debacle. He ate heartily, greedily, as if he had just stumbled out of some godforsaken wilderness, having been lost for weeks—which, in a way, he felt he had. For the boy, this first day working on the rig had been his summiting of Everest and the mess his triumphant return to basecamp, most of his black, frostbitten fingers and toes still attached.

He also had someone other than Peter to sit with.

Work ethic

Over the following days he learned that he was a terrible offsider. Mostly because of his age, which put him at a disadvantage, a stark physical and mental disparity between him and the men he was working with, unavoidable because of biology and inexperience. Neph had never really worked before—real work, hard work, long hours—except for a few casual jobs, some hours after school in his parents' pushbike shop and a few days of house painting when he left school, and some labouring, brick cleaning, putting up antennas with a mate. Jobs where he acted entitled, lazy, or that he was not particularly good at or cut out for physically. And he hadn't worked for long stretches, no more than a few days at a time. There had been no daily grind, no rat race, and he didn't hate Mondays. And having completed his final school year, he had bummed for a good eight months of what was an unofficial gap year. Seriously bummed: his mind and body were in the early stages of an almost irreparable atrophy by the time he got the job. But he did get the job, and suddenly he was going to be working fourteen twelve-hour shifts in a row, with hard labour, no shift change, and practically no sleep.

For most, this is precisely what work is—the everyday, the norm, how a living is earned. It is how bills are paid, how food and shelter are provided. For him, this sense of domestic responsibility was unimaginably foreign, having never paid a bill, bought food, or even considered how he might be sheltered.

He was weak, lazy, slow, and clumsy. He didn't use his body, his hands, his weight right. He moved without urgency or purpose. And he was moody, angry, impulsive, stupid, and uninterested—

A Boy Miner

not unusual for a teenager; for someone alienating themselves from themselves, the schizoid desire for both individualisation *and* assimilation, all at once wanting to forge themselves anew, define their generation. The lyrics of Rage Against the Machine in his ear: 'Fuck you, I won't do what you tell me.' Even if he didn't know what it was that he wanted not to be told to do—the confused indifference and disenfranchisement of the nineties' teen. Others in his ear: Slayer, Sepultura, Pantera, Cannibal Corpse, Nirvana, Soundgarden, Pearl Jam, Tool, Korn—a who's who for the angry young man. Kurt Cobain may have taken his life with a shotgun a few years prior to the boy's entry into mining, but his legacy of apathy, cynicism, and grunge melancholia was alive and kicking, particularly in Mandurah, a small town where it took time for the rest of the world to arrive. Neph was that teen spirit and wore it as overtly as the flannelette shirt tied about his waist and Chuck Taylor All-stars on his feet. At the mine, as a miner, he was an interloper, an imposter. More a tourist, wall-eyed, happy-snapping the sights, but not one of the people, the culture. He may have never properly adjusted to the circumstances, nor really tried, which made it all the more difficult.

And his was a different working experience to his mates; some had gone to university or TAFE to study the new thing called Information Technology. For them a few lack-lustre grades was no big deal and could even be seen as part of a necessary trajectory for personal growth and responsibility. Nor was it like his other mates who had taken on apprenticeships as sparkies, roofies, or diesel mechanics, where a clear and important hierarchal relationship between the master and the apprentice is forged, with the apprentice paid a much lower wage as they learn their trade, perfecting their skills over several years. From the start he was paid the same as the more experienced offsiders, bringing with it the same workload expectations. There was no probation period or structured learning process. No concessions, even if he was Neph. He had a few days to get it right. More importantly, he had a few days to adjust to the FIFO lifestyle—get his head right. Lee would be his mentor for the rig; Dave, a father, became his mentor for everything away from it.

By the end of the first week he was shuffling around like an old man, his body aching from each day of lifting rods, from standing most of the day, awakening unused muscles, his back aching, hard to straighten out, shocks of pain in his wrists, all the while denied time to recuperate.

It was hard. Hard for him. Although not as hard as others had it. There were blokes doing four-and-one, living only a fifth of their lives. And not as hard as others that have mined in the past, such as the Welsh coal miners that he read about in Orwell's *Road to Wigan Pier*, on their knees, shovelling coal like the devil, and their 'button backs'—callouses from their vertebrae banging on the low beams of the tunnel as they walked, bent almost double, down the mine. There were the blood diamond miners in Africa—slaves, children. Or Kalgoorlie's own Paddy Hannan, the immortalised Irishman, pushing into the harshness of what would become the Goldfields. He wasn't them, hadn't experienced their hardship. Or he had no comparison to what hardship really was. Didn't know any different. He hadn't fought in a war, hadn't made the fatalistic decision of bayonet or bullet; hadn't fled a war, unlike one of the

Croat miners at Bronzewing who had survived the Croatian War of Independence. The boy hadn't lived through the Depression, been forced to eat mouldy bread, or stand in line for days for a job that doesn't exist; never experienced civil unrest at the bloodied blade of a machete; never retrieved bodies or their parts from the rubble of an earthquake or the silencing mud of a landslide. This was as close as most Australian white-privileged, first-world, lower-middle class, (mostly) able-bodied, heterosexual, parents-still-together, long-haired Gen X males would get to anything that resembled adversity. He was going to be building character like nobody's business.

Home

The second week was much the same as the first. And time did proceed, lame and stumbling, shift after shift. He was improving and Dave was helping him less and less, steadily transitioning back to his job as drill fitter.

With three shifts to go he let himself get too excited. Getting ahead of himself, began packing his bag. By the second last shift he had refocussed, just keeping it together. And then, the last. He thought it would never come—the final shift of the first swing. But it did come.

They finished a few hours earlier on the last shift to catch the plane, which was arriving soon. He showered at the mine, and went back to camp, where he showered again, before dressing in his civvies for his return to Perth. He would shower a third time at home, just to be sure that he had left the mine where it was. Even then, friends and family noticed a faint chemical odour lingering about him; and he still had traces of black grease that sat under his fingernails and in the sudden new creases and tiny wrinkles of his hands, like spider webs spun from charred silk.

He had been especially careful of staying clean on the day he was going home, keeping the mud and himself separate, desperately tiptoeing his way to the untainted sanctuary of the city. At the mine and at the camp, over the past two weeks, it had been a continuous battle, skipping over puddles, finding unmuddied tracks in the buildings, kicking his shoes off at the entrance of the donga. And above all being mindful of everything he touched or leaned on. The boy had learned this lesson when he flew in. Having met with Peter and collected his bag, the boy headed to the bus, reaching for the handle to enter when his hand squelched into a thick glob of mud that had flicked up as the bus made its way to the airstrip. He withdrew the hand, recoiling more from the cold of the mud than the mud itself. Not wanting to spoil his civvies, he walked around with the dirtied left hand held up in front of him, in limbo, like he was in the middle of waving to someone he recognised, or waving at someone he misrecognised, now only half-committed to the gesture, all the while keeping his right hand clean for shaking other hands.

He waited for the plane, amazed when it landed, like an apparition, shimmering from the heat, the anticipation rising, now loud and real. A perfect landing. He felt guilty as the new arrivals, stone-faced, exited the plane. Tired-looking, cigarettes at the ready, even if they had to wait for the camp before lighting up. Two of the longest weeks since he stepped off that plane. He would be unrecognisable, a stranger, if somehow the boy from the past were to meet his present self as they crossed paths on the red tarmac.

The cross-shifts spoke to each other, giving them the state of the rig and anything else worth noting. Neph kept quiet, hiding in the back, nothing of importance to add, and also not wanting to reveal the shameless, contorted grin stuck fast on his face, set as a stone gargoyle, as if the wind had changed.

The plane heading home was again only half-filled with men. As spruced up as they can get. Faces clean-shaven, a hint of aftershave fighting against the smoke and drink. Other dreadful smells emanating from abused bodies. Some of the men were drunk, chatty, and horny, which was directed almost exclusively at the air hostess—a different woman from his flight there—who maintained her grace, even if this was the least exotic trip any air hostess should ever be forced to take. She wore her false smile well, feigning interest in the fawning men. Kept herself light-hearted and accepting, even when she overheard that the game keeping them amused was trying to guess what colour underwear she had on underneath her modest airline uniform.

Again he couldn't sleep, as he watched the red plains become yellow and green and then the magnificence of the city, returned to Earth, even if its steel and glass and bitumen and fast-moving cars felt momentarily estranged, having wandered out of the desert.

They landed and trammed their way to the little satellite airport.

Waiting for their bags, Lee came up to him. 'You coming back?'

'Maybe.'

'You'll be back,' said Dave, who had also made his way over. Dave seemed to believe the words, but in the way that you might tell the terminally ill that they will soon be on the mend, back on their feet.

Maybe.

He was picked up by one of his very good mates, who drove him back to Mandurah, to his parents' home. Neph, mute for a fortnight, wouldn't shut up, except when he bought three cartons of Victoria Bitter and shoved the neck of a stubby into his mouth. He was as frenzied as a child tearing open presents on Christmas morning: there was a giddiness about him, a madman mistakenly let loose from the asylum. Or someone who had cheated death and had only just now found the map for living.

For the first time in a long time, he was not unpleasant to be around: energetic and positive, the hopeless stagnation of the past six months suddenly gone from his eyes. He was all smiles when he saw his parents—surely a stranger in their home.

He had some money, too, from the first week of work, and did some shopping: first, a Sony CD Walkman so that he could listen to his music in his donga, and some CDs. He spent most of the rest of his first pay packet on drink, generous with his money, happy to shout his friends at the pub, which was still very much a novelty, having all turned eighteen that year. No question that he owed them. And while he was suddenly wealthy, they were relatively poor from study or the meagre wage afforded an apprentice; or from being unemployed, just as he had been only a fortnight ago.

He flew in on Wednesdays but it felt like Friday night, the potent joy that marks the beginning of the weekend. For his mates it was still Wednesday, and they had work or study the next day. This meant little to him: he was home, ready to tie one on, and they would need a better excuse for not coming to the pub directly. This became the incontrovertible routine for almost every night on his break: drinking excessively until closing, sleeping on the lounge of anyone's house, and embracing a guilt-free hangover as he watched those who worked go to work.

Despite this sudden benevolence, and the joy and magnanimity he assumed he brought to his mates, they would soon be looking to the calendar, ready to circle his departure date.

Prodigal son

Dave and Lee didn't really think he was coming back, that he had it in him to go another swing; neither did the rest of the crew who had spotted the skinny, miserable-looking kid darting his way around the camp and mine site. And he was sheepish when Dave, Lee, Horse and some of the other drillers made a point of it, with well-meaning jibes and incredulous faces, as he met them in the lounge area waiting for the plane.

'Hey Dave, old mate came back. Didn't think you had it in you, Neph. Must have liked the money, eh?' Lee happy because he had seen some promise and had already invested too much time into the boy.

'Yeah, something like that,' he said with a guarded wry smile, knowing that this was easily top of the list of reasons. But it was more than this: the week's break had given him time and distance to process and debrief, and eventually lead him to the unexpected conclusion that maybe he could do this, see it out for a bit longer. The horrific stories he told at home had metamorphosed into fond memories and tales of survival, something to laugh about even if he couldn't remember laughing once while he was away. Time enough had passed to let humour tickle the belly of even the most gloomy tales.

Belonging to the workforce also gave him a new sense of self. Of contribution and purpose. Even seeing the big chunk of money taken for tax made him feel good. Also for the first time in a long time, he felt pride.

And, of course, again, he came back for the money, which was really very good, and of which he reminded himself as often as possible. As such, he had been in better spirits for his return, right up until he saw the terminal for his departure from Perth.

When he got back, Dave was back to being the full-time drill fitter, leaving Neph with Lee. Seemingly he was now capable enough to do it alone, the week off revitalising his fledgling body. There was also very little he could do wrong on the rig, which is to say that he was on a short leash, and the tasks were fairly straightforward once all the other factors had been taken out of them.

He was beginning to find his place, his mining legs. In that fortnight's stint he worked a little harder, got a little better, adjusted and acclimatised. His arms had new definition and his legs no longer ached from standing most of the shift. He got stronger, wirier, more capable, but stayed about the same modest weight.

The soft hands from when he first felt the cold metal of the rod were now swollen with chunks of callous, as if stung by bees. He became familiar with the drilling process, with the rig, and his tasks, developed a rhythm as he pulled the rods, and a style, the way he flicked the clamps around the outer tube, the way he swung the rods, tapped the core out. There was also an increased sense of synchronicity between him and Lee. Lee may have lamented having the boy assigned to his rig, but within those first two stints he had moulded him well enough to help him earn some good metreage. No longer was the boy 'fucking the dog,' which is to say he was no longer going too slow, or being inattentive. Sometimes, after a good day's metres, they might even have been considered to be 'killing the pig,' which is to say they were killing the pig.

Isolation

Even if he wanted to, there was no way of leaving the camp other than the plane, no cars or public transport. And there was nowhere to go anyway. Just the camp and the mine. At the end of each shift, after dinner, he went directly to his room, where he would read the sports magazine he brought with him for the plane ride, poring over every column, no matter how little he understood or cared for the sport in question. There was an antenna port in his donga but no TV. He would have to bring his own, which he could have easily done; and there were lots of channels, pay TV and regular. He never did bring one though—never thought he would be there long enough: Pete had told him that contract renewals weren't always guaranteed, and he assumed that soon enough he would either be sacked or quit. The room, therefore, was his sanctuary, his hiding place, a bunker, but it wasn't home, so he never thought to make it homely.

The only connection between those at the camp and the outside world were the payphones, where they could talk to remote, faintly metallic voices at the end of the phone line, made more distant by the impossibility of traversing the deserts that lie between them. Not an international call but it felt as if oceans separated them.

He made his first call, to his mum, on the second night of the first stint, between dinner and getting to sleep. There were eight or so outdoor payphones spread out over the Bronzewing camp, catering for hundreds of workers, which made for rush-hour traffic and peak times. He would learn that even when he avoided the busiest periods, there would be a wait, sometimes thirty minutes or more. Time spent pushing around cigarette butts and dead insects with his shoe, studying the contours of his footprint in the dust, watching the trails of ants. Waiting for a phone meant keeping a place in the queue, which looked less like the dinner queue and more like a few desperate individuals randomly scattered at a distance of twenty to thirty metres around the phone, circling like wolves. They took cover behind dongas or scrub during the day, in the shadows at night, not wanting to pressure those on the phones, allowing them their time. But they also made sure their presence was known to those on the phone and to others waiting in the queue by moving in and out of the caller's view, or with intermittent guileless scraping of the gravel with their foot, or a sharp clearing of the throat, spitting an emphysematic ball of phlegm, all within earshot of the caller. He did this too, and felt bad for it each time, but not bad enough to never do it again. One night, as he spoke on the phone, out of the corner of his eye, he saw the lighting of a cigarette, the sinister glow of the red embers rising and falling in the shadows. He was certain that the hint of smoke wafting in his direction was purposeful. Never really alone at the camp site.

A ten-dollar phone card went quickly for the caller, the machine automatically punching a hole in the card every few minutes, and the little screen on the phone counting it down for him. Time was slowed for everyone else, punching holes in their store of patience.

FIFO relationships could be described in similar terms—of distance, waiting, and growing impatience. Fathers waiting around wanting to speak to their children at home, anxious to call within the small window between the end of shift and the kids' bedtimes. A quick hello. 'How was school today?' 'Have you been a good boy for Mummy?' The tired young minds of their children, distracted, and hardly enthusiastic, losing connection with the bodiless voice of their father. It turned out that he hadn't been the only one that had cried up there.

The camp, a life-raft in a desert ocean; and also, like a life-raft, its occupants were necessarily confined within close quarters, trapped together until rescued by the plane. Forced to eat together, drink together, head out and return to work together. They had to get along. If there were disagreements, then it was best to tackle the issue head on, sometimes in a punch-up, and clear the air. He heard of at least two occasions where this had been the preferred option, with one leading to a sacking when one of the blokes fell through a glass door and almost bled to death. Amicable social interaction wasn't compulsory, but it helped make time at camp more agreeable.

Not that he didn't feel lonely, even when he was rubbing shoulders at dinner and breakfast, on buses, in change rooms. He didn't go to the wet mess except to get his phonecards, keeping to himself in his donga. If you looked for him you might catch glimpses of him, fast-walking, staying direct in his movements, occupying himself by creating routines: washing his overalls, socks and underwear, drying them in the dryers, preparing for the following shift, packing his crib bag. Working hard on being comfortable on his own, his company not as good as any, but enough to get by.

He would have company soon though: his cousin Steven, or Boof, as he was called by friends and family because of his largish head, was coming to work the drills also. He was Peter's stepson. They were of the same age, eighteen years old, Neph being older than Boof by only a month, but from when they were young, the boy had always looked up to and loved Boof as if he were an older brother. Boof made him feel confident and brave when he was around him. He learned from Boof, Boof being the most worldly and experienced person the boy had ever known. This despite Boof growing up in the Goldfields' town of Norseman and then Geraldton, and having never been out of the state, let alone the country. He was that kid that had heard and seen it all before. Street-wise and cocky. Had watched a bunch of R-rated movies. Called his friends 'mates.' Could kick a footy a mile.

It should have been the other way round: Boof should have come here first, paved the way, and his cousin would follow. A few months away. Until then, the boy dedicated himself to going it alone.

Two months and Underground
September 1996

It took three swings to finish off the holes in the pit, before finally being ready to take the Onram underground. Working in the relatively normal environment of the 'surface' had made his adjustment to the rig a little easier. The underground, though, was unlike anything he knew or could prepare for. For one, most obviously, there was no natural light, neither from the sun nor the moon, and he needed his caplamp fastened to the top of his hardhat, which, like a torch, lit up only a small yellow circle, a few feet wide, in front of him. Where he looked is what he saw. He had seen some of the underground during his induction: they went down during the day, the daylight blinding them when they resurfaced. However, on their proper day shifts and because of the short winter days, they headed down when it was still dark outside and stayed underground for twelve hours, including lunch, which they took by retreating to the underground crib/refuge room—a walled-off cuddy, with a thick, steel door that he had to stoop to get through. The crib room was well lit with fluorescent lights, and had a fridge for food, an urn, and benches and tables to eat at. The crib room was also the designated safe place at 1230, which was the official firing time for both day and night shift. The drives being fired were a kilometre or so down from the crib room, and the explosions sounded more like a series of pops than a singular bang, the reverberations dulled as if in a wartime bunker. Small fragments of rock and dust would still loosen and fall between the mesh pinned to the ceiling. They would pause as the charges went off and look up, suspiciously. The crib room was safe, but it was instinctual to do so—to see what might be brought down upon their heads; and maybe their concerns were even a little justified, especially since some of the worst cracks in the mine were there, and because the occasional dollar-sized shard fell from the ceiling, making a splash in his Styrofoam cup of coffee.

At the end of the shift they exited the portal, again in the dark, the night sky indistinguishable from the underground, except for a few faint stars and the orange glow of the refinery's lights. Hypothetically, it was possible for him to not see the sun for the seven days he was on day shift, living nocturnally, like they were mushrooms, emptied of chlorophyll, just as their new, verdant overalls soon faded to grey. Luckily, every few days there was some reason to head to the surface—a new drill bit, more core trays—giving him the opportunity to feel the sun and natural breeze on his face, reminding him that daylight still existed.

The absence of light temporarily distracted him from the increased dangers of working underground. When he first got to the underground drill site, Lee immediately handed him a scaling bar, which was a longer crowbar—six foot or more—for prying rocks off the walls that may have loosened during a blast. Small rocks, shards, but also the bigger rocks—slabs weighing hundreds of kilograms that would crush a man, his hardhat as good as a hairnet. At the beginning of each shift, they scanned the walls for widening cracks, hitting rocks to hear if they rang out firmly or were dull and therefore loose.

Working made him forget the danger, focussing on the rig,

getting their metres. Only every now and again did he really think of where he was, hundreds of metres underground, rock pressing down, like when he dove too deep into the pool, the weight of the water pushing on him, making his ears pop from changing atmospheres. It was a fifteen-minute drive from the drill rigs to the surface, up the only road and out. This was the primary, underground-specific danger. They could flee in any direction if something went wrong on the surface; in the underground, however, up and out was not always an option. If a truck or other machine crashed on the decline, blocking it, caught on fire, they would need to climb hundreds of metres up the escape route ladders to get to a level above or, better, all the way to the surface. The ventilation of the mine came from huge fans on the surface that sucked air down the decline and then up through vertical shafts. There were also the smaller fans on the decline, which pushed air through big canvas vent bags into the drives, like the ducting of air conditioners in a roof cavity. If there were a fire, the best way to stop the smoke flooding the mine was to cut the power to both the surface and the underground fans, which also meant cutting the supply of fresh air coming from the surface. This is when the self-rescuers were needed, as they made their way in the utes or on foot to the Fresh Air Bases or up though the escape routes.

    He wondered what would happen, how he would handle being tested in a real emergency situation, if he could climb all those ladders, with all his gear and his gumboots; if there were smoke and he couldn't see, would he be able to blindly feel his way along the wall, making his way up and out of the mine? Or would he curl up in a ball and wait in the darkness? They hadn't had a drill or simulation of it, other than putting the self-rescuer on during their induction, which he was comfortable doing on the surface, in daylight, where it was safe as houses. But the daylight didn't come any further once they turned that first corner heading down into the underground, replaced by a darkness that was only intermittently broken up by the occasional fluorescent lights above power boxes or those hanging from the backs.

Later, in some downtime, he walked down a disused drive and turned off his caplamp to see how dark it really was. It sucked the air out of him, his body rejecting it, as if he were in limbo, with only the uneven ground keeping him tethered to his sense of space, swaying as if at sea, keeping still so that he didn't fall. He removed his earplugs too, listening to running water, a babbling stream through the rock. The cold, damp smell of broken rock, like limestone or brick dust, reminded him of the absence of the perfumes of natural life, the tang of a sea breeze, the swirling, clinging B.O. of humanity.

This was the dark side of the moon.

It felt like a game to see how long he could keep his lamp off, thrilling, unnatural, the absence of all light, unable to see his hand reaching out in front of him for a wall, attempting to contradict his memory, which told him a wall wasn't there. He made it almost a minute before a slight panic trembled through him at the thought of his caplamp not coming back on. He had no glow sticks he could crack, like those he had seen in the movies, in case of his caplamp failing. No spare battery or globe. Only the reflective strips of his overalls would save him, and even then he needed someone else's caplamp or a ute's headlights to shine his way and illuminate him.

The caplamp did come on, the sudden walls jumping out in

front of him, like God creating the universe out of nothingness. He walked out of the drive with a quickened step, as if he had seen a ghost, knowing full well that he didn't believe in ghosts.

◉

The underground had its own climate, and stayed about the same temperature, whether it was minus two degrees or forty degrees Celsius on the surface. It was hotter in some drives, or at the faces, which became stagnant and humid, the fresh cool air only travelling as far as the ventilation allowed. This was especially where the bogger—which was like a front-end loader but flattened and elongated for the underground—and trucks were working, pumping out heat and diesel fumes. Dark patches of sweat would gather quickly; he could feel it run down the inside of the thick overalls.

Taking the bad with the good: there were no insects or flies, no life at all—too hard for anything to live on rock alone. Of course, no sunburn—no tans either, evidenced so starkly in the showers. And there was little to no dust, with sprinkler systems set up to dampen the decline and drives. Only in a blast was the dust an issue. It lay thick on the rock pile, which he heard could be deadly, like the splinters of asbestos, if not watered down. It was grey too, like asbestos. But who was to know its real effects: the boy had a blood nose every other day, but this was likely from the dust on both the surface and underground. And most others were busy filling their lungs with cigarettes, such that a few puffs of poisonous mining dust was possibly the least of their worries.

Even if he was improving as an offsider he still managed to fuck up several times within the first month of being underground, black eyes, overshadowing his most pedestrian triumphs and burgeoning confidence. Once was when he tried to syphon degreaser out of a drum by sucking on a bit of hose. He'd seen Lee do it and thought he would have a go himself. But the physics was all wrong, vacuums and pressures, and by the end he had swallowed a cupful of the spirit-like liquid but had none in the container. It didn't affect anyone except himself, losing his sense of taste for a few days, his tongue and gums numbed.

Two other incidents occurred when he was driving the ute, which he had done his best to avoid, fearing the tight, unmoving rock walls, the trucks, the darkness, and the rabbit-hole labyrinth ready to ensnare him. The underground resembled a kind of anarchy; no place for a boy who may have passed his driving test and been handed a freshly-laminated driver's license—his pimpled face in the corner, marked with his silly kid's version of a signature—but still had next to no driving experience, having never had a car of his own.

The first incident of the two occurred when he drove down the decline by himself for the first time. He had made his way out of the underground easy enough, safe in knowing that if he kept driving upwards he would eventually break through to the surface. The only thing he feared as he headed up the decline was running into a truck coming down the decline, not understanding the levels they were calling out. The rumbling that sounded like a tidal wave, an avalanche, coming around the corners which made

A Boy Miner

him think of when he played hide and seek as a child, running to hide, to find a spot, knowing that they were coming, thrilling and terrifying all at once.

Heading down the hole was different. The oncoming trucks were slower and he had more time to back the ute up to an empty drive. But his sense of direction was darkly muddled as he headed into the belly. He hadn't paid much attention to where they were going each time they had gone down or up—nothing to do with him—and sitting in the back of the ute, facing backwards under the roll cage, meant that everything was reversed. This was part of the reason why he became disorientated and made a wrong turn at a junction, veering left instead of right towards the rigs. He barrelled down the decline for what seemed an overly long time, deeper and deeper underground. There were no markers he recognised, just infinite grey walls spiralling downwards, broken only by the occasional drive extending into darkness. He saw no trucks either, and no utes. His gut told him that he should turn around, but was unable to will himself to do so. He wanted to assure himself, be confident, like a footy player centring himself to kick the winning goal after the siren, trying to quieten the ego talking him down.

Suddenly, emerging from the black nothingness, were two men shouting at him, heard above the motor of the ute and his earplugs, waving their caplamps and arms, signalling him to stop. He jumped on the brakes just before running into the backend of a jumbo—a strange, futuristic machine the size of a bogger, but instead of a bucket it had two long hydraulic boom arms with giant hammer drills attached, capable of drilling holes almost five metres deep. He just pulled up in time at the end of a locked-up skid. There may have been literal warning signs that the jumbo was ahead, but the mine was littered with them, rendering them altogether meaningless.

It was the kind and sympathetic jumbo offsider—the nipper—a huge man, mid- twenties, a tormented look on his face, that first alerted him of his error: 'You just drove over the fuckin' jumbo cable. What the fuck are you doing here?'

'I am looking for the drill rigs,' he answered with quavering defensiveness, as if to say it wasn't his fault that they weren't down there. Someone must have moved them.

'Well they're not fuckin' here, are they?'

By now the jumbo operator, Rambo, so-called because of his uncanny resemblance to the square-jawed face, mullet, and bulging physique of Sylvester Stallone, had arrived, ready to contribute to the conversation: 'Hey, fuckwit. You know how much it costs to repair a jumbo cable?'

A jumbo cable, as he was educated through an angry impromptu lesson, is a very large electrical cable, 70mm or more in diameter, running from the power box to the jumbo that if cut or crushed needs to have all of the wiring individually reconnected. The jumbo cable itself was expensive, but it was the down time for the repair that was most costly.

The cable was fine, which would be one of the few times that fortune would pardon him. He backed the ute out and they passed the cable over the top as he drove under, all the while shaking their heads like they were mourning some inexplicable tragedy, brought down on them by a cruel, unseen god.

The second driving incident was potentially more dangerous than expensive. This time the ute was filled with the drillers and

A Boy Miner

offsiders in the front and back. He had long been curious to see how far it was to drive to the rigs, and now had an opportunity to find out. As he entered the portal and the straight of the decline, he stuck his hand through the gap in the steering wheel to press the 'trip' button on the dash, resetting it to zeroes. He was still fumbling for the button, bumpy and dark as the decline was, when the first bend approached. Instinctively he turned the steering wheel to make the corner, his arm still poking through the steering wheel, which resulted in catching himself in an arm-bar and becoming unable to turn the wheel far enough to make the bend. Releasing his arm would steer them straight into the wall. Instead, he jumped on the brakes, again skidding for fifteen metres in a straight line, before pulling the ute up just in time, the bull bar coming to rest gently on the wall. His flimsy excuse was that he hadn't been driving very long. Again, men were shaking dumbfounded heads, and all but shook their fists at the heavens, which seemed even further away than usual.

In the underground he would also learn how others worked, finally able to see other rigs, their drillers and offsiders. He watched Bob, in his fifties, Old Bob, working on the big LM75 rig twenty metres away, in a cuddy across the decline. He was bald except for a few curly grey tufts at the sides, and not much of a body, with skinny legs and arms, no chest, and a round, fecund beer belly—more E.T.: the Extra-Terrestrial than hard-bitten miner. Despite his age, Bob was still spry and ambitious; he went *hard*, in drinking, smoking, and working—even wore a homemade t-shirt that read 'Harden up, fuck ya' on the front, and 'Get hard'

on the back, which he sported on days when he was at his most hungover, rubbing his throbbing forehead, scrunching up his face like he was looking into a harsh light, chastising himself for having been lured to the wet mess once again to soak himself to the bone in cans of piss.

    Between runs, Neph watched Bob busy himself, cleaning core, cleaning core trays, cleaning the rig. Watched him paint it too, using up a whole box of white spray cans. He tidied and made the workplace safe, pre-empted possible hold-ups to the process and created a routine that ensured maximum efficiency of the drilling process from the initial pinning of the rig to the final survey of the hole. The rig, the core, the area around it was his space, and the driller was privileged in being able to operate it. All with a smile and a cigarette hanging loose from his lips, thankful for the opportunity afforded him, chances fewer and fewer with age, something Neph knew nothing about. More importantly, Neph saw how at ease Bob was in knowing the ins and outs of the rig, and in ensuring its smooth and untroubled operation. He envied him this and set about emulating him. Keeping busy also made the time tick over faster, taking his mind off both his watch and his groan-hungry stomach.

    Pride was one thing, but money was another. He worked harder because he could earn more. On top of a flat rate, they were paid by the metre of core drilled: one dollar per metre for the offsider; four dollars per metre for the driller. The difference between getting twenty and thirty metres a shift over the fortnight was $140; $560 for the driller. The position of driller was where the money was. Lee made a point of it: if he wanted to become a driller, work the levers, not the rods, and earn more money, he was going to have to not only learn about the rig but *want* to learn—to ask questions instead of waiting to be taught. Be ambitious, proactive. Only then would he maybe be considered for a promotion somewhere down the line. This of course would require a complete overhaul of his attitude from moody, arrogant, and indifferent, to enthusiastic, attentive, and grateful in the face of adversity. They would have better luck turning Andy Warhol into a Navy Seal.

Shift Change

When Lee and Neph took the rig underground, they were also placed on the normal roster when they flew in—seven night shifts followed by seven day shifts—which also meant they could join the shift change with the rest of the drilling crew, the mining crew celebrating at a different part of the mess. Coming off night shift, it was eight in the morning, which, in the bush, was as good a time as any to start drinking, shift change or not. They loaded up a few empty bins with ice and four or five blocks of warm beer between the seven of them: Neph, Lee, Dave, Horse, Bob, Frank, and Stuart, a driller with the voice and poise of a Shakespearean actor.

His first lukewarm VB tinny was unimpressive and he downed it recklessly. And then another, and another. For the first half an hour he drank and listened, letting the beers sink in, loosening him up, relaxing the tightness of his face. Then he smiled; and then he laughed. He hadn't laughed for the three stints he was there. Not because Lee and Dave weren't funny, teasing and mocking each other for most of the shift. He just didn't know if it was for him to join in, like he was merely an audience to their show. He also didn't know how to act when they made fun of him, gentle and harmless, at his expense, roasting him, mostly because of his youth. Besides, as far as he was concerned, there was no time for joking at the rigs, making about as much sense as laughing whilst on fire.

Such a surprise when the boy suddenly spoke, bubbling up like a belch. Full sentences, subject and predicate, grammatically correct for the most part. So different to the soft monosyllabic yes or no responses he had uttered for most of the time he had been there. He had a deep voice, spoke quickly, deliriously, and earnestly, and revealed some snippets of himself. He had ideas, opinions, stuck by them. Like 'What was the point in voting—they are as bad as one another.' He knew as much about politics as he did how the brain worked, but it had nevertheless been at the forefront of his mind given that now eighteen he was expected to register to vote, which seemed to have encumbered him no end. Even if they were mostly the fatuous views of a teenager boy, there was at least some substance to him, hidden behind the determined yet wearying scowl. He was like a stale bottle of cheap piss that had been standing on the shelf for a few years—dust on its shoulders, the corners of the label coming away—which curiously opened like champagne—all pop, bubbles, and celebration.

Only temporarily though, as by the following morning, at breakfast before the day shift, fizz had given way to flatness and he recapped himself, albeit a little less dusty, having finally met his crew. He was finally welcomed—finally allowed himself to be welcomed—even if it was three swings overdue.

A Boy Miner

Narratives of mining

Sisyphus, the existential hero of Greek mythology, was condemned to repeat forever the same meaningless task of pushing a boulder up a mountain, only to see it roll down again. Sisyphus would return to the bottom of the mountain and begin the process again, with no end. The French Algerian philosopher Albert Camus cites this myth as exemplifying the human condition. The absurdity of striving for unachievable goals—like sweeping up downy feathers, watching them eddy away with each push of the broom. Or of achieving goals only to find that new goals present themselves, such that no meaningful presence is realised. It is this allegory that exemplifies the narrative of the mining process, which is both beautifully simple and mind-deadeningly repetitive. Maybe not quite Sisyphean, but the labour of moving rock from the bottom of something to the top of something is almost certainly the same. In this, mining was admirable in its ancient, practical goals: dig a hole and get the rock. Simple, clear, tangible. The outcome could be held in the hands, like baking a cake, building a house, or having a baby. There is no theory, no greater moral to the story, no ideology at work, no questions about deeper meaning. The big names of philosophy—Socrates, Plato, Aristotle, Descartes, Nietzsche, Sartre, Camus, Derrida—didn't come down the hole. They talked about it, argued, dialogued, fought for moral rights, revealed truths, but, like the light, didn't travel that far, only peering from the surface, safe and content in the abstraction of thought.

Rock was dug up from the ground—end of story. If there was more to the story, such as the refining of the ore—gold, nickel, alumina, diamonds—and the various processes that followed, or issues such as capitalism, exploitation, sustainability, pollution, then they were of little importance or interest to the blue-collar sensibilities of the miner, alienated as they were from the end product of the thing they were mining. Unionless and vulnerable and set to making as much money as their bodies and the company's fickle contracts would allow. Get down that hole and dig.

The preamble to the story of both underground and open-pit mines is exploration drilling, which takes place on the surface. Kilometres-deep vertical holes are drilled down to find the ore seams to determine the mineral and its quality, before a map is created for the mine. Following this, a small or large pit is dug and a portal cut into the wall. The portal leads to the underground decline, the tunnelled highway, winding its way down into the earth, with drives branching off from it towards the ore seams. From the moment the surface of the earth is broken and the decline begun, the process is always the same: the jumbo drills a matrix of holes, outlined in spray paint on the wall; the charge-up guy loads the holes with explosives and fires the wall; the wall explodes into a pile of rock; the bogger comes in and bogs out the dirt, loads it into trucks until it is clear; the jumbo returns and drills holes into the wall again; the cycle continues. In between the bogger's clearing and the jumbo's drilling, the service crew extends the ventilation, water and compressed air lines, power boxes and electric cables.

The narrative thus takes the form of the simplest plot: there is a problem (of rock in the way); and there is a resolution (where rock is moved out of the way). The problem then repeats itself.

But Sisyphus casts the shadow of repetition and cycles

not only on the workings of the mine—it falls on the miners themselves, creating the same familiar subplots and character arcs. The most recognisable is the cycle of working life in general: earn money, spend money, earn money, spend money. At the camp, FIFO workers spent relatively little money on site: all their meals are supplied, they are accommodated, clothed. There is nowhere to go to spend money—no supermarkets, department stores. And, relatively speaking, they can't drink too much, and even if they did, the beer is cheaper than the pubs at home.

So different on break, though, as a miner's possibilities for consumption become far greater. Like little boys with their pocket money, embarking on a lolly and videogame spending spree. Mostly booze, but also shameless materialism: cars, boys' toys, objects. For some of the bachelors, coming home to an empty fridge was excuse enough to eat out for every meal. For a few, the first night began at Burswood Casino and finished at Langtrees, where they could spend a good chunk of their pay on prostitutes, firm in the belief that a steady girlfriend was too great a burden, and because they had become too feral to be of sociable company anyway.

The break was made for excess. One of the fitters, Micko, single, early-twenties, said he took pills—ecstasy—almost every night on his break. He said it was okay because they were out of his system within twenty-four hours, and wouldn't be pulled up if they dropped a drug test on them when they flew in. Neph asked if it was a good idea, because of health issues, damage to the brain. Micko just shrugged his shoulders as if he'd never considered it before. As if the boy were proposing they invest in a racehorse or timeshare together. Left the conversation unconvinced, both of them.

For others, far sadder subplots determined them: get married, get divorced; get married, get divorced. Which created other related subplots: earn money, pay alimony and child support; earn money, pay alimony and child support. The relationships of FIFO seemed doomed, and having a happy, functional family almost an impossibility. Divorce was not a matter of if, but when. An inevitable end and beginning to their circumstances. Circumstances in which the father was away for two to four weeks at a time—a father *in absentia*, doing his parenting over the phone. Circumstances where the mother assumes the role of a single parent, widowed, with no respite from all the hardships and frustrations and responsibilities that it brings: solely in charge of cooking, cleaning, shopping, driving, putting out the bins, paying bills, taking the kids to sport on the weekends, to the dentist, to the doctor, the first and only respondent to emergencies, alone during their pregnancies, at check ups and scans, loathe to get sick. Compelled to rely on sympathetic friends and family—if they are not too proud. Which necessarily also makes them stronger. For many women, like their foremothers, they were condemned to follow these men, stand by them, wait for them. More than a century on, they were the modern incarnation of Henry Lawson's drover's wife, the husband driven away by his work, the wife left to maintain their home life.

When father is away, mother is regarded as a stingy disciplinarian, yelling at the kids, doling out punishments, depriving them of their wants. But when father returns, the world is temporarily undone: the father, both wealthy and guilty because of his absence, showers his children with elaborate presents. Routines, bed times, and food habits are all disregarded; they were vacationing at Disneyland for all they knew. Over time, the mother finds her routine to make her time alone easier; over time, better that the father stays away.

The boy's own absurd subplot hinged on a similar reciprocating conflict that arose from his separation from home for weeks at a time. It was within months that he came to realise that the more he was away from normal society, the more he preferred the mine; the more he stayed at the mine, the less he fit into normal society. But when he was at the mine he was unhappy and longed for home; when he was home, he was alone, out of step and unhappy, and wanted to return to the mine. Each was romanticised in its absence. A catch-22 that would make Joseph Heller proud. Even the definition of fly-in, fly-out had become ambiguous. 'In' he assumed meant home, interior, within, the heart, and 'out' meant the mine, exterior, otherness. But he began to hear people say they were flying 'in' to the mine and 'out' to home. It depended on how he looked at it, but how he looked at it was becoming less uncertain.

Within the first few months he had begun to lose touch, particularly before Boof had joined him, which was most noticeable on his break. With what people normally do during the day; what they do at night. He swore more frequently and inappropriately, unable to switch from a mining vocabulary to the more polite discourse of home. And he drank too much. Every night was either a party, or a session, or a few drinks, or a bender, or any excuse to keep the good time going, making the most of the manic break.

Out of joint. A misfit of routine. When he met friends, especially those not immediate in his life, they asked questions like 'So, when are you heading back?' Innocent questions, without malice, but they reflected a way of thinking about him and their relationship to him—of how he entered and exited their lives. Not reliable as a friend, to be there, for the good times or bad. Always looking forward, towards him flying out (or in), beginning the next swing. No one was asking him when he got in, a question that implied his break had begun and was open-ended still, available to plan and catch-up, even if the fly-out (in) day was unequivocally determined.

He'd already seen the evidence of the tragic, lonely narratives that the older men had lived—some not so old. Worn-out men, still mining because they had no other skill set, labourers, all of them, from the drill offsider to the jumbo operator. Some worked away because no one wanted them at home anymore. Their kids hated them, their wives hated them. FIFO may have started out as a temporary solution—a way of making quick cash—but over time and through habit, it had metamorphosed into a permanent lifestyle choice. Some preferred the FIFO life because they could hang out with old mates, smoke and drink, speak their minds, as if it were an extended boy's weekend. It was a return to a life less complicated, free of relationship woes, political correctness, and social mores.

From the casual drinkers he could distil a few alcoholics. High functioning, never missed a shift, no matter how beaten up they were. Like Lethal, on charge-up, who would stagger in, long blonde hair, a thin, muscular body, pale blue eyes looking like piss-holes in the snow, a guttural muttering voice. He drank heavily at the end of every shift but was never breathalysed in the morning—did too good a job. There were a few of them, grumbling through the start of the shift, working off their hangovers, penitent, sweating out their vice, revitalising themselves to once again get back on the piss, walking into the wet mess like a legend.

Some didn't understand the world outside of a mining camp, as if it were utterly foreign, passed them by too quickly. Instead, they embraced the outback's old-world familiarity where men were men and that's all that mattered. Most smoked—packets of cigarettes a day—just to pass the time, like a hobby, a distraction. They would huddle together offering cigarettes and lighters to each other, smoking without affectation, skilled and seasoned. The boy not fussed by the fog that he would wander in and out of— not fussed like he would be now. He expected that few would live long lives. Or they would be punished by living forever, retiring only when they were forced to. Theirs was a sacrifice, taking care of their families. No longer able to parent, but capable of making money. A martyrdom. Which Neph already understood and admired. And they *should* be understood and admired for it, although he wasn't sure many of them thought much on their sacrifice anymore, a consequence of the apathy and indifference that tumoured in them, as well as the dysfunction, depression, and mental illnesses that permeated the everyday. Harden up, fuck ya.

Each man handled himself differently, coped in his own way. But there were still perceptible character types from the homogenous FIFO mass. Types of men that shared personalities, attitudes, and values. Such as those who fit easily in to mining and the FIFO life, like it was the same as any normal kind of job. They enjoyed it and would happily keep doing it—the extended boy's weekend types, preferring male company over women's, where they could talk about the simpler things in life: fishing, cars, gambling. Hardened men, working class, bikies, ex-sailors, bushmen, bearded, purposefully ugly. Cheap blue-green tattoos—home-made—which were still symbols of rebellion more than fashion or desperate symbols of masculinity. They were the 'manliest' men, most suited to the place and didn't necessarily want to go home. And there was no façade: they were the round pegs in the round hole. Often, they were also the ones no longer wanted at home, the family reducing them to a smelly, lumpy-cushioned piece of furniture, dragged back out from the curb-side rubbish, and sat in a corner of the living room for the week's R and R. For some of the fathers, the break was no longer their own, only good for doing chores and paying bills, unable to find themselves at home. Embittered, they reciprocated in kind, unashamedly confessing that they hate their partners and that they hate their kids. 'Cunts, the lot of 'em.' It was to the youngest in the crew that they could lament, catching the boy's ear because he was expected to listen, pay attention to his elders, in case he learned something about life, maybe even something about mining. No need to tell the aged who already knew and no longer wanted to hear it. They may have started FIFO with good intentions, but now their time away from home bled resentment.

    There were also those who fit the FIFO lifestyle but didn't necessarily enjoy it—those types that also didn't fit into normal society and carried with them a prickly misanthropy wherever they went. Unpleasant types at the mine and at home, happy to stay out of the way, finding fewer and fewer haunts for their kind to feel comfortable in.

    There were those who, by the look of them, didn't appear to fit in to mining or FIFO at all; the professional types that seemed

A Boy Miner

more suited to accounting, politics, or academia— too polite and too educated. Of these, there were some that enjoyed it too much, treating it as if they were seeking real life experience at a fortnight-long boot camp away from the monotony of a white-collar suburban lifestyle. They didn't smoke, had a few beers only. And they did their job well, and with sickening and peculiar enthusiasm, like that of a Nazi SS officer whistling contentedly as he cleans his Walther P38. James Woodman, or Wood duck as some called him, was the exemplar. He had a sensible haircut, perfect set of teeth, was educated, articulate, and unironically liked to wear 'happy' pants, a throwback to the '80s. When he swore, it sounded forced, the tone and timbre all wrong. He was nice, white bread, the grader operator and sometimes truck driver. And completely incomprehensible. Neph would see him at the gym and each time James would smile and greet him earnestly, just as he did with each individual at the start of the shift. He was immanently likeable, and enviable for a demeanour so adjusted, acclimatised, despite what the boy interpreted as their unfavourable circumstances; never frustrated, irked, burdened by mistakes. James called him Neph without any sense of meanness or derision. A good friend.

There was another character type that he recognised, one that, over recent decades, may have swelled: those that *acted* like they fit in and *acted* like they enjoyed it. They were those men that aspired towards an image of manliness, not because they wanted to but because they were expected to. They *played* the mythical Aussie battler, fighting against white-collar oppression, or the fantastical Hollywood images, such as the gangster or the heroic-yet-distant American cowboy. They displayed men's habits: drinking, smoking, profanity, misogyny, but gave themselves away with elaborate and colourful sleeve tattoos, white teeth, fashionable haircuts, and expensive designer underwear. Others were less obvious and could fall into other categories of men, but shared the same willingness to appear to embrace isolation from society. More importantly, they embraced isolation from themselves, repressing feelings and thoughts that may contradict their image, or may make it more difficult for them to maintain their image. They were the real martyrs in that they gave themselves up completely at the mine by becoming flat, two-dimensional characters, leaving their third dimensions at home—the dimension that their family loved and cherished. The flesh that lay beneath the tattooed skin. Even more disparate if they had kids. They had men's responsibilities: providing for their families; sacrificing time with their families *for* their families. Which meant coming home from work, not back to see their little ones, running into their arms, but to the empty donga. And children grow up quickly, minds and bodies maturing too fast; easy to miss those unrepeatable milestones—first steps, first words, and father's days, and taking the training wheels off, and awards ceremonies, and performances—missing the *becoming* of their children, when they are away two thirds of their lifetime. They would need to make peace with this, bury it deep, and convince themselves that the secondary moments and everything between the firsts was just as important. Try and forget that that part of the life even exists. It was a single man's game they said whenever they stepped outside of themselves and the situation to think about it. But there were very few single men; fewer that didn't have a kid by some previous, failed relationship.

Neph, who was single and didn't have kids, fit into this category too, of not fitting in. Except that everyone saw him for who he really was—he didn't fit in and didn't enjoy it, and didn't hide it, even if with each swing it was becoming the most homely place for him. There was no façade, or at least he made a poor show of it. His sincerity ran deep, heart-on-sleeve-type stuff, but without the passion or fervour or tangible direction that goes with it. This was his authentic character: his sincere, joyful, emotional, better self. But it was not for here at the mine. And it was not for home either, his authentic character haunted by the spectre of the mine—the spectre of flying back—which could at any moment strangle the life out of who he longed to be.

He saw these character types and their stories, playing out like a Greek tragedy, predetermined from the start; he saw them clearly, with strong outlines, and detailed. And he feared that, by small increments, he would come to assimilate, embrace this life, a stereotype in the camp society. Above all he feared living a vague, self-perpetuating narrative, guided by an arrow that was no longer pointing towards the target at which it was first fired; pointing away from the end that so many had initially envisioned when they boarded their first flight to the desert.

He had always been guilty of plagiarising the lives of others. Absorbing biases and prejudices, taking on his family's characteristics and their past by proxy; the town he lived in, the people he knew, *their* likes and dislikes, all came to influence and oftentimes unconsciously dictate how he lead his life, his world views, ideologies, and hobbies. And he defended them blindly, with prejudice, and often hypocritically, as if the town in which he grew up and the interests he pursued were obviously superior to all other towns and all other possible interests. And, so, the boy was Catholic because his father was Catholic. He played squash because his father played squash. He supported the blue and white of the East Freo Sharks because his father supported the blue and white of the East Freo Sharks—wore Ron Alexander's number on his long-sleeve guernsey as a kid, even if he didn't really have much of a clue as to who 'Big Ron' was. More importantly, he was too empathetic and too honest because his mother was too empathetic and too honest. As he grew older he adapted his prejudices just to be accepted and liked—to be heard even if it was the voice of another.

But, now, he would decide on his own, more definitive story. One with a decisive ending: he would buy a house, pay it off, and get out; he would cross the great Australian Dream off his list. He came to this decision around three months in, when he bought his car outright, paying cash: a 1985 Toyota Forerunner, which he loved like no other object in his life. Not the newest or most expensive car, but it was a four-wheel drive and he could go anywhere he wanted. From there, the next goal was owning a house, which meant a longer-term commitment, seeing beyond the next swing. This, he assumed, is what men do, an old-fashioned nuclear family sensibility with no real foundation to it other than it seemed the logical progression that comes with wanting to establish a comfortable future, with a family, a dog, a neat suburban life. Someone else's middle-class story, to be sure, but he was content to also make it his. It was his fundamental project, which is to say it would be the fundamental way in which he would comport himself towards the life he had chosen. Not just a house, but a way of being and becoming, a shadowy image of himself in an equally shadowy future, unable to make himself out, as yet unrecognisable.

At about the same time, he passed up his deferred university placement. It seemed fate and a steady income had decided that he would not be a civil engineer.

Three months and Boof's arrival
October 1996

Just as he was when he met Peter for the first time at the mine, Neph was amazed when Boof, his cousin, finally arrived. Finally someone he knew and who knew him. Boof had flown in when Neph was starting day shift and they met in the mess that night, Boof looking comfortable, sitting with Peter who had also flown in especially. It took all his strength to stop himself from running up to Boof and embracing him, holding on tight as if Boof were a lifebuoy ring tossed to those who are drowning.

Even though their mothers were sisters, they didn't look like family, bearing little resemblance to each other in appearance or temperament, attributable to their different paternal lineage. Boof was confident, funny, interesting, and, having finally grown into his head, was well built, and good-looking. He had sandy blonde hair, blue eyes, and long eyelashes. Girls loved him. Not quite a troublemaker, but capable of petty insubordination, a mediocre delinquent. Cheeky and confident and subtly precocious. In contrast, Neph had a Woody Allen-style neuroticism about him, was skinny, with a big, bent nose that wouldn't be denied its place.

Similar in other ways. Like a faint mono-brow threatening to reveal the Neanderthal that lies within each boy and man. And just as Neph had been in his first weeks, Boof was lazy and privileged. But being Pete's stepson afforded him greater leniency than Neph. Also because, where Neph's laziness was coupled with a miserable attitude that earned derision from his driller, Boof's laziness was coupled with a demeanour that had found a perfect balance between carefree indifference and entitled arrogance, which was both endearing and enigmatic, and thus excusable.

Boof didn't struggle with camp life. He had been at boarding school for his high school years and was thus accustomed to being away from home. And he already knew some of the drillers there—Frank, Bob, both of whom had lived in Norseman—and some others that were mates of Peter, who was looking increasingly like a Godfatherly mob boss, hiring his friends and family for his goons, Neph, of course, being one of them.

But Boof did struggle with the heavy lifting. He had gone straight onto the bigger LM75 rig with the heavier rods, which had been set up across the decline from the Onram. Neph had always thought Boof to be unnaturally strong for his age, but when Boof had a 300-metre rod pull in his first week, Neph could see that he was flagging before he had even reached the halfway mark, arms trembling, clumsy in his movements on the platform, sweating heavy through his overalls, and an unfamiliar look of seriousness that told that he wasn't comfortable. Boof was on his own up there—the rod pull was the job for one offsider, each twenty-three kilogram rod lifted by one person, regardless of whether the offsider weighed 65kg, a welterweight, or 130kg, a super heavyweight, like he guessed Horse weighed. They could take turns, the driller and the offsider—100m/700-odd kilograms each—but could not share the weight of the individual rod. And only if the driller felt like it.

When he saw the difficulty that Boof was having, Neph

A Boy Miner

couldn't help but feel better for his own struggles with the lifting. At the same time, it redoubled his concerns of rod pulling on the LM75, which he was sure to be assigned to soon.

Boof's arrival galvanised the boy. Suddenly he was more confident, spoke more, branched out, could be himself more, and he became more sociable. More sociable although the two boys stuck to themselves, Neph no longer the only kid at the boring adults' party. They kicked the football under the spotlights of the green oval, the yellow Sherrin occasionally disappearing beyond the scope of the lights into the dark of the scrub. They went to the gym, the boy stronger than he had ever been, bench-pressing over half his weight, but still well under Boof's PB.

On a Saturday night after a day shift, Bob invited them both to watch cricket in his room. It was now December, summer, the season just starting. Bob in his chair, Neph and Boof sitting on Bob's bed, backs against the thin wall, reminding him of his first night when his neighbour invited two mates back to his donga for their shift change. The small donga looking far smaller with company. Other than Boof's, Bob's was the only other room he had seen the interior of. There were nude centrefolds tacked to every wall, a stack of 'stick books' from which the centrefolds had been pulled, but also on top of his little bar-fridge Bob had a book, Wilbur Smith, *The Seventh Scroll*, a romance-adventure novel set in present-day Egypt. Reading to escape, even if it was from one desert to another. It seemed contrary to what he knew of Bob, from the centrefolds, his drinking and smoking, his 'harden up fuck ya' ethos printed large on his t-shirts; but it also contradicted what he understood as the common belief that literature was a subject for girls: girls do English, boys do science. Not that Neph was all that great at science but he had as good as failed English at high school. And yet Bob was a man and Bob read books.

'I'm almost done with it if you want to borrow it,' Bob said, seeing the boy eyeing it.

He would, given permission to borrow a book, but more importantly to engage in literature. First some Wilbur Smith, and then, upon another recommendation from Bluelight, another man from the cross shift, some Irvine Welsh, before, finally, Orwell's *1984* which seemed to awaken an intellectualism that he had been craving. Other books would come, classics, modern classics, the postmodern, as would a more critical and discerning mind.

They drank enthusiastically as they watched the cricket, the empty cans stacked like tenpins on the floor, having quickly filled Bob's little bin. They had work the next day, but when the game finished and Bob kicked them out to go to bed, Boof and Neph headed to the wet mess, Neph for the first time outside of shift-change. There they had more beer, played pinball, the anxiety of the working day replaced with the dread of the unruly steel ball falling between the flippers. And they also shared in some laughs that belonged just to them. They drank to closing before wandering into the dark to their respective rooms.

Neph never slept so soundly at the camp, a dreamless sleep, his unconscious blissfully unconscious, utterly dead to his anxieties, right up until a rude banging on his door and Lee shouting, 'Neph, you in there?' It was 520am. He shot up, yelled an incomprehensible response, and launched out of bed, narrowly avoiding stepping in a neat pile of vomit that had somehow slunk its way into his room overnight. It was hard to tell if he had done it when he first entered his room from the wet mess or simply leaned over from his bed in the middle of the night. Possibly the alarm had sounded and during the action of punching it out he had casually opened his mouth, expelled, and immediately dropped back into the black abyss of drunken sleep.

There was not much he could do in the way of a clean-up, so he grabbed his gear (a nod to his preparedness) and staggered to the buses, happy to skip breakfast because of the pounding in his head and the poison that was still sloshing around in his stomach; this despite the evidence of him emptying his guts during the night. When he got to the buses he saw that both were full, the men waiting, but the driver's seat in one of them was empty. In his affected state, he assumed that, as some sort of penance for being last to the bus, he was the designated driver of the twenty-seater minibus. So he jumped in the driver's seat, started the bus, eventually figured how to close the bi-folding passenger door, and, unlicensed, drove them very slowly to the mine, the sky half-lit in the summer morning. Every member of the crew remained silent, even seemed to revel in the knowledge that the actual bus driver was still finishing his breakfast, and was now in need of a lift himself.

Boof confessed later that he had mistakenly slept in someone else's room for the night. The room owner was on break, or was on the opposite shift and the door was left unlocked. They all look the same, the dongas, from the outside anyway. Only his early morning need for a piss alerted him to waking in the stranger's bed and got him up in time. And whilst Neph was being woken up by Lee, before drunk-driving the crew to the mine, Boof was cosied up in a corner of the bus, snatching a few more sobering nods.

Neither of them were of any use that day, barely able to lift their heads let alone their arms for rod pulls; for the rest of the time they lay in dusty corners of the drill site like rag-bags. Boof spewed most of the day, making himself sick to rid his gut-demons. Under instruction, having disclosed his misfortune, Neph borrowed one of the bosses' utes at crib time to return to camp and clean up his room before the 'not-my-job' cleaners found his mess, alerted the camp manager, and got him kicked off site. He did and when he had finished, he got his lunch from the mess. As he ate he vowed to keep his drinking binges to shift changes and his breaks only, never again wanting to feel that way at work, or to put his job in jeopardy. He was also thankful that he hadn't made Boof's mistake of waking in someone else's room; indeed, it wouldn't have been Lee banging on his door to wake him but the owner of the room. An ugly scene: someone's been sleeping in their bed; and worse, someone's been spilling their porridge on the carpet.

Mine Hierarchies

If it wasn't evident from the start when he saw Mick the truck driver being toured about the mine by the shift boss, and at the segregated shift change, it became even more obvious over the following months that the mine had several tacitly-understood hierarchies which were casually or strictly adhered to by almost everyone there. One of the clearest and indeed most reasonable divisions existed between the underground crew—which included the Eltin miners and drillers—and the surface crew—which included the geologists, engineers, and other educated types, all of

A Boy Miner

whom worked for GCM—Great Central Miners—the owners of the mine. Despite being from different companies, they all worked at the mine, lived at the camp, and shared the same FIFO roster; and yet there was still a strong sense of class stratification—a literal upstairs/downstairs situation.

Unlike the GCM college boys (and some girls), a miner didn't need to have completed high school or have any other skills, needing only to pass a health check and a drug test, and have a police clearance and a valid driver's licence. They could get their tickets to drive trucks, boggers, and other heavy machinery on site. Even then, there wasn't always a formal test. Essentially, they were well-paid labourers; they worked hard, got filthy from dust and sweat, and gave up their backs for the cause. Mostly they were working class, from generations that had done the same. They wouldn't have a clue about the best private schools and universities, where to summer in Europe. Given other choices, opportunities, they still might shrug their shoulders as if to say 'what is it to me'—other people's business. This is their lot so just get on. Some came from other jobs, skilled in other ways, never having intended on becoming a miner. Such as K-Mart, a goliath of a man who, prior to his mine-change, had been a manager at K-Mart, his namesake; and Bluelight, who gave up on being a cop. Even his uncle Peter was a butcher by trade. The money in mining was good—better than any trade or unskilled position; and if someone knew someone, then it would do for a while or longer.

The geos, engineers, and others were the privileged middle class. Every now and then they came underground, but they spent their time almost exclusively on the surface, and, as was built up in the minds of the miners, dedicated their time to fucking the dog. They worked only during the day, in air-conditioning, sitting at computers playing solitaire, occasionally examining some core, looking at maps, drinking coffee, bludging, and getting paid more for it.

One of the geos didn't help their cause when he fainted during the screening of an OHS video warning of the dangers of eye injuries. It was intentionally shocking, complete with gruesome close-ups of an inch-long nail embedded halfway into some poor bastard's eyeball. Despite spending most of his time getting a tan on the surface, the geo's face went very white, and then he wobbled, before falling forwards, arms still crossed, completely out to it. He came to almost as soon as his face hit the lino. Unharmed, he sheepishly went to get some air. Nothing was said, but it did well to reaffirm the miners' views of the surface dwellers as silver-spooned layabouts.

Neph himself had been feeling increasingly queasy during the video. Half way in, he had broken out in a sweat and was looking to take a seat in one of the few available chairs, just in case he too pitched himself onto the floor. He found one, and not wanting his girlish weakness, unbefitting of a miner, to be discovered, he leaned forward in the chair, feigning the need to get a better view of what was one of the most-interesting and important safety messages he had seen; even if his focus was only on the antenna perched atop the TV. And although he was more than ready to blackout like the fallen geo, he rode it out, not looking away from that antenna for a second, successfully upholding the alpha-male image of the miners—the hard-working desert proletariat.

Ironically, the gruesomeness of the close-ups may have caused him to completely miss the point of the video, as within a few

A Boy Miner

weeks, when hitting the teeth of a drill bit with a rasp to sharpen it up, without his safety glasses, a tiny shard of metal struck his eye and became lodged. It was more uncomfortable than painful, like a grain of sand hidden between his eyeball and the cup that holds it. For days he washed his eye, trying to flush it out without success. By the fourth day he went to the camp nurse, reluctantly because of how he had sustained the injury. On close inspection, it was but a scratch and would heal within a week or so, with no permanent damage. It was a relief but also a significant revelation of something that had eluded him until now: he hadn't worn his safety glasses because none of the miners wore safety glasses, almost as if they were merely a suggestion and not compulsory, especially on night shift when the big bosses weren't around. To do so was almost a show of cowardice: 'safety' was for women and geos and poofs and OHS clowns. There was also an element of risk and danger in shirking Personal Protective Equipment, as if losing an eye or a finger was somehow a necessary sacrifice to becoming a man. A seat belt was a slight on one's driving capabilities.

It was the same when they were waiting for the plane—a misguided bravado when the plane landed and came to a stop some fifty metres away, propeller engines still roaring as it wound down. They would stand there, facing it, arms folded or hands in pockets, without plugs or fingers in their ears to mute the sound, decibel levels over a hundred. Their posture and austere faces were an attempt to look hard, as if to show that they had done their time and had earned their break; that they had stood in line long enough and now it was their turn on the merry-go-round. Or they were a Kiwi rugby team, shoulder to shoulder, about to break into a Haka to intimidate their opposition. Any attempt to stop the damaging noise was a show of physical weakness (which, again, ironically, was precisely the issue as they were partly deaf already and didn't know that it was damaging). Even though it was unpleasant and, as evidenced by the deaf older miners, most likely harmful, Neph imitated them as best he could, keeping his arms folded in his best tough-guy stance. It was easy to conform to the group no matter how injurious. And wanting to belong may have been hazardous, but wanting to belong with the people he spent two thirds of his life with was nevertheless essential.

Yet the scratching of his eye was cause for taking a bold step away from both the boy he was and the man he was trying to impersonate. Having almost gone blind in one eye, and not ready to lose another of his senses, he began to see how ridiculous it really was. He spotted those fringe types that did plug their ears, despite the implications. He also wore his safety glasses, would continue to wear his seat belt, and he would plug his ears against deafness, even if he were disgracing the mining tradition in his feminine safety conscientiousness. Sacrifice was expected of the job, but at least he could choose to sacrifice only for the mine. Doing it at the airstrip was on his own time.

But this need to fit the mould of the miner mattered very little anyway, as he wasn't really a miner. Not as understood by the *miners*, who, in a secondary level of class division, separated themselves from the *drillers*. Although they all went underground, wore the same uniform, and belonged to the same company, the drillers and miners were of different castes, and had little much to do with each other, even if they were both essential parts to the mechanism: without drillers there would be no mining; without mining there would be no point in drilling. The miners outnumbered the drillers, two, maybe three to one; and like any minority, the drillers faced unwarranted prejudices, or worse, were invisible wherever they stood.

He experienced it first hand when Lee asked him to flag down a truck to borrow their radio and contact the shift boss. The power had switched off and drilling had come to a stop. It was Jim 'Bulldog' Honey that stopped for him—a cantankerous former shift boss, in his sixties, slumming it on the trucks until a space opened up on a jumbo. Jim did call the shift boss, told him that there was 'some driller' that needed help. Neph was waiting, listening for the shift boss's response, still holding onto the truck's hand rail, until Jim leaned out of the window, staring at him with the black beady eyes of a magpie hidden deep within the folds of his bulldog face, and stated unequivocally: 'Let go of my truck.' The boy did. And Jim drove away.

The animosity and division between the miners and drillers had several unstated reasons, some more credible than others, which is not to say they were really credible at all. The least was that the drillers were not directly involved with the mining of the mine—the removal of rock. They worked in the *mine* (noun) but the drillers were *drilling* (verb) and not actually *mining* (verb). Like the drillers on the surface, they were merely the preface to the real story: a preamble, the foreplay to the action of the mine, where real things got done. The miners were the FBI taking over an unsolved murder investigation from the plucky but inconsequential small-town cop. No one ever went from mining to drilling; it was always the other way.

The more credible reason for the division was very much related to the first: the drillers never seemed to be *moving* or *progressing* the cause, or at least not in an immediately tangible way like the mining team did: extending drives, making tunnels big enough to drive trucks into, creating mountains of rock. Evidence of the miner's activity was everything and everywhere—the drillers' far less obvious or impressive. Big is beautiful. In contrast, a drill rig could stay in the same place for months, drilling sometimes ten or more holes, each taking from a few days to a week to complete. During that time, the driller would for the most part sit in a beaten-up office chair, at his control panel, and his offsider would likely be seated next to him on a lesser chair (or milk crate) of his own, watching the rods bore into the wall, up to half an hour at a time, waiting for the end of the run. From a distance, the driller and his offsider looked as if engrossed in some kind of staring contest, the loser being the first to look away from the hole. Sometimes the driller and his offsider were caught playing night shift 'noddy'—a game of solitaire fought between the player and the need for sleep. It began when their head slowly dropped forward, eyes half closed, until their chin almost came to rest on their chest, waking them just enough to lift their heavy head. An exercise in futility, as, like a vertical pendulum, their head would pause for an imperceptible moment, before swinging the other way, back towards the ground. The boy played often, losing to himself each time. Occasionally, in a strange synchronicity, the driller and offsider would sometimes nod along together, as if engaged in a most-agreeable conversation with the rig in front of them. Stumbling upon the driller and offsider passed out with the rods still spinning was like boarding a ghost ship, the murdered helmsman splayed over the wheel of the ship, his captain, laid out beside him on the deck, pooled in blood, clutching a blinded telescope.

For these reasons and others, each group—drillers and miners—stuck to their own, demarcating themselves, with only the most senior and experienced drillers being accepted amongst the upper end of the working mining class. He had his place, and he stuck to it and his own kind. In a lonely place like a mining camp, acceptance was a cherished fortune, and he needed to find it wherever possible.

Camp societies

The class divisions of the mine site and the underground were clearly defined by the individual's job title and were the source of mostly unfounded animosity. Yet, within the camp itself, there were no such distinct hierarchies or social divisions. Neph did live in the lowly-regarded Bronx area of the camp, the implication being that the newcomers were to be marginalised, sequestered to the ghettos, away and out of sight of the chosen ones. But it didn't mean all that much—there were no escalated crime rates, or heavier traffic, intrusions from industry, urban pollution, or lack of quality services. No one was privileged with river or seaside views. The Bronx was further from the mess, but it was also further from the wet mess and the loud and yobbish behaviour that it sometimes brought.

The camp was a commune, individuals thrown together regardless of their job at the mine. As weird and isolated as any Jonestown, the Kool-Aid at the ready. They woke together, ate together, drove to work together, worked together, and flew in and out together. Even if they brought their trivial divisions back from the mine, there was no segregation; no distance except the thin wall between their rooms.

There were no real possessions at the camp site either. No objects to be fetishized—a socialist paradise, where a man could be measured by who he was, not what he owned. Or it was the stuff of dystopian fiction, where freedom and identity are surrendered to a faceless bureaucracy—uniformed drones for Big Brother.

The dongas were humble and sparse, furnished like a monk's residence, or a prison cell, or a poor man's attempt at minimalism. Besides Bob's and Boof's, Neph caught glimpses of the insides of other dongas: photos of families, cars, or centrefolds, blue-tacked to the wall. Mismatched linen. Odd pieces of stationery. Pulpy, travel-worn, dog-eared books, shoved into bags, read and discarded or passed on. Letters from home. A single pair of shoes. A pile of dirty clothes for washing; and washing powder.

Some of the miners had more extravagant items in their room—a slightly larger TV, or more diverse collection of dirty magazines—but they were hardly impressive. Filling a room needed to be done piecemeal because of the size and weight restrictions of the plane. No one had a shed, or workshop, or man cave to retreat to, no pool room to show off trophies or mementos. There were no cars, no gadgets or gizmos. For this reason, almost none locked their doors, the irony not lost on him as he remembered his terrible first night and his misplaced key. He had his Sony Walkman CD player and some CDs. None worth stealing though as most there were listening to Country and Western, Barnesey or Farnsey, not grunge and death metal.

A Boy Miner

The same could be said of their possessions at home, all of which meant very little at the camp. A pair of brand new jet-skis was of no value in the middle of a desert. It didn't impress if someone lived on the beach, had views of the city, or a pool out the back. What was best about home was that it wasn't the camp; that it had his friends and family, his bed, his room, his space, and the freedom of movement beyond the camp's confines. All the rest was window dressing.

Just as relationships were romanticised in their absence, so was their home life. Everything that hinted at their existence away from the camp could easily have been pure fiction—fantasies spun by seasoned storytellers. Houses were bigger, friends were friendlier, lives enviable. He was often the audience for many of these stories—he was a good listener in that he didn't much talk back or have stories of his own. Even some of the miners spoke to him, finally accepting him as a regular, seeing him as a captive audience: 'Oh, you're still here? Well let me tell you something...'

One of the older miners, twice-divorced, was most happy to regale to anyone naïve enough to stand still and listen for a few minutes about how every two or three years he would buy a brand-spanking, high-powered, top-of-the-wozza, flared and spoiled Holden Commodore. Only a sixteen-year-old boy on his L-plates would be impressed by such boasting. It may have been boasting but it may have also been bluffing: the boy never *saw* the swathe of brand-new Commodores—just talk for all he knew, insecure puffery. Just as he never saw the houses, boats, or any of the luxuries that suggested a wealthier, excessive lifestyle. It could have all been fantasy, made up to impress. The most important thing was to keep home and the camp separate, all the better to maintain the fiction.

Some tried hard to realise the fantasy of living an upper-middle-class lifestyle, the upwardly mobile, hitherto unattainable; mining money gained them entry into highish society or enabled them to afford the same indulgences, proving that they were as successful as any executive businessman, any university graduate, or entrepreneur.

Paul, a truck driver, knew this better than most. He was older than Neph by almost ten years, but they were the same in that they were both of average height, scrawny. And like Neph, he lived in Mandurah, itself trying to imitate a more sophisticated and refined lifestyle, having ripped up much of the central farming land and frantically excavated innumerable canals, as if looking for its very own Tutankhamun. Paul lived on the canals, never really affording it, faking a tenuous residence amongst many who had bought theirs merely for a holiday home.

He looked old for his age, like he had lost a lot of weight fast; and he was jittery, most likely on the gear—speed or similar. He supposed this after seeing Paul on the minibus at 520am on a day shift, ready to go to the mine site, wildly air-drumming and tapping his legs to Savage Garden's 'I Want You' (May 1996) being played on the radio, continuing his drumming well after the song had ended, all the way through the back announcements and the 530am news report. Maybe it wasn't drugs, maybe it was buckets of Nescafe Blend 43, but it seemed inconceivable that at that time in the morning anyone could be anything other than glue-eyed and clumsy as a newborn.

When Neph and Boof bumped into Paul at the shops on their break, it was clear that he had aspirations beyond those of the typical working class. He was wearing tired blue jeans, thongs, and an Eltin-logoed polo shirt—the kind they gave when they reached lost time injury free milestones. He could have stepped out of the minibus at camp, about to head to the mess. They started to chat in the middle of one of the malls at the Mandurah Forum, one of their routine destinations. Before either of them had even attempted a greeting, before even acknowledging the recognition of each other, Paul pulled a wad of cash from his jeans pocket and proceeded to dextrously fan out a few thousand dollars in front of their eyes, as if he were a street magician about to ask them to pick a card, all the while, in a poor show of conspicuousness, his wild unblinking eyes darting all around, scanning to see who was watching, wanting them to see, and not wanting them to see.

'Just won this on the horses. Not bad, eh?' he said, his eyes now fixed on them, imploring eyes, bruised all around for what looked like a lack of sleep.

Of course the two boys agreed, their faces lighting up from the cash, having never seen so much in one hit. Boof particularly, having also enjoyed an occasional punt on whatever could be punted on. He understood completely.

'I'm buying a Porsche,' Paul bragged, his big jumble of teeth on show, as he reluctantly put the cash away, still eyeing them for their reactions, which were far more important than the car itself. It wasn't new, fifteen years old or thereabouts, but it was going to cost about twenty thousand dollars, which the amount of cash he held in front of them would be put towards. Cheaper than a new Commodore, but classier, chicer, and would be appreciated by those who know.

In the curvaceous shape of a luxury (second-hand) sports

car, Paul was founding his increased sense of social status. It was a symbol of his entry into a world longed for by those whose mediocre circumstances would never have allowed such movement up the social strata. In place of old-money inheritance, education, privilege, or connections, Paul's only resort was to put his faith in chance—a big win—which, like a lotto win, was always the newest of money. Neph understood this completely. New or old money, a Porsche signified that he was in the game. He could say that he had a Porsche, just like any wanker dentist or GP or lawyer would. A class-struggle chip on his shoulder. Hard to tell if he was sticking it to the man, taking them down a peg, or wanting to *be* the man and raise himself up one or two.

The other thing about a Porsche was that he could drive it around all break, up and down the coast from beach carpark to beach carpark and back again. And to the Forum, back and forth across the bridges, to the Ravenswood Hotel on the weekend. Maybe even a trip up to the city. And everyone could see his wealth—a mobile proclamation of the self-made man. And although he could have been sleeping in it at night for all they knew, Paul was winning, and seemingly ahead of most of the pack.

But Paul wasn't to know that the dice were loaded; he didn't know that the world was cannily engineered to maintain the social status quo, keeping people like him in the place that he should be, had been, and always will be. This is to say that he didn't know that the dream would be short-lived, as in less than a month he crashed his Porsche. Didn't write it off completely, but it was cheaper to wreck it than fix it. Ever the gambler, he hadn't taken the chance on insuring it either and the money he had so proudly displayed like a peacock's tail was gone.

A Boy Miner

When he heard, Neph felt sick with proxy heart pains at the thought of such a setback, like someone close to him had died unexpectedly—had died too young. It would take at least another year at the mine to recoup a loss that big. Paul, though, took it in on his gaunting chin; it was the natural course of things: of winning some and losing some, and where progress is measured only by keeping a seat at the table. Even if he were fighting a system that is temperate, disinterested, faceless, and global. Even if he were waging against a system that plays a short-odds, long-term game; a system that has existed long before him and will exist long after him. His big win, his Porsche, was evidence that it was carnivalesque, a moment for reversed fortunes, but only temporarily, before order is restored. His smile was genuine and excited—this is what life is about, this was everything. Which meant he would be fated like many career miners, living hand-to-mouth, telling fantastic stories, animated by quick eyes and talk, but nothing of real value to show for it, be it family or objects, imagined or otherwise.

Six Months and a Merry Bronzewing Christmas
December 1996

The three-week turnarounds began to add up, and Christmas was soon approaching. Having started in July, he didn't have much leave accrued, and even if he did ask to have Christmas off he would likely be refused. Those that came before him had priority and without holidays he had only a one-in-three chance that Christmas would coincide with his break. These were the same odds for any other meaningful events—Easter, birthdays, anniversaries, concerts, the AFL Grand Final, the Boxing Day Test. To take one day off necessarily meant taking a whole week off. A third of the mine would be lucky to have Christmas at home, even if, by the look of their faces, no-one seemed to have had any real luck their whole lives. He would be home for New Year's Eve, which was a consolation.

The mine put on a feast, breakfast and dinner, including trays of seafood, fish, prawns, and even baby octopus, which he had never tried before. Many got crook guts, the food being too rich. He got crook guts when he reheated the octopus in the microwave for crib that night, rendering them rubbery and dubious.

He went the back way to avoid the wet mess the morning of Christmas. Lee and Dave and the rest of the drilling crew invited him to go, with drinks being shouted by the company. And it was hot and a beer would have tasted sweet. And even though Boof was going, it felt as if celebrating with strangers would make him realise what he was missing at home. Instead, he snuck away after breakfast, straight to bed, and hopefully to sleep through the day and work the night through to Boxing Day, as if it had never happened.

In his feeling sorry for himself, he didn't even think of all the dads there. He knew Dave had young kids. Didn't think of how they might be feeling, missing their kids, missing watching them open their presents, the surprises, expectations. Helping with the Lego. Assembling Barbie's dreamhouse. Adjusting the seat of a new bike. Wish Dad was here. Maybe next Christmas. A phone call would have to do, longer lines than any other day. Kids reluctant to talk, dragged from their gifts to talk to someone who seemed to care more about work than being with them at Christmas. He still seemed closer to those kids at home—still a boy—than the dads—the men—at the mine.

His mum had sent through a care package; sent it through with Frank who had temporarily changed to a different roster. It came on Christmas Eve when Frank flew in, Frank who had three young kids at home. Frank told him that it was in his room and that the door was unlocked. Neph had asked for one thing—a book, Anne Rice. And when he entered Frank's room he assumed it would be easy to find, given that it wasn't too small and there were not many hiding spaces in the straightforward donga. But it wasn't easy to find, and he started to search a little more frantically and then in a panic as if this care package—a pulpy vampire novel—were the most crucial object ever given him. Like it was a kidney transplant, or the phone number of a girl he liked. He was tearing Frank's place apart, ransacking like a clumsy thief, knocking over empty bottles, his laundry powder, messing up the disorder of Frank's desk. Eventually, all but defeated, he looked in the only place left unravaged: Frank's fridge. There it sat, wrapped in a plastic bag, the book he had asked for and some chocolate bars, which explained why it was in the fridge—exactly where a kidney for transplant should be. A wave of calm and relief coursed through him, and he tidied the room as best he could, except for a little pile of the spilled laundry powder, impossible to pick up with his fingers alone.

He blamed Christmas for his hysteria. The goodwill and the expectations and the tenderness of family were impossible for him there. Knowing it was going on everywhere except there. The best thing for him was for the goings on of the world—regardless of whether they were celebrations or commiserations—to be kept from him. He would rather live by his roster only, ahistorically, his weeks at the mine as good as a void in time with no meaning or importance other than the passing of a shift. If Christmas or birthdays happen to fall on his break, then he would enjoy them as happy coincidences—luck would be on his side; if not, if the swings didn't go his way, then wipe their existence from his memory, and remove all calendars. Let him get on with it, earn his money, unhindered and unburdened by the plenitude of life outside.

○

Christmas passed and he flew home for New Year's Eve. More importantly, he met a pretty girl on New Year's Eve, Emma, with beautiful big eyes and long dark hair, and a mischievous vampish smile. They met at a mutual friend's parents' party, in a way reminiscent of a less romantic version of the John Hughes film, *Sixteen Candles*. He was Molly Ringwald. He had been drinking since landing mid-afternoon and was loud and uncensored. *Sixteen Stubbies*. For this, he was rightly kicked out of the party by the host's parents. Like a naughty child punished with a time-out. It wasn't even 10pm and he didn't want to go home until the midnight countdown, so he set himself to sobering up outside on the curb. She had come to console him. They spoke for a bit in hushed tones. Nothing deep and meaningful; instead, together, they constructed an apology that would allow him back in. It succeeded. At midnight they kissed.

He had only the week to establish a relationship between them before flying away for two weeks. So they got to know each other by phone, where they spoke to each other's disembodied voice, unable to touch or kiss or hold each other. They could not see each other, absorb their facial features, their bodies, skin.

He had no photos—Emma's face was a collage of partial angles, glimpses, vague memories, taken from what had been only fleeting experiences together from those last few days of his break. An identikit image of a fleeing shoplifter.

On the phone, he realised very quickly that they were both shy, and both inexperienced in relationships. Strangers forced to dance steps that neither of them knew. She would also come to realise very quickly that his personality on break was far different from when he was away. At home he had been funny and full of stories; he did things, shouted drinks, made himself the centre of attention, went out, smiled, laughed. He flew out, leaving her with this impression. But it was incomplete. When he phoned her from camp, he was silent and had nothing much to tell. Each day was the same as the last, their phone conversations a repeated series of insipid questions:

'What did you do today?'

'Drilled some core.'

'Anything exciting happen?'

'Almost drove everyone into the wall whilst checking the odometer reading. What about you?'

'Not much, went to work.'

Of course, he could give her a more detailed rundown of his day:

> 4.30am: woken up by horrible alarm. Shovelled sleep out of eyes
>
> 5.00am: ate breakfast: eggs, bacon, patented Coco Pops/Nutrigrain combination
>
> 5.20am: in bus for work
>
> 6.00am: headed down hole (almost killed everyone)

6.30am: first run 2.4m
7.00am: 1.4m
7.15am: 0.5m
7.40am: 3.0m (yay!)
Etc.
12.30pm: ate lunch in underground crib hut
1.00pm: recommenced drilling
1.15pm: 1.5m
Etc.
5.45pm: exit hole
6.00pm: showered (hiding body)
6.30pm: ate epicurean mixed bag
6.45pm: put overalls et al. in washing machine
6.50pm: waited in line to call you
7.15pm: called you, explained day in vivid detail
7.35pm: put overalls et al. in dryer
8.30pm: removed overalls et al. from dryer
8.45pm: went to bed
9.45pm: fell asleep

He didn't tell her this. Instead, in those few moments, with carefully selected words, he would need to tell her who he was. His likes or dislikes, which were often exaggerated: likes morphed into loves; dislikes into hates. They both did this, along with some exaggerated laughing, conscientious listening. More than this, they needed to identify the extraordinary moments of themselves, romanticise themselves, which was to isolate specific parts from the whole of themselves, to show that they were interesting enough to create the desire to keep a relationship going—for her to put her life on hold for two weeks at a time. But he wasn't interesting, and maybe at that time, or because of him, she wasn't either.

They said more in the letters they wrote each other, where time and imagination allowed them the chance to voice what they properly felt. The heightened emotions of teenagers. Polarised intensities. True love. Crushes. Between shifts, in his room, he would be hunched over the little school desk writing letters, his headphones on, removed completely from his situation. Like some eccentric, penning the minutiae of his hapless life. There was little in the way of simple everyday speech in what he wrote—it was emotional, unmasked. He wrote angst-ridden poetry, getting his emotions out of him, Jackson Pollock-like, like spitting poison sucked out of a snakebite, but lacking nuance or subtlety, with its forced rhymes and clichés, enjambments to nowhere, alliteration and assonance all awry. Even so, between the emotional adolescent convulsions, there was something much sweeter and earnest in the letters—the earnest conversation he could have with her as long as she wasn't sitting in front of him, meeting his eyes, there to question him, make him self-conscious. He read her letters when he flew back to the mine, over and over, like a desert-island castaway would a message from a bottle. But the letters were also fictions. They each reread them, holding on to the lifeless ink-dry words, as a vivid eternal present, like a tiny portrait in a heart-shaped locket. So different when he came home, bringing with him the reality of the FIFO world: through triviality, through drink, tainting moments, time proceeding, through happy-tipsy, melancholy-drunk, and indifferent-passing out.

Absence made the heart grow fonder, but it had also grown jealous and paranoid and fragile, which was common in such isolation. He promised to call at a prearranged day and time, which fell within the hour he had between eating dinner and trying to get to sleep. She promised to be at home on that designated day and time. He would be waiting for the phone to free up. And he hoped she would be waiting by her phone, looking forward to his call. And as each minute passed beyond the nominated time, eavesdropping to hear conversations coming to a close—which was easy to do, open as the booths were to allow for the heat and the smokers—shuffling his feet, eyeing would-be queue-jumpers, he imagined only that she would be growing impatient, flicking through an old address book, or tidying up the kitchen, listening for the trill of the phone, but eventually giving it up to go out; or off to bed, the phone off the hook, now too late to call.

He imagined that she was thinking of other things, wanting other things; that she would be heading out with her friends to do the things that eighteen-year-old girls should be doing. That she was meeting guys who were *present*, their smiling mouths, kissable lips, and kind eyes in front of her, their laughter real and strong, unmediated, instead of tempered and immaterial through a phone line. In the queue, he had too much time to think on these things, succumbing to the meanderings of a tepid self-esteem.

Other times he got to the phone on time only to find she wasn't home, having waited and rehearsed what he would say. Letting the phone ring out two, three times. He could try again, but he would need to relinquish his place in the queue, and step away from the phone booth, conceding awkwardly to the next in line, to again hide in plain sight. Like everyone at home, she wasn't to know what each of them went through to make their calls. No one at home had much of an idea of anything they were doing.

With each subsequent break they should have been growing

closer, more intimate, moulding their being around each other's; instead, they became further estranged, drifting away, such that by the third time he was home, their nascent relationship had run its course, bringing their short story to an end. Maybe it was better that way. Easy to feel when living this way. Too hard to maintain a relationship; even harder to properly start one.

The LM75

He finally got his chance on the LM75. One of the drillers had moved on, his offsider promoted. Along the way Lee and Dave had shifted rosters, as did Horse and Stuart. Frank and Bob stayed. Robbo was brought in to work on the Onram, Boof his offsider. And within the shuffle, Neph suddenly found himself on one of the big rigs, to work on it but to learn it too. He was sorry to see Lee and Dave go, Lee especially since they had made a good team. And sorry to leave the familiarity of offsiding the Onram.

The anxiety toward the LM75 was a combination of fears and a lack of choice. There was peer pressure, where everybody else was doing it so he should be able to do it too. It was a line that was drawn, where he was still the skinny kid, capable on the Onram, but not fit to be a called a 'real' driller's offsider unless he could work the LM75. If not, he would instead be a driller's offsider with an asterisk, a caveat, suggesting that he could only work on certain size drills. He was fearful of physically 'hitting the wall' before he had even lifted the first rod. It was the fear of being trapped on the platform next to the drill. It reminded him of when he rode a big rollercoaster for the first time, locked in the carriage as it made its slow ascent for the initial big drop, having to face his fear surrounded by strangers, without options, without choice. This was his test.

But the anxiety was for nothing as he found is body was now more adept than he could have expected and he handled the rods and the workload. Just as he had handled the rollercoaster; loved it so much he rode it another five times in a row. It was all technique with the heavier rods: finding pivot points, fulcrums, using momentum. Just as it was for the Onram, the weight was on the wrists and forearms, as was the action of unscrewing or screwing the thread out of or into the other rod. But heavier and more cumbersome, and his back, shoulders, and stomach muscles were strained as never before. He didn't have much of an excuse for not being capable as he had seen Frank the Smurf cope well enough; Frank would lever the heavy rods, holding them in the crook of his arm, and throw them over, an ungraceful struggle, but nevertheless getting it done. Just as he had seen with Dave the fitter when he first began on the Onram, Frank demonstrating the wisdom of age as opposed to the brutal showiness of youth.

His driller was John A, who had come over from another shift. Not the worst driller to offside—decent enough bloke—though infamously lazy, not one to leave his control panel unless absolutely necessary. He had a touch of the statesman about him. He was very well groomed, with thick lush dark hair and an impeccably manicured beard, and his overalls were mostly unblemished. He looked as if he would be more at home in a suit and tie, polished Italian shoes, cufflinks, gold. Neph couldn't imagine he had ever offsided.

A Boy Miner

If on the off chance John was needed to attend to problems with the rig or assist Neph, he would reluctantly grab at things—core, the stuffing box, drill bits—with only his forefinger and thumb, like he was picking up a cooked sausage from a still-lit barbecue. He did this also with the levers, as if they were foreign each time he grabbed them, looking at them as opposed to intuitively knowing them, having to take his eyes off the rods each time to find them. He wasn't keen to help with the rod pulls either. And he didn't like to get wet, which sometimes happened when drilling up-holes. Not that anyone wanted to get wet, their overalls chafing on sweat rash and jock itch, and the wet socks in their boots becoming ripe for tinea, trench foot, and other foot-related maladies. But John seemed to dislike it especially, as much as a wicked witch trembles at the approach of a monsoon. The boy was on his own when he took the backend rod off the rod string to let the thousands of litres of water drain out, like the opening of a sidewalk fire hydrant. And like happy kids playing in the heavy gush on a summer's day, he would be soaked, each run, ten or more times in a shift. Overalls and jocks and socks and boots.

John was safe at the control panel, yet on occasion he was needed to help release the sometimes-stubborn hose from the stuffing box to let the water drain. Avoiding the drenching meant crafting a technique for redirecting the water, as powerful as a fire hose attached to the hydrant, after disconnecting the high-pressure fitting. But there was a miscommunication of the method, which involved the boy, the torque created by a twelve-inch set of stilsons, John A's fingers, and two hard places. John A screamed like Neph had never heard a man scream before, and snatched the stilsons off the boy, very nearly belting him across his pimply face with them, his eyes a psychotic glaze. Instead, he threw them out into the drive, the boy collecting them later when the dust had settled. The boy not entirely remorseful.

John A solved the problem of the water very simply and cleverly by moving the control panel a few steps further away from the rig—not too far that he couldn't see the turning of the rods and the water return, but far enough so that it would be too long a walk to come assist his offsider, and also too far for the spray to reach.

Neph was left by himself on the platform to take a bath each run, which he accepted as his lot as an offsider, knowing that each soaking, taken unquestionably and dutifully, brought him another step closer to the levers.

A picnic
April 1997

It was autumn and the weather was becoming milder, the bright light of the days was growing shorter such that the heat was no longer completely unbearable. There had also been some rain that had done well to settle the dust. Conditions just right for a shift-change road trip and a picnic in the bush. The six of them, Neph, Boof, Frank, Bob, Robbo, and John A, borrowed two utes, loaded up some bins with ice, VB and EB, found a piece of metal for a hotplate, requested a tray of sausages and bread from the mess, and headed out bush, directed only by an approximation from the sun—west maybe, the general direction of home.

Proper bush, some twenty kilometres from camp, without any obvious sign of human life, not a red-gravel road, not even a fence, which seemed the most rudimentary sign of the civilisation he had known. For the ten months or more that he had been there, he had never considered the possibility of venturing beyond the confines of the camp or the mine site. He had no means, hobbled as they were until the plane returned. And there seemed no place to go—nowhere except into the solitude of the outback. Off map, off grid. Try your luck.

It was an hour of aimless, wandering driving, weaving in and out of scrub, climbing over rocks, pushing the vehicle's capabilities, until they found the nothingness they were after. The camp and mine were in the middle of nothingness, but now they had found the untouched nothingness—untouched country as far they could tell. There is nothing more tainting than the infrastructure of a mine. Nothing more blighting. But some way, over the long horizon, they were far enough beyond and could experience the outback authentically and better know the bush's romance.

They found trees for shade, rocks to sit on, firewood, and set up the hotplate. Cooked the sausages until they were brown and black, a stick for tongs. A few sliced onions and tomato sauce to add some culture. Ate it all and sat in the shade, filled bellies, with good momentum in their drinking. Doing nothing except swatting away the little bush flies, catch and release, or rolling them between fingers, dropping the silent, tiny bundle of wings, eyes, and legs to the dirt beneath them.

Free to wonder. Marvelled at the ancientness and the quiet. The beer had made the boy ponderous and emotional, silent. Listening as he liked to do, wondering where other's thoughts came from. Hearing the men talk, Frank and Bob the most conversive, learning some important things and others not. They forgot the mine and, unpretentious, entertained the possibility that maybe not even the first peoples of Australia had trod this fraction of Earth.

'Look at those rocks. They're just sittin' there,' Robbo breaking the silence, pointing at nearby balancing rocks, some the size of cars, stacked as if by a giant.

'Yeah, they're just sittin' there,' echoed Frank, half-mockingly, as if Robbo's observation was too 'philosophical.' He needed to be hung shit on, affectionately though, because he was well liked—he was a country boy, and softer, in a kind and gentle way, some of his good manners still intact. They laughed and it became a catchphrase for a stint or two. Either way, it was important that they disrupted the increasingly sombre mood. They couldn't get too introspective. With a week to go, there was little value in thinking deeply, or thinking beyond the present. For Neph, introspection was a millstone around the neck, putting a slump in the shoulders, pulling the features of his face toward the ground.

They joked about The Granites gold mine being just over that rise. That they had gone so far from camp that it was close—in the middle of nowhere and lost in the outback. Really they were picnicking very much to the left of it, The Granites being still over two thousand kilometres away, abandoned in the true middle of nowhere—the Tanami desert. They joked because there were rumours that the Bronzewing contract wasn't going to be renewed and The Granites, considered one of the worst FIFO jobs available, was one of only a handful of Eltin's contracts. He didn't know that the discussion was a foreshadowing of what was to come for him, creating a myth and prophecy that he would soon fulfil, willingly even. If only he could see, just over that rise, only then may it not have been possible, as only then would he know that this was not quite the worst of it.

PART 2
Silver Swan

A Boy Miner

July 1997

He was at Bronzewing for a year, from July to July. The rumours were confirmed: Eltin lost the contract to a different mining company. Packed it all up, sea containers and semitrailers. But the workers were long gone before the machinery. The whole Bronzewing crew would need to find work at one of Eltin's other mines. They didn't go to The Granites, though. Some of the more experienced drillers, Frank, Robbo, and John, went to the Argyle diamond mine, famed as one of the best FIFO camps in Australia. First class. Crayfish at least once a week he heard. En suite rooms they said.

The only option for him and Boof was Silver Swan, some fifty kilometres north of Kalgoorlie. He had a choice, though. He could choose not to go. But he would go because he wanted money for the home he had set himself to buy. And the thought of going home with no prospect and no direction, returning to an aimless stagnant life, having to reinvent himself, struck an existential nerve. Which is to say that, ultimately, it was the fear of freedom that motioned him towards Kalgoorlie.

Kalgoorlie was the only choice for him and Boof because they were two of the last to join the crew at Bronzewing and therefore had the least say in their destination. Or it was because it was a town job and they would both need to move there, which was easier for them given they were young and didn't have families, even if Kalgoorlie was perfect for a mining family: home every day, playing with the kids, dinners together, enjoying the semblance of normalcy that FIFO families could not.

They did a final four-week swing at Bronzewing, made as

much money as possible, which near crippled him physically and psychologically, a few weeks home and then away. Bronzewing was gold, where the ore was hard and the water ran white. Silver Swan was nickel, where the ore was soft, and the water ran black. It was a 'wet' mine, not as wet as some, like Boddington in the south west of WA, where a few of the drillers had been, but there was a steady flow of saltwater running out of the up holes, which would soak them, making their overalls as uncomfortably stiff as a starched collar when they dried out.

He would be the driller, Boof his offsider.

Kalgoorlie was a town plagued by ephemerality, playing to the tune of swings and roundabouts. It could be baking hot and bone dry in the summer, creating floats of dust; and, in winter, nights cold enough to leave blinding frost on the car windscreen, forcing him to stick his head out the window as he drove, snot trailing like a pennant from his nose because of a head cold he caught within a few weeks of their arrival. It could be drunken, loud, and yobbish at one moment; hungover, silent, and repentant the next. It was a place where intergenerational poverty rubbed shoulders with sudden wealth. This was a town determined by another repetitive mining narrative: boom and bust, and boom again. Breathing in and out like a dusty set of lungs, exhausting itself before being revitalised, sucking in the life of a new find: a teasing nugget; an untapped ore seam; a suddenly-useful metal or mineral to mine.

These contradictions and oppositions belonged not only to the life of the town—the diagnosis would also be his. It suited

A Boy Miner

him, having been living a bipolar existence between the mania of his R-and-R and the depressive stint at the mine. Not only his—certainly the same cloud shadowed many of the townspeople—the exasperated and the revitalised, temporary and permanent alike. Kalgoorlie was as close as a miner could get to being wedded to the land. The farmer has his patch, tilling the same for generations; even the fishermen have theirs, anchored to a familiar seabed and the volumes of water and currents that lay above it. With only a few exceptions, a few towns, the miner was a nomad, a transient, but as stubborn as any farmer or fisherman if he chooses to plot a history, dig in for the long haul.

He and Boof packed what they could in the back of the boy's Forerunner and drove—still drunk from their leaving party the night before—the six hundred kilometres to Kal. The Great Eastern Highway almost took the same kind of route as the plane to Bronzewing, only now they could see up close how the land changed, the relief of driving the countryside as opposed to the topography of flight. His earliest memory of the highway was when he was six years old, his brother three years old, his parents leaving Kalgoorlie to start their new life in Mandurah. In a white Kingswood. On the side of the road, an eagle, wings spread, perched on a dead kangaroo, more than a metre tall in a child's eye, guarding its feed, eyeing each vehicle that dared to pass. The longest journey. He thought every blue sign with a 'P' meant Perth—not 'P' for parking—a child's introduction to tragedy. Finally coming over the range, Greenmount, and instantly beguiled by the city lights, as big as the Earth from orbit.

And eventually a toe in the ocean for the first time.

Nineteen years old and still the longest journey, and this time in the wrong direction, the Forerunner struggling to get up and over the Darling Range. The further the distance from home, the longer it would take to return. Also, the less likely they were to return until something better came along.

His uncle Peter had been staying at the Boulder caravan park, which may have been another reason as to why they were there: he could keep a close eye over them and be on hand to put out any spot-fires they were likely to light. And it was Pete that booked a room for them upstairs at the iconic Exchange Hotel, standing tall on the corner of Hannan Street and Boulder Road. Built in 1900, it was as close to an historic building as Western Australia could get. It was temporary until they found a fully-furnished rental with a fridge, beds, and other furniture. They were treating Kal almost as if it were a camp job—not expecting to settle in, one long indefinite stint—and brought with them only clothes, bedding, their football, and other random impractical bits and pieces.

They entered the Exchange, pushing through the flapping doors of The Wild West Saloon front bar, wearied as any ranging cowboy from the long drive, and were not unpleasantly surprised to find a young woman, dressed only in her lingerie, serving at the bar, utterly casual and unabashed, as if it were the most ordinary thing. As normal as him pulling on his overalls before a shift. For the young boy, inexperienced in both women and drink, the marriage of the two was a revelation. As if it took uncanny business savvy and innovation to think of combining two of man's greatest weaknesses. The financial acumen of a pervy Einstein. The revolutionary foresight of a lascivious Copernicus or Newton.

'Hey, you two! Goan' put some shoes on if you wanna be in here,' the skimpy said, pointing with her delicate chin at their bare feet. About their age but beyond their years in knowing things. Caught off guard, the abrupt Siren sounds snapping them out of their slack-jawed gawking, they promptly went to the car, like good boys, doing just as they were told. When they returned, they asked about their room, and she took it upon herself to direct them, still in her lingerie, whereby they followed her lovely bare bottom up the grand old staircase to their room. She left them there, a tour of the room clearly outside the scope of her duties. They threw a few of their belongings on the two single beds, and, impressed by the size of the room, but unimpressed by the run-down and outdated décor and flaking paintwork, decided that the best thing for it was to hurry back downstairs and take a stool at the bar. By the end of the night, quite drunk and smiling idiotically from the onslaught of semi-nudity, they both felt that maybe the move wouldn't be so bad at all.

As was Kalgoorlie's way, this sanguine mood was contradicted the following morning, initially by the crust of a hangover, and then when the car didn't start. It was the alternator; $600 to repair—a dollar for each kilometre they had driven. They would already be getting paid less for the shorter shifts and for being a town job, which meant being able to come home each night. And with the rent, fuel, and drinking that was to come, it was clear that

Kalgoorlie would be a static event in his story—an interlude, like the one on his first day at Bronzewing when he locked himself out of his donga, delaying his opportunity to find solace. However, this Kalgoorlie interlude was more like that of a long film, ostensibly designed to sell overpriced buckets of yellow-flavoured popcorn and flat, watered-down Coke.

Renting

They stayed a week at the Exchange, trying to fall asleep to the raucous sounds of the pub beneath them with the dull booming of the band playing to midnight and beyond. After each shift they drank at the bar, in the small window between working and a compulsory first-aid course they had to take over a few nights. When they ate, it was pre-cooked chickens, unbuttered bread, milk, and cereal, using paper plates and bowls and plastic utensils. When they moved to their rental they lived on steak and salad, ham and salad sandwiches, pies, and cereal. Their culinary inventiveness was solely dependent on how many dishes were needed. If they could, they would have bought a hundred disposable frypans. With no more ready-to-eat dinners from the mess at Bronzewing, it was an unwanted reality check. They were two domestically-unprepared bachelors desperately missing their taken-for-granted mums.

Their rental was a two-storey yellow brick townhouse, circa 1970s, on Carrington Street, just around the corner from the boy's childhood home on Balfour Street—a fibro house, painted in a similar shade of yellow, with a long red gravel back yard running to the back alley behind the rows of houses. There had also been an above-ground pool; and, of all things, a stable for his father's horse, which was run about as often as a half-done car restoration.

The townhouse on Carrington was one of four, with the other three seemingly unoccupied—symptomatic of a hot and cold pseudo-ghost town. It had typical Kalgoorlie landscaping: a wide expanse of red gravel out the front, enough to park four or five cars; in the little courtyard out the back, there were shoulder-high weeds—wild oats—reaching towards the fold-up washing line. Inside, there were an open-plan living room and kitchen, and two rooms on the second storey, accessed via a spiral staircase; so tight was the spiral's geometry that there was a precarious three-step drop around the centre column about halfway up. Begged for them to tumble down it, and on a few occasions they obliged.

It was agreed that Boof, having had more girlfriends than his cousin, would take the main room with the queen-sized bed, the rub being that it was open on the mezzanine floor, which would have been awkward if he did indeed find himself a girlfriend. The boy would take the smaller, enclosed room with the bunk bed—the kind that would have made his ten-year-old self very jealous, but would surely disconcert any female who may dare to come home with him. He slept on the bottom bunk, and used the top bunk for a shelf.

It was July and winter-desert cold, dipping below freezing in the night, taking them both by surprise. Amongst their first purchases were electric blankets which took some time to heat up but made the nights bearable. He would discover some three months later, after receiving an excessive first power bill, that Boof had solved the problem by keeping his blanket running from the day they bought them. And whilst the boy shivered away each night, goose-pimpled like an uncooked Christmas turkey, waiting for the electric blanket beneath him to warm up, it seemed his cousin, canny in his forethought, was already there, cosy, sweating even, for the heat.

Silver Swan

To get to Silver Swan, they took a company coaster bus, which left from the depot just off Hay Street in North Kal. It was about a fifty-kilometre drive, heading northeast from Kalgoorlie, firstly on bitumen of the Goldfields Highway, past the Superpit and the Broad Arrow pub, before turning onto an unsealed road, which took them to the mine. The long journey gave them time to sleep, which was only occasionally disrupted at night by suicidal kangaroos darting from out of the darkness into the oncoming headlights, with more than one cleaned up by the bus's unforgiving bull bar, their remains later scraped and hosed off like they were bugs. From Silver Swan, looking south, in the night sky, the glow of orange lights of Kanowna Belle made it feel like they had company in the bush.

It was eight-hour shifts, broken up into morning, afternoon, and night shifts, with a bit over an hour added each way for the drive to the depot and then the mine. They didn't stop for lunch as the firing times were too far down in the mine to affect them. Hungry as they were by the end of the shift, it was a welcome break from the twelve-hour shifts of Bronzewing and close to the normal length of a working day, and at least one week out of the three they went to work at about the same time as everyone else.

A Boy Miner

The Onram

'Yeah, I been here my whole life. Been at Silver Swan since it started. Changed since then.' Coatsy, one of the older drillers on the cross shift, their first shift, telling them how it is. A bushie from way back, squinting through Coke-bottle glasses, reeking of old smoke. Thumbs hooked into his belt. He had three stiff black hairs growing out from on top of his nose, each nearly a centimetre long and thick as the wiry threads of a toilet brush. It wouldn't take much to pluck them out. But he didn't. Which made the boy uneasy. 'Make sure you don't push it too hard. Ground's different here and they're keeping score on how many bits we are going through. Tight bastards.'

Silver Swan wasn't a big operation: they had just the one drill rig with six members on the drill team across three shifts, and nowhere to hide if someone fucked up. Just him and Boof representing the drillers on their shift. No onsite drill supervisor either, Peter popping in only occasionally; just a shift boss who acknowledged their presence as two bodies in the mine, two name tags on the wall, but not much beyond that. Strangers at the mine, the only ones to come from Bronzewing. He brought his overalls and hardhat from Bronzewing to Silver Swan, but was nevertheless stripped of his Bronzewing identity. No one called him Neph at the mine; and even though the nickname was at first intended as mockery, it had defined for him a place. He had even written it in permanent marker on his hardhat. It had tied him to a community—a familial gesture that signified acceptance, belonging. And after a year it was no longer mockery that kept his nickname—it had worn in, like his overalls, such that, like so many nicknames, the origins were no longer essential to the nicknamed. At Silver Swan, he scratched off the permanent marker, not wanting to have to explain its meaning and once again be defined by it; instead he wanted some meaning through his work.

He found himself missing his companions from Bronzewing, which felt like longing and guilt: he should have appreciated them more, enjoyed their good company; he should have been more open and let them know him—been more generous with himself and more understanding, just as they had been to him. He should have stopped playing the foolish kid. Taken a leap of faith.

For the first week, the two of them worked alternating shifts. The boy was refamiliarising himself with the Onram rig which had been brought over from Bronzewing along with some leftover hardhats, belts, gumboots, and bags. It seemed he had unwittingly picked up how to run the rig through immersion, like a prisoner absorbing the foreign language of his captors. Boof was temporarily offsiding for Coatsy. When they were put together, with the boy in charge, there was an awkwardness between them. Their longstanding relationship, in which his cousin Boof had also assumed the role of an older, wiser brother had been upturned. Even if they were driller and offsider in name only, there was the spectre of a hierarchical power shift that would take a while to get used to. Pete must have assumed that the boy's extra three months of experience made a difference. Maybe there was a hint more assertiveness in the boy. Maybe Peter didn't want to look to be playing favourites by putting his stepson ahead of his step-nephew. They were silent on the issue, with Boof neither agreeing nor disagreeing that that was the way it should be.

○

It seemed everyone had forgotten how young and relatively inexperienced they were, the boy with the responsibility of a driller for the first time. And even if he knew how to get the rods spinning and drilling, there were other tasks he hadn't attempted without Lee or Dave there to guide him, such as moving the rig to a new site, which they had to do within the first month at Silver Swan. To begin with he would need to learn how to drive and operate the IT—an Integrated Tool carrier—which was like a frontend loader to which they could attach forks or a 2.5x1.5m basket on the front that they worked out of. It was a twenty-minute crash course, and he was handed a 'verbal' ticket at the end of it. They used the forks to lift and transport the rig in its three pieces. They got it there, after a few near misses, avoiding trucks and walls, but found that there were no power services at their site, and the water line and vent bag also needed extending. The shift boss said he would organise the sparky to get the power up but the service crew for the water and ventilation were busy. And the shift boss could care less about their metreage so if they wanted they should have a go at it themselves using the basket. Until that shift neither of them had driven the IT, let alone looked at how to extend the vent bag or attach twenty or more metres of 70mm poly pipe to extend the water line. It took them all shift—finding a spare IT basket, the poly pipe, the vent bag and the tools to do it—what would have taken the service crew an hour or two. Unhappy because of the metres lost to the hold-up, the boy wrote in his end-of-shift notes that 'It would be handy if the services were ready before we got to the site.' A fair enough statement, just trying to do his job, with the expectation that others would do theirs. The mine manager, Urquhart, a tall, lean man with bristling eyebrows and moustache, perpetually disgruntled, didn't see it that way, when, the following morning, seething through straight clenched teeth, he told the boy, 'It would be *handy* if you two got your shit together and stopped fucking around.' From then on, at the end of every shift, the boy was both contrite and succinct with his notes, keeping it to just two words: 'Everything ok.'

Town job

Together they were a team, driller and offsider, working together, relying on each other for their pay, their metres, just as Lee and Neph had relied on each other. And like Lee and Neph, they would frustrate each other, have personality conflicts, which was sometimes difficult for a camp job, but usually fine for a town job: unlike a camp, when something went wrong, problems with the rig, maybe a disagreement between parties, it could be left at the mine, readdressed, if not already forgotten, the following day. Each could go to his respective home, to sympathetic family and friends, telling it in their own words, or find time to themselves to work through it. Kal was a town job, but he and Boof may as well have been back at Bronzewing. Worse than a mining camp as there were only the two of them, living in the same house, where they ate together, watched TV together, drove together, shopped together, chose their vegetables together, their dishwashing liquid. Conjoined twins would have more time to themselves.

It would have been a revealing test for even the most loving

A Boy Miner

marriage, let alone a friendship. That they were related was likely the only thing that kept them from smothering each other with a pillow as they slept. Boof would find that his cousin was not always pleasant to live with: the anxieties, bouts of depression, mood swings, prolonged silences, the stinginess. Boof was hard too mostly because of his relaxed attitude, which continued to endear and frustrate. And he could be careless, like when he forgot that he had left the solitary front key in the metre box. Only when a power outage gave them reason to check the metre box for a shorted fuse, most likely the result of Boof's forever-running electric blanket, did they find the missing key. It wouldn't have been too big a deal, except for them only being able to get into the house through the back door for the two months the key was missing. They were too young and stupid to ask for a second set, fearing they would need to pay for it. In an increasingly tempestuous relationship such as theirs, the smallest aggravations were the flapping of butterfly wings setting off hurricanes of silence between them.

Which is why they had to find ways to remind them of themselves, their friendship. Getting pissed on Saturday night could always, at least temporarily, reunite them as a happy couple: playing doubles in pool at Paddy's Ale House; shouting each other drinks; dancing together at Judd's in the way that drunken fools dance together; being stupid together. They were excused, even nurtured in Kal for their drinking, as long as they didn't pick fights and were respectful to the bar staff. They were mostly happy drunks, talkative, open, looking only for amusement. Their first encounter at the Exchange was a novelty—a must-see for the tourist—but within a few months, they felt like true locals as they scampered from pub to pub. It had become routine, which is not to say that it became tedious or boring, only that it felt like a responsibility to the community—a social obligation, no different to joining the local primary school's PTA or donating blood; as if it were the duty of a Kalgoorlie resident to continue its drunken legacy. They knew the jukeboxes, they knew the beers, the vagaries of the pool tables, and they knew the dancefloors. At the pubs they looked settled and at home, present in the moment, eyes only for their beer. Knew the etiquette. Lay your beer on its side when you are done. Leave it for the bar mat to soak up the dregs.

On a Saturday night, at what would normally be dinner-time, staggering their way to the pub, the boy made a wager with Boof that he could touch the lower awning at the front of a laundrette on Boulder Road. They were as well dressed as their sparse wardrobes allowed, and had been drinking for most of the afternoon. He made his attempt from a ten-step run-up before making his leap from his good leg. But he stumbled, as if he had taken off from fresh-laid concrete, which made for an awkward landing, sending him rolling along the hard pavement, painlessly because of the drink. Eventually, after pointing at him and crying from laughing so hard, Boof composed himself to see if he was okay. He was, although his clean, whitish polo shirt and jeans were tainted with red dirt and blood. There was no point going home as he had only the one pair of jeans and his only other shirt was a Hawaiian print, light blue, with palm trees, little boats, and surfboards, his favourite, but the irony was beginning to wear thin.

If he was disgraced it lasted only a week, as the following Saturday, at the same place, and at about the same time, reminded like a sober moment of déjà vu of the previous week's follies, his cousin decided he would also try to reach the awning. He gave himself a long run-up before making what seemed a promising leap, but he too came up short, fell awkwardly and went cartwheeling along the pavement. The boy pointed and cried and laughed, as if watching a replay of the week before, seeing himself as Boof had seen him. Mirrors of each other, brought together and comforted in the sharing of something so trivial and so essential to who and where they were in that moment. Of no consequence to strangers, no lack of tomfoolery in Kal, but it was these silly stories, memories, that they could retell again and again that confirmed the love they had for each other, even when forgetful, as sometimes they were.

Drinking brought them together, as did another pastime, just as crucial for maintaining their relationship: their dedicated watching of soapies on TV: *Heartbreak High* at 6pm, followed by *Neighbours* at 630pm, and finally *Home and Away* at 7pm. They watched them together on the strange hammock chairs that came with the rental, sitting close up to the small 12-inch TV that the boy had bought (which Boof named BTATV—Brett's Tight-Ass TV), as they ate their dinner. These popular, vacuous programs played the important role of normalising them and of maintaining their connection to the kind of society they had left, albeit a far less sexy and dramatic version than that on the TV. Each show represented something that was absent in their lives: *Heartbreak High* reminded them of the high-school youth that mining had stolen from them; *Neighbours* and the residents of Ramsay Street gave them the sense of community they were missing; and *Home and Away* allowed them to vicariously live in the beachside town of

Summer Bay, much like the one they'd left behind.

But the TV played an even greater part in their togetherness: it also filled the role of a third roommate, a talkative interlocutor flooding the vacuum of silence between them with drama, sport, and irrelevant ads about sheep-dip and combine harvesters. With the TV babbling away, they needn't feel compelled to converse with each other, like strangers might feel compelled; they didn't even need to look at each other. It spoke to them, informing them, bringing newness to their lives. Only when it was switched off for sleep or work did they return to the reality of where they were, the place they were in, and the same face they saw for close to sixteen hours a day.

They still needed each other, though the boy probably needed Boof more than Boof needed him. Having made up their minds not to stay long in Kal also meant making as few attempts as possible to integrate themselves into the community outside of the pubs. They hadn't caught up with the miners from their shift, hardly having a chance to know them. And they didn't see the drillers from their cross-shift. They didn't have a phone and didn't have anyone's phone numbers if it ever came to that. The boy had a video rental card—essential in a town with only two TV channels—and some utility bills in his name, but that was all.

Creeping

FIFO and the excesses of the breaks between stints had left him unprepared for town life. There was a way of living FIFO that was out-of-step with everyone at home. Never too familiar at home, enough to get by, maintain old relationships, reassure others of his existence. But Kalgoorlie didn't seem the best place to reconnect and reintegrate into everyday society. He may have even regressed, as within months, he was infected by an unsettling creepiness; a zombie, lurching his way from awkward social interaction to awkward social interaction, unable to interact with the living community outside of the pub's sanctuary, missing social cues, misinterpreting tones of conversation, unable to distinguish polite conversation from austere conversation. Maybe he had always been like this and Kalgoorlie had just thrown it into greater relief. If he had a theme song, background music, then it would have been Radiohead's 'Creep'; the beautiful pain of Thom Yorke's voice could be his own. Not that Boof was fairing any better; despite his better looks and natural charm, he was still hanging out with his cousin, drinking together until closing time.

They had help in losing touch. In September, on AFL Grand Final day, they paid an entry fee to some bloke's shed where they had topless waitresses serving them drinks and a sometimes stripper/sometimes 'prossie' come do a 'fruit and veg' show at half time. There were twenty men. No women or children. All of which seemed increasingly normal.

It was worse around women, so removed was he from female company outside of skimpies and strippers. In that first week, accommodated at the hotel, drinking at the long Exchange bar, he would fall in love over and over again—a superficial, pubescent, boner-driven love. The skimpies made him feel familiar, at ease and at home, calling him 'honey', 'sweetie', and 'darling'; from the very first round they remembered the beer he drank, paid attention to him, listening to his occasional dribblings, answering his small-talk-type questions, deflecting his deeper probings.

Short, meaningless, and insincere conversations, mostly held across a bar, one eye on the muted footy being played on the pub's TV. Just as they did with the older men who talked endlessly about their glory days, how things have changed, how much hair they once had, recapturing the fragments of their youth. It was a coquettish art, weaving fantasies into the hearts and minds of attention-starved men. The smallest of gestures enlarged in the minds of the unwanted and unappreciated.

It worked well on him because he was shy, quiet, unassuming and very dull; drink, though, as it is for so many, was a tonic, a personality elixir, as he imagined, and as he was told by others who found his liquored-up self endearing. This was his alter ego; his unconscious, real, suppressed self surfacing, as authentic as a Freudian slip, giving him the courage to talk to women. At home, on his breaks from Bronzewing, when he was pissed, the girls he knew seemed to want to talk to him. And he would listen intently, hanging on their words, so different, so much more interesting than blokey conversations. From his male friends he learned how to tell a Ford XD Falcon from an XE or XF by looking at the shape of the taillights. There was more to them as well but overall the focus was cars, girls and drinking.

Women spoke to him when he was pissed; and because it worked, he reckoned that the drunker he was, the more interesting he became. He would be the drunkest, the first to crack a beer and, if still standing, the last to leave—an Aussie hero, really. But they didn't all like that, not relationship material, not willing to consider him outside of getting pissed, giving him a wide berth—like dog shit on the pavement. But he liked being drunk and liked himself when he was drunk. And he was stubborn, and wouldn't change, and didn't learn. Easier to say fuck it all, and go the other way: avoid women, avoid the possibility of being rebuffed again and again. The mining camp was the perfect place for this kind of attitude—for angry, avoidant behaviour, which he had found so comforting and destructive. He couldn't avoid others so easily in a town job. So he stuck with the women who were paid to pay emotional attention to him as they poured him drinks, engaging him in light conversation, playing the role they played. But their greater part was just being there, with him at the bar, watching him and many like him unravel, sharing in the tragedy.

Such a strange and tenuous relationship across the bar, demarcating public and professional lives. Private lives. Public lives. Transgressing, overstepping. Misinterpreting demarcations. He struck up a conversation with a woman at the nightclub late on a Friday night. They had met earlier that day, when he and Boof had been lunching at The Foundry—half pub, half strip club—on Boulder Road. Which is to say they had foregone lunch to begin drinking at midday. He won a competition to guess one of the strippers' height and weight and was rewarded with a hipflask-sized bottle of vodka, which she presented to him with a kiss on the cheek, followed by a short, half-hearted, public lap dance. The dance part was the steps of the routine, the gyrations, hair flicks, boobs and bottom wiggling. Rehearsed and automatic. A strange intimacy. As if knowing her height and weight had given them some familiarity. Later, when he spotted her that night, standing alone, when she had come to the nightclub, not as a stripper, but an ordinarily-dressed woman, having a fun night out with friends, he figured that his victory was reason enough to approach her.

'Remember me from the pub today, when I guessed your

measurements?'

The slurring introduction oozed out of his mouth, like so much shit. He had to say it loud too and up close because of the music. It could have been the same music from the strip club earlier that day. But, here, they were much further apart.

She looked at him, a vague recognition, before looking away to compose herself, before condescending to look at him again. 'We don't talk about work when we're not at work.'

The smiling, semi-enthusiastic persona that accompanied the semi-enthusiastic lap-dance from earlier in the day had quickly dissolved, revealing a hardening and weariness in her face, aging it as if in a quickened time-lapse; as if her professional smile, the one she wore at work, was the only thing holding her youthfulness together; the only thing that connected increasingly disparate photos from her childhood to now. It was the kind of wear that came from patrons doing just what he was doing now: hitting on her, lusting after her, falling in love with her. The kind of wear that came from patrons holding reality up to her, reflected in their sleazy faces, like his sleazy face, reminding her of a life and the people she wanted to leave behind the blacked-out windows of the strip club, if only for a moment. In their eyes—those at the pub, hiding within—she was necessarily one-dimensional, a caricature, ostensibly without a home, family, or deeper human qualities, incapable of empathy. Academically, she was an *object* for *objectification* by his leering *subjective gaze*. He had done this, rendering her a blank slate on which to carve some ridiculous fantasy of his own.

He was sincere, though, in this moment, at the nightclub, on her break; sincere in wanting to know more about her, away from the pub. Not everything—not about the faint pregnancy stretch marks and caesarean scar he had seen earlier in the day; not the particulars of the job—the whys and whens; just enough to possibly humanise them both, give flesh and nuance to their characters.

This is what he wanted. But he was sober enough to realise that her reply had been both a sound piece of advice and more than a definitive conclusion to the interaction.

He should have kept to himself and his beer, where he and many others were most comfortable. Isolated but in familiar company. Hiding behind his glass, keeping it close to his lips, money safely on the bar, ready for the next.

○

He was able to regain some sense of his old self with the chance meeting of some mates from back home in Mandurah, mostly from high school, young like himself, and a few girls he knew but had never spoken to. Quentin, Geoff, Brad, Kate G, Kristy. Some were working in the Superpit, others at nearby mines, or the railway. Before Kalgoorlie he might have considered some of them barely acquaintances. But Kalgoorlie and much of the Goldfields are places for second chances and they soon became new close friends, so important in this alien town, creating their own exclusive ex-pat community, a Mandurah diaspora of temporary citizens. It did well also to ease some of the tension between himself and Boof, giving them someone else to talk to.

They were often sporadic encounters, as they had no means of communication other than popping around to each other's houses. Maybe home, maybe not, the shift-work not aligning, with almost no one in Kal working just weekdays, nine to five. A randomness to it. Sometimes the best way to meet each other was to head to the pub and hope to find them there.

When they did meet, they drank, Fridays and Saturdays, as good as corpses on Sundays if they weren't working. They shared a tent at the Kalgoorlie Cup, where the boy didn't see a single race and got lost on the walk home. Only on a handful of occasions did they consciously make an effort to avoid the pub and try something different. They took a drive to an abandoned pit, dirt roads, hidden deep in the bush. It had filled like a dam and they swam in it. It took a week to get rid of the smell of chemicals from their skin and hair.

Underneath the façade of drink, there was more to Kalgoorlie, a sense of community similar to that of any country town, which maybe they would have seen, if only they didn't always have a foot out the door, ready to make their retreat to the coast.

Limbo
August 1997

Even if they were looking west, he began to feel increasingly sentimental towards Kalgoorlie. Visiting his old school, Kalgoorlie Catholic School, with memories of bitumen playgrounds and almost every child running around with betadine on their skinned knees. He reminisced about his old home, vague memories of the waterpark and a playground with a huge metal slide that burned like hell in the summer. Now he enjoyed the pubs, the atmosphere tailored to young men, which he had taken to with gusto. In his blood. But in himself he still felt that he was contradicting his blood. Familiar and unfamiliar. *Heimlich*—homeliness—and *unheimlich*—unhomeliness.

It was a glancing blow to his face from a hi-lift 'kangaroo' jack arm—the kangaroo's tail—that further revealed his contrariness. His contrary blood now running from his eyebrow. Just the slightest trickle, a dampness really. He felt for it, along the socket's bony ridge, to find the evidence to justify the sudden shock and sharp, ringing pain from it.

It was late on a Friday night, early Saturday morning, nearing 1am, a few months in at Silver Swan. He and Boof had been tasked with taking a brand new drill rig underground. The old Onram rig was retired when the new rig was shipped in, all shiny with its polished aluminium, fresh warning stickers and tags still attached. It was a smaller rig than the Onram and was fitted to a trailer about the size for transporting a medium-sized car. Small but nevertheless expensive, costing upwards of $100,000, which in 1997 was about the price of a luxury European car. They were two nineteen-year-olds, teenage boys, with less than two years' driving experience between them, towing a trailer carrying a just-rolled-out-of-the-factory Porsche 911—the kind Paul the truck driver would have wagered everything for—into the rock-lined bowels of an underground nickel mine.

Halfway into the journey they had to pull off the main decline to let a loaded truck pass as it made its way lazily to the surface. They could have asked for the other traffic to give them a clear path down the decline but they had always been told that trucks have the right of way—keep the dirt moving. It could also have been interpreted as a shameful admission that they didn't know how to reverse a trailer; which may have been true, given that neither of them had ever reversed a trailer on the surface, on flat ground, let alone underground onto an inclined plane, in the dark. Men can reverse trailers; boys let men do it for them.

When the way was clear, they began reversing, maybe too quickly, as almost immediately the trailer ran over rock about the size of a football, causing it to lift and then drop and bounce on its heavy springs. They didn't notice the rock when they pulled in, and it possibly had rolled out of the back of the passing truck.

A sudden release in the weight at the back of the ute hinted that something very bad had happened. The confirmation was the awful vision in the rear-view mirror of the trailer and the rig rolling backwards, away from the ute, at a walking pace, growing smaller, before crashing into the opposite wall of the decline, and finally coming to rest. It all happened noiselessly because of the two-metre diameter ventilation fan, roaring like a jet turbine above them. His earplugs had also dulled the sound; all except his quickened heartbeat throbbing heavy in his ears, which seemed to be amplified by the foam plugs. His mouth gaped silently, not because of the fan, but because words were failing to capture it.

The boys looked at each other, eyes wide, his hands still at ten and two on the steering wheel, before flinging the ute doors open to see what had happened. A brief autopsy of the wreck revealed that, having hooked the trailer onto the tow-ball of the ute, neither of them had released the latch to lock the coupling. Nor had either of them thought to shackle the trailer to the ute with the back-up safety chains, which would have kept the ute tethered to the rig in the instance that it accidently came undone. Just like they would have kept it tethered in this instance. The weight of the trailer and the angle of the decline had somehow kept them attached for the journey down. Pulling off of the decline onto the flat of the drive, it seemed, had finally upset the delicate balance.

They shouted sombre, reluctant accusations toward each other:

'I thought you did it.'

'I thought *you* did it.'

Guilty both; and, anyway, there was no time to further the argument, nor nit-pick the details of how it came to be: the trailer was blocking the decline—the only way up or down—holding up the oncoming traffic. They were less concerned about the loaded trucks heading up than the empty trucks returning down the hole, at speed. Imagining they couldn't brake in time, would smash them and the rig all to pieces. He alerted the shift boss, the trucks, and anyone else with an ear to the two-way radio, and lied, telling only that the decline was temporarily blocked. He didn't wait for a response or couldn't hear the response. It was just him and Boof that would need to solve it; even if their first solution was to leave the rig where it was, take the ute to the surface, tag off, return home, collect their things, and head east towards the flattened horizon, never to be heard from or seen again.

Instead they took the second, more conscientious solution, which was to get the rig off the decline as quickly and quietly as possible, transport it to their site, set it up and begin drilling, without drawing a great deal of attention. As if nothing had happened.

As was the case for most of the underground, they were working in the dark, except for their caplamps. And the trailer couldn't be hitched back on easily: everywhere was uneven surfaces and at an angle because of the decline; and the ute's tow ball sat higher than the trailer coupling. With the rig on the trailer, it was too heavy to lift or move by hand; only by manually jacking it up with the high-lift jack would it be possible for the two to align.

They found a spot on the trailer to get some purchase and leverage, and the boy started pumping the long jack arm frantically. Every move had urgency, but his was a headless-chook urgency—like he was spinning plates for the first time, and blinkered like a jittery racehorse. With each minute passing as they toiled with the rig, their mistake would more likely be found out, and as quick as the ripples from a stone thrown in a pond the story would be disseminated through the ranks, eventually finding the ears of the charmless mine manager.

The jack took the weight, and with a barely-audible groan the trailer started to lift, by increments measured in millimetres, despite the laboured, arcing crank of the metre-long jack arm. But something slipped, the rig on unsteady ground, and the unweighted bar flung back, striking him across the eye, sending his safety glasses and hardhat flying. The hardhat was tethered to him by the cap lamp cord and the battery pack fastened to his belt, and like a yo-yo recoiled back to rest at his feet. It was Chaplinesque, flawlessly overlaying tragedy with comedy.

He dabbed at the wound with his dirty trembling fingers, assessing it—a moment for calm and pause. But then, the flick of a switch, calm gave way to rage, eyes only for a scapegoat on which to enact a measure of vengeance. Not the truck-driver. Not Boof. Instead, he picked up the hardhat laying at his feet, in both hands, like he was holding a severed head, and screamed at it, his voice breaking under the strain, yet still silent under the fan, before hurling it away, so hard that it hurt in the socket of his shoulder. Again, the hardhat yo-yoed back, and again came to rest smugly at his feet. An object not so easily dismissed. So helplessly overwhelmed by objects—rocks, trailers, jacks, hardhats.

Boof was doing *his* best to be like an object, attempting to blend into the petrified wall, even if the reflective bands on his overalls and his cap lamp easily gave him away. Boof was bearing witness to the dumb show of his cousin's implosion and found himself torn between comforting him in this dire situation, and keeping a safe distance to avoid becoming collateral damage. Certainly the intensity in the boy's eyes had been a clear and unequivocal warning to stay out of the way. And although the boy was only twenty-nine days older than Boof, he carried the weight of responsibility, him being the driller and Boof his offsider. It was on the boy's shoulders and for this he felt he must bear it alone. Boof's crucial role in all of this was to be present and to share in the disaster. Sharing was not halving, not quite an unburdening— it was common witnessing, of being present with others, which served well to dissipate some of the tension of the terrible moment. Common witnessing which also denied the boy the opportunity for self-loathing and crumbling into a pile of despair.

It was the shift boss that rescued them; with his cool head and common sense they got the rig reattached. Properly this time, the boy making a pathetic show of attaching the chains himself as if to say 'lesson learned, won't happen again.' They moved the rig to unblock the decline but the shift boss wouldn't let them take it to the site. Instead they brought it to the surface where they left it with the fitters to figure out. They waited in the surface crib room for the shift to end, six or so hours, unable to work and unable to go home until the charter bus came to pick them all up. With no managers on site for the Friday night shift, they also weren't asked to explain themselves—just sit and let their imaginations unravel their fates.

They had even more time for imagining once home, dreading the reaming that was coming to them. They couldn't be contacted by phone. And he didn't have the stomach to contact the mine, or his uncle, or home. In those moments, he was like Schrödinger observing his cat, uncertain of his fate: either they were fired, or they would be given a second chance. Either the cat was dead, or it wasn't—it could go either way. And not knowing, not observing, not looking to determine theirs or the cat's fate, the in-between, the multiple, was the preferable option.

Hay Street

The half-empty stubby slowly rolled along the bar, pouring beer as it went. He watched it, wondering, like a mirror of his fate, to which side of the bar it would fall. The barmaid watched it also, right up until it fell on her side. It was John, one of the truck drivers from Silver Swan, who showed the most interest, having been the one that rolled it.

They were upstairs at Sylvester's nightclub, at a small bar towards the back of the club. Boof was elsewhere. Earlier in the day, the Saturday morning following the incident, they drank and drank, drinking in silence, and then they each went their own way, unusually separate. In the few hours together following the incident, there had been a fork in their emotional reactions: Boof's face didn't seem to be a mirror of his own—they were not sympathetic, sharing the same grief; instead, Boof's face was a reflection of

A Boy Miner

the grief the boy was making his own, empathetic, but unable to understand the greater crisis that grew within the existential part of the boy's mind—the part concerned with meaning, the unseeable future, the regrets of the past, inevitable death. Now, the boy on his own, making the most of it by bingeing on vodka shots and VB in the hope of quietening his anguish, and to suppress thoughts of what the next week would be. Which is when he met John—a not-quite-stranger and a welcome distraction. The boy was looking for a new friend. Drink wasn't enough to quell the tightness in his chest. But John and his hijinks could do the trick.

He was frustratingly good-looking, for a man, his face put together the way it should be, physically fit, a perfect set of white teeth, maybe a little short. If he had been born in the right circumstances, which is to say not in the very uncosmopolitain Kalgoorlie, and a foot taller, he could have been an actor or modelled—clothes, fragrances, mining equipment—or at least entertained them as possible career choices. He would be discovered whilst walking in a mall. Just not one in Kalgoorlie.

He thought that John would be fighting women off at the nightclub. They could be superficial too, as any man, he hoped. And, yet, at one in the morning, John was on his own, well-pissed, and yelling obscenities at anyone that looked his way, crook-eyed or otherwise. Having grown up in the outback, he had taken on the worst that an isolated life could bring—as primitive as an upright ape wielding a cow's thighbone.

Both seemed to be enjoying themselves, talking shit, as boys and men can—a bit about mining, a bit about everything else—until John had done what he did with the stubby. He had leaned forward, resting his elbow on the bar, and stared at the barmaid as it rolled, unmoving, intimidating, waiting for a reaction. It was uncomfortable for the boy—something sinister and violent lay behind John's beautiful, blue eyes—malevolence bleeding into brilliance. The moment revealed itself as a demonstration of the worst ways that a man could hold power over a woman—of size and strength and fear. The boy should have said something, his conscience signalling to him that it was all wrong, the atmosphere jarred from minding its own business. He should have said something; or pushed him, or punched him. But he didn't. A useless bystander, rubbernecking, caught between laughing it off as a drunken prank and remonstrating against the abhorrent behaviour. It was a moment for fitting in, picking a side; and it was a sad revelation of the boy's character—of cowardice and contradiction—that he kept himself to himself. Theory before practice.

Fortunately and unfortunately, the barmaid had seen it all before. Unable to stop the bottle smashing to the floor, she glared back at John, unfazed, as if anticipating his behaviour—had sized him up long before. John got a more animated response from a very large Maori bouncer who, without malice or violence, escorted them politely out of the club.

Neither argued, guilty as charged, and moved on quietly. For the boy, it was a very good reason to call it a night, go home, vomit, and snore through to Sunday lunch. But John had already decided what lay ahead of them: he was going to the Hay Street knock shops and he wanted the boy to come with him. He sweetened the deal by offering to pay—the kind of reckless generosity only the drunk can enact. The boy agreed, still not ready to be alone with his thoughts, reminding him of what he had done. He would go, though not as a patron, but as a concerned citizen, a chaperone, looking out for a mate, to make sure John got there safely. Or as a keen observer, as if he were gathering research for his sociology thesis, better to make sense of the human condition.

It would normally be less than a ten-minute sober walk, but John was slowing them down, and it was a bitterly cold night, so the boy, the soberer of the two, found an abandoned shopping trolley, and pushed him the rest of the way. And so they went shopping for a woman. More specifically, a supermodel, an Elle McPherson-type, top-shelf-gourmet-free-range, as was John's request.

They would surely have been loud, their raised, drunken voices hootin' and hollerin', and the trolley's mesh vibrating like a cymbal crescendo, its hard-rubber castor wheels grinding along the bitumen. Only when they came to the first brothel did they lower their voices, speaking in conspiratorial whispers, deciding on the best door to choose. They had driven past them every day in the bus to work—unassuming, indifferent little sheds, much like the others on the same street; by night, though, during business hours, they revealed themselves, lit up like Christmas trees, bringing good cheer by satisfying the needs of lonely hard-working men in the mostly womanless town.

From the street, he could see some of the women in the windows; others were lingering at the front door where they smoked and talked, or looked bored from waiting, some with coats over their mostly-bare skin, guarding against the cold. By now it was very late and the singles from the pubs and nightclubs who were still capable of performing sex had probably found some willing partner to spend the night with; the incapable rest were most likely passed out in a flaccid heap at home, on the street, or in the lock-up, sleeping like the dead. A few would try and salvage the night by heading for a sure thing at Hay Street, as much a beloved historical landmark as it was a strip of socially-bankrupt whorehouses. If skimpies created a fantasy for clients, encouraging the possibility of forming a relationship with a sexy, talkative, interested woman, then the women here represented the sobering reality of an end-of-night, last-resort, chuck-it-on-the-credit card, drunken, and most likely, inconclusive fuck.

They spoke at length, but despite the concerted discussion, they randomly selected a place and entered. The foyer area was plush and luxurious in a gaudy way, still fashionable for the 1970s. It seemed right though, outdated and outmoded, and undeniably nostalgic. They stood close to the entrance, unsure of the procedure, like walk-ins waiting for a maître d to escort them to a table. The boy, a stand-out letch, worked hard at concealing it, careful not to eye the women for too long, even if this was one of the only places that such perversion was acceptable, if not encouraged. He can look; he *should* look. He shouldn't buy an apple without checking for bruises. The conflict within him was palpable.

Time enough to collect themselves before they were approached by the brothel's madam—a much older woman, in her sixties, regally dressed in a three-quarter length black oriental robe, cinched around her waist. Her long, straightened blonde hair attempted to contradict her age, but the deep creases at her mouth and brow, her yellowed teeth, and thick make-up, more appropriate for a pantomime, revealed the truth. Although it was close to 2am, she was eating a bowl of corn flakes, soggy as if having been forgotten. She introduced herself and took a spoonful of the yellow mush. A rivulet of milk ran slowly down her chin.

A Boy Miner

'See this here,' she said, pointing to a piece of jewellery in her eyebrow—a solid gold telephone receiver. 'Because I'm a call girl,' just in case they didn't understand. Her face lit up as she spoke of it, a proud symbol of her history in the industry. Despite the aging hair and makeup, there was an undimmed light in her eyes that had somehow also endured this same history. This was her place, her home, and the women all her daughters to watch and guard over against men who were both their most important saviour and their greatest threat.

'Cool,' was the boy's reflex response, struggling to find much else to say.

She quickly worked them out and saw that this wasn't John's first time; but the wide-eyed, nervous, out-of-town-looking boy would need some coaxing if she was going to squeeze something out of him. Ghost-like, she glided over to him, too close, even in these boundaryless circumstances, and ran her hand gently down the boy's arm, from his shoulder to his elbow, where it lingered. It was an unmistakeably sensual act, to set him at ease and warm him up, automatic and rehearsed just as the steps of the stripper's lap dance had been. And although for some it may have been somewhat effective, the forty years' age gap, the stench of stale cigarettes on her breath, the undabbed milk on her chin, and the sorry-looking cornflakes had all conspired against his usually enthusiastic libido.

John was quiet, still surveying the room, now on his best behaviour, the jocularity of the journey in the shopping trolley all but gone. So the boy became the spokesperson, or his agent, or whatever the counterpart of a madam or pimp was. 'We are looking for an Elle McPherson. Him, I mean. Not me.' Quick to distance himself, respect for women and all that, as if he wasn't depraved. As if his head wasn't filled with filth and bestial desires. A fiend masquerading as a feminist. He knew full well he was one of the worst.

Her face dropped when she heard the self-righteous caveat at the end of his proposal. Like the stripper he approached at the nightclub, her real self was temporarily unveiled. She had been wasting her time with a sanctimonious and clearly hypocritical little boy, and turned her attention to John, her face quickly returning to its former demeanour: 'Yes, we have an Elle McPherson. She is busy and you'll need to wait. Take a seat.'

They sat on tired lounges and waited, as instructed, with two other gentlemen, where they were offered drinks and watched the lingerie-clad women play some very skilled pool, biding their time between clients. Occasionally, when the game ended, the pool cue racked, the boy was approached by one of the players. She would lean in and ask if he wanted to come on a date. Ever the eunuch, he would decline, telling her he was just here supporting his friend. Untroubled, she graciously moved on to the next waiting client. Ten minutes later, another pool game won, she sauntered over to see if he had changed his mind.

The casual atmosphere disarmed any questions of morality or breaking of taboos that may have plagued his conscience about paying for sex. If anything, he grew sympathetic towards the less attractive women, or the older women who were rebuffed more than the younger girls. He felt sorry for them—hoped that more work would come their way. Like they were the owners of a struggling restaurant. But they seemed indifferent, detached, recognising that very few men were coming to a brothel in the hopes of finding a glowing personality, to see past the woman's age, her imperfections, looking for someone with inner beauty. Some men wanted to talk, happy to pay for conversation or counsel. Almost exclusively, though, it was the body that was being borrowed. No place to be precious or self-conscious about the skin and flesh that housed their reputed better selves. Better to play the part, separate mind from body. A Cartesian dualism if there ever was one.

They waited an hour, time enough to drink a few sobering beers, until a beautiful brunette finally walked out, black lingerie and heels. Except for a wide, toothy smile, her face looked nothing like Elle, but she was she was tall, leggy, and had long hair. The madam pointed John out to her and she gestured for him to follow; he did, without so much as a backwards glance at his impotent sidekick.

In John's absence, the boy felt his presence had suddenly become offensive and unwelcome. It revealed itself as another pivotal moment, of condoning or reproving John's behaviour, of whether he should follow John's lead or decide for himself. He could stay and pay a woman for sex; certainly he had a credit card and his dick was beginning to show more interest. And so much of popular culture told him it was permissible. Prostitution was without question immoral, the exception being when it is a young man's first sexual experience, which is so often portrayed as a comical rite of passage. The boy would emerge a man, hailed to the cheers of his drunken mates; in the background, leaning in the doorway of the boudoir, a much older woman, fishnet stockings and camisole, would be smiling knowingly, counting out notes in her hand, assured that she had once again played a fundamental role in the tradition.

But the boy had done the maths, both moral and financial,

and chosen his particular kind of martyrdom whereby virtue and frugality always have the final word. He left unsatisfied, with a twenty-minute walk home in near-freezing temperatures ahead of him. He cut a sad, sexless figure, dressed only in jeans and polo shirt, hands in pockets to keep warm, his back seizing up from the cold, to the point that his shoulder blades were almost touching. It was enough time to contemplate how snug and content John would be; enough time to contemplate how frigid and unfeeling his unplugged electric blanket would be. If he were to tell the story, he would say that it was for moral reasons that he didn't stay. Truth be told, it was the money and not knowing if he still had a job that kept him from taking the plunge.

The following day, hungover, a wintery Sunday morning, in a wandering despair, he found himself barefoot, wearing only t-shirt and shorts, standing at the corner of Hannan and Wilson streets, looking up, looking out, imploring the universe to speak; searching for something to explain why he had come here, why he was so useless, ill-fitted. This was limbo, his lowest ebb, needing reassurance that all 'this' served some purpose. Part of the bigger picture. On the true path.

He found no answers, the universe responding only with the familiar grunting drones of the diesel motors of red-mud-stained four-wheel drives departing and returning from mines. Across the road, the bronze statue of Paddy Hannan, sitting with his water bag, his back to the boy, was also keeping life's secrets to himself.

Eventually, after standing there had taken time enough, in the wake of a silent transcendence, he returned home to the TV and

A Boy Miner

Boof, his awful wife, to carry on.

Everything ok.

◉

Back to the mine on Monday morning, nervous and sickly hungover from another night's drinking at home. And they were reamed by Urquhart. A drive train had been damaged, something like $30,000 to repair, and no back-up rig for two to three weeks whilst parts were sought. Nothing worse than a machine not working. No uncertainty anymore: Schrödinger's cat was dead.

That should have been the end of it, the straw that broke the camel's back. And it had just about finished him; finished him in the sense that he could no longer play his part as stolid, hard-working miner, contributing to the common cause. It was a moment for change. Whether they were fired or quit, now was the time to take their lives in a new direction. The boy knew this wasn't his place, regardless of whether he was born here, lived here, had a lineage that rooted its way through the red dirt of the Goldfields. This was not his place, not his job, not him. And they should have been fired, anyway, using up all their chances in one unshackling, no matter the earnest entreaties Pete must have been making on their behalf. This wasn't for them. Time to give something else a go. Boof had always wanted to be a cop—follow in his biological father's footsteps. The boy would write romantic poetry questioning the purpose of existence whilst waiting in line at Centrelink.

To be fired would be best. To be sent home, their tails between their legs, would not be a failure. They were still young; still young enough that their mistakes did not determine them. They could hope to learn something from it, become more mature for the experience. More character building.

But they were not fired. Instead, they were punished by being allowed to keep their jobs. And for those weeks when the rig was being worked on, they were on penance, on the surface, where menial unnecessary tasks were undertaken. Just as they were menial and unnecessary—him and Boof, both. They were not quite the two biggest fuckups the long history of mining had ever seen—they hadn't injured or killed anyone and there were far more important and expensive machines to break. Not the biggest fuckups, but certainly somewhere in the middle of the long list.

Time to leave
December 1997

Uncle Pete popped by, unannounced, for morning tea on a Sunday, early December. The weather was heating up, the gravel drying in the front yard; the caked mud that had fallen off in lumps from fourbies in the street was being ground back into the bitumen, before the dust was swept down the street with the warm easterly winds.

They were both sleeping when Pete banged on the glass sliding door. They didn't look too good, judging by Pete's reaction as they made their way gingerly down the spiral staircase, as good a hangover as any.

Peter, smiling, like a sometimes teetotaller can when in the company of the hungover. 'You boys look like shit.'

They agreed. Nodding only, not especially chatty for now. It took Boof what felt like half an hour to make them all a cup of tea, like he was pottering around in someone else's kitchen. Only six months there, but Kalgoorlie was taking its toll, getting some good mileage out of them, leaving them threadbare.

Although unwelcome, Pete's impromptu visit brought with it good news. He was there to let them know that a FIFO job had come available at The Granites Gold mine—the stories of which had caused the boy so much dread. It was timely news though, the new FIFO job, as they were more than ready to pack it up and return home: they didn't speak much to each other anymore, and living outside of a camp didn't suit them. The kicker was that they had also been burgled a few weeks earlier: the boy's clothes stolen from the line, Boof's wallet, and a six-pack of stubbies from the fridge. And they weren't making any money. The new job was also a possible explanation for why they had kept their current jobs: Pete was always intending to move them on and get them out of the rough bristles of Urquhart's militant moustache.

They cleaned the rental of six months' worth of bachelor indolence, vacuumed the carpets for the first time, whipper-snippered the weeds out of the back, and loaded the car, leaving whatever couldn't fit. Back to their friends and families. Back to their homes. Back to Summer Bay and Ramsey Street.

Kalgoorlie, though, would have one last jibe—a departure tax—as only minutes into the six-hour trip, not even halfway to Coolgardie, the car stereo suddenly cut out, stopped dead, just as the car had done six months earlier when they first arrived at The Exchange—the alternator arrival tax. A quiet descended on the car, made worse by the absence of BTATV's welcome banter. They could have pulled over and fiddled around with it, maybe something obvious under the bonnet, a wire come loose, but they weren't stopping for nothing. Keep the car rolling and get out of dodge. The saving grace was that the aging Toyota was not air-conditioned, which meant they had to roll down the windows to avoid cooking inside from the December heat. For the length of the trip, driving at a bit over 110 km/hour, foot to the floor, they listened only to the cyclonic buffeting of the wind filling the void. The six months in each other's pockets had all but used up their friendship. As if it were a finite object that could be worn down, a coin passed back and forth between their mine-gritty hands, eventually smoothed from rubbing the engraved numbers away, leaving only bare worthless metal. What should have been a lifetime of quality intermittent companionship had been condensed into half a year and consequently exhausted.

From there the two boys took somewhat different paths. Boof announced that he wasn't going to The Granites; he was going to return to Kalgoorlie to drill and to make a proper life of it. He had seen something in Kalgoorlie, some possibility that the boy hadn't. Maybe the boy had been holding him back; maybe Boof had realised that they had very different goals, and needed space, a separation, to see what lay outside of their little marital union. Which is to say they had a break-up, Boof giving custody of the football to the boy.

Boof continued on at Silver Swan, bought a house in Kalgoorlie, got married properly, had kids, got into trouble, and then got out of trouble. For the boy, the fly-in-fly-out drilling position meant he would be able to earn some real money again and restart his narrative, 'kick it in the guts', and maybe even bring it to a close. See the ordeal to its proper end.

PART 3

The Granites

A Boy Miner

January, 1998

If he had done his homework, just once looked at an atlas, any map, he would have learned that The Granites gold mine was a long ways away, laying beneath the Tanami desert in the Northern Territory, about 500 kilometres north-west of Alice Springs, itself 3500 kilometres east of Perth, 1500 kilometres north of Adelaide, 2700 kilometers west of Sydney and 1500 kilometres south of Darwin. A blank empty space of yellow-brown, with no relief in sight.

And as he stepped off the plane onto the baking red tarmac he also learned that it was hot, average annual temperatures in the high thirties, which would leave him with an indelible dread towards the approach of summer. Parts of the year, it could be fifty degrees in the shade; at others it could rain for three days or more without a break. But mostly it was dry and dusty, which, when coupled with strong winds, could stir up colossal dust cyclones, set to journey across the red plains. He witnessed one cyclone, so wide it engulfed an entire workshop—an industrial-sized shed, capable of servicing five 40-tonne dump trucks at a time. For him, it was a chance encounter, an exceptional moment of enchantment, disrupting the mundanity of the mine site. For the cyclone, it seemed a conscious targeted attempt to defeat a civilisation that had arrogantly blundered its way into the outback, overreaching what man should be capable of. It was unsuccessful, because of man's weightiness and immovability, and so it quickly moved on, frustrated, into the anonymous desert, soon to lose its bluster.

Like the Nullarbor, it was laser-level flat in all directions.

Able to watch the full sun rise and the full sun set, unobstructed by any landmark, as if he were standing on the deck of a cargo ship in the middle of a becalmed Indian Ocean. But it wasn't an ocean—it was a mass of dry dusty soil, bulldust, softer than beach sand, which felt like he was treading water with each step. When wet, it was as slippery as grease. An ice-skater in gumboots making his unsteady way across a frozen red pond.

Other parts of the dirt were covered by thick, knee-high spinifex, stiff and ugly.

He saw it up close, not long after he got there, when he took a walk out from the camp, towards an old windmill, a remnant of the early pioneering days. He followed the thin dirt paths cut through the spinifex hedge, listening to myriad unseen lizards, goannas, all manner of banished creatures, scuttling in short bursts, like the sharp crumpling of newspaper, as they moved effortlessly through the labyrinth of their homes. Half a kilometre out from camp, a black snake blocked his way, one-and-a-half metres, taking up most of the path, sunning itself for the morning warmth. The boy jumped into the hedge, taking a wide berth around it, slowly, fighting against the tide of the scrub, like wading through floating swathes of seaweed, all the while keeping an eye to it, just as it was keeping an eye to him. The unseen dangers seemed less a concern than the ones clear in front of him, preferring the scaly devils he didn't know.

The highest points of the landscape, found further from the camp, were giant termite mounds, metres high, rising up in all directions, as if evidence of a triumphant civilisation. Millions of ants, peacefully colonising the outback, mining the outback, beautifying instead of pillaging.

A Boy Miner

A pack of dingoes haunted the mine's rubbish dump at night, their eyes illuminated by the ute's headlights as they panned across them. Tongues lolling, skinny dogs, ribs on show, thin fur, surviving. On the drive to camp, wild camels were seen following the highway to nowhere in particular, more adept than any to be directionless in the outback. There were also crows, or ravens as the Canadians called them. 'Faark' the crows would caw, as if they too couldn't believe men were out there.

Some of the smaller creatures were more game, like the bug that crawled into his ear one night as he slept in his donga. He woke to a loud and horrifying scratching at his eardrum, deep inside his head. He panicked, fearing he would be deafened by its clawing; or worse, it would burrow into his brain to lay eggs—a staple of horror films and urban legends, old wives' tales for scaring children. For five minutes he tried unsuccessfully to dig it out with his little finger, useless nails bitten down, the bug nestled deeper than his finger could reach, until finally pouring water into his tilted ear, eventually drowning it, but still stuck. The camp nurse flushed out the corpse of an underwhelming flea-sized insect the following day, which neither justified the noise nor the angst it had caused. For a good month he continued to finger his ear, scratching at a phantom itch, paranoid about the vengeful offspring it may have left behind.

The intrusion of wildlife became more biblical when a locust plague descended on The Granites, the air awash with flying exoskeletons. He had never cared for crickets or grasshoppers, for no proper reason other than their unpredictability. His aversion had been tested in his first few months at Bronzewing, when, sitting in the tray of the ute, journeying with Bob and Horse down the hole to the rigs, he espied a single locust, some four inches long in the body, clinging to the inside of the roll cage surrounding them, not two feet from him and at his eye level. He set about willing it telepathically to maintain its position: to not embarrass him in front of the men. But it didn't listen. Taking fright at the increasing darkness, it sprung from its place and flew directly at him, madly aflutter, before coming to rest on his face, just under his right eye, partially obscuring his view with its papery wings. He could feel its legs sticking to him, grabbing at his cheek, squeezing gently, like checking the ripeness of a peach. He sat still, stalwart, pausing long enough to calm himself, before casually brushing the thing away, overcoming the pathetic challenge to his manhood.

It had been a single locust at Bronzewing. The Granites it seemed had the rest. A few days and the plague moved on, leaving an apocalypse of a million corpses strewn everywhere, having drunk from pools of diesel, oil, and hydraulic fluid, or from being crushed under the weight of boots and vehicles, or smashed into windscreens and grills. Most were swept up into neat piles, or consumed by ants, unmourned and unmissed.

From the moment he stepped off the plane at The Granites, it was revealed to him an inescapable and essential truth: that all in life is relational. You cannot truly know something until there is some other thing to compare it to. Meaning is founded on what it is not. Meaning is founded on an absence. Philosophers already knew this. Linguists and cultural theorists. Anyone that has aged should know this. Relationality is the foundation of identity, place, time. Every moment, every action, only makes sense afterwards when it cannot be changed—when experience becomes determined by the future, and its meaning revealed only in hindsight, founding a new sense of objectivity.

This is a roundabout way of saying that he shouldn't have gone to Bronzewing first. The offal that was Bronzewing had retrospectively metamorphosed into a thick, marbled rib-eye steak, because The Granites was a lean, stringy piece of dried beef jerky, sticking in his throat. If there were a worse place than The Granites, then The Granites' status would be similarly elevated, a hindquarter lamb chop, mutton. Even if he had hated it, loathed flying in, and found the work hard, Bronzewing had suddenly taken on a romantic image, which is to say a fallacy, which battled between his understanding of the memories of how he felt when he was there and how he felt now in its absence. Time had passed and those memories, both best and worst, seemed to have become charged with new importance and emotion. Vivid, as if redrawn with a sharpened pencil and rendered in a way that drew colour from the dun everydayness.

He learned this when he got to The Granites, and it was reaffirmed on the same night that he learned that there was no God. An early evening, twilight, walking back to his donga, he could see the full sun setting to the west and, in the same view, storm clouds a bit to the north. Two completely different weather systems were being held up against each other in contrast. The expanse of the outback meant that he could watch the rain come, like a rectangular, metallic-grey smudge, a stroke of a wide paintbrush, isolated. Like the clouds were a basin, and a plug had been pulled to let the water out. Or like a cartoon in which the downtrodden move about their day with their own personal rain cloud hanging over their head, whilst everyone else is bathed in sunlight and fortune. Amidst the cloud, lightning was sparking from the friction, touching the earth, and had set off a scrub fire: the two clouds—storm and smoke—intermingled seamlessly. As he watched, the clouds also took fire, reds pinks and orange, lilac and lavender, putting on a mostly unseen and unappreciated show. No one else around. Just for him.

The moment swelled within him, hurt in his chest and gut. The sickness of confronting the sublime and profound. Maybe he was bearing witness to a religious experience. That this could only have been God's work—the otherworldly intruding into his. Away from cities and people, the natural world was spread before him, transcending humanity and civilisation. Far from an idyll, an Eden, but no less magnificent. More magnificent because of the contrast with the darkening monochromatic red flatness that lay beneath. And this was the point of it all. This was how God was speaking to him. So loud when contrasted with the silence he felt on that street corner in Kalgoorlie.

But the Agnostic in him rejected it, bucked, truths like walls fortifying against this default line of thinking, crowding out these spiritual intrusions, wrestling him back down to earth. He had lost his head for a moment there. Falling back on passed-down beliefs. And he questioned: for this, this beauty and this feeling, does God need to exist? Must there be a connection to this God? To this spirit? Maybe? Undecided. The fence sitter. But he was already listing away from faith as the holistic explanation for all that was inexplicable.

Only later, amongst stronger-willed friends and colleagues, when he found confidence and conviction in defining himself as an atheist and secular humanist, badges of the triumph of the rational, would he finally decide that there was no God—the lingering remnants of faith from his religious childhood all but evaporated, the big book as fanciful as his vampire stories. No longer was he the terrified eight-year-old boy that prayed to an omniscient God to forgive him for saying 'shit' for the first time. The showy customs of saying Grace at dinner-time, occasionally attending Midnight Mass at Christmas, were now altogether meaningless. There was no God; his increasingly austere rationalism told him so. An unwelcome truth, but nevertheless embracing it, purposefully biting into the bruise of an apple. Trees of knowledge and forbidden fruit. There was no God. There were only atoms and elements. Gold. Nickel. Carbon. His soul returned to dirt, diamonds embedded in the teeth of a diamond drill bit.

Not all was lost in the desert of nihilism. Undeniably, there *was* emotion, pure human emotion that had been nurtured through his very individual experiences that made moments so charged, just as the storm clouds were charged in *this* moment at the lonely camp. Elation was something he felt from within, in his body, viscerally, heart and guts. Belonged to him and his existence. It was his to recognise and feel and examine. As he did so, the moment emptied itself of its ecstatic wonder. The sun hiding itself away for the blue then black night. And elation gave way to cold reality and loneliness and despair at not being able to share the experience. Needing someone to turn to, his love, to say 'Isn't it beautiful,' and all would be well in the world. He wished Boof could be here, as mates again, to take on The Granites together. The moment in the desert was emptied of its romance and he came to himself, and back to his room, to empty his crib bag, wash his clothes, write a little in his letters, listen to some music, and keep emotion at a comfortable distance, at home, where he was himself.

But those moments, where he knew he was unhappy, returned to him as fond memories, distorted by nostalgia, reinterpreting his mistaken naiveté. The same could be said for his time in Kalgoorlie. Good memories were as good as any he had had in his relatively short life, his even-shorter 'adult' life, but the bad ones were flickering back and forth, bad to good, and back again, undecided and schizoid. Relational. Absence and presence. He was uncertain, remembering the experience, and then only remembering the experience of remembering the experience, playing games with the past.

On their desert-wandering picnic at Bronzewing, shift-change drunk, they had joked about The Granites—the worst mine that Eltin was contracted to. At Kalgoorlie he heard other rumours. About 'hot-bedding', which meant sharing a room with their cross-shift, sleeping in the same bed. About the mad Croatian mine manager: you had to drink with him, be seen at the bar, or risk being fired.

They proved untrue, the rumours—a bogeyman for frightening children. But there were differences that were going to be hard to adapt to. Instead of the one-and-a-half-hour flight from Perth to Bronzewing, it was a six-hour flight, which included a refuelling stopover at Kalgoorlie. They left Perth just before four in the morning, a sting for anyone expected to give them a lift to the airport. Already tired, he did sleep on the plane but was jolted awake at Kalgoorlie, and then again as they hit the airstrip at The Granites. The flight to The Granites was also more unreliable: having agonised if the Bronzewing plane was late by even ten minutes, at The Granites he agonised at the possibility of the plane being late by hours or even days if the seasonal rain had flooded the dirt runway. Instead of a ten-minute bus ride from the Bronzewing camp to the mine, the bus ride from The Granites camp to the mine was close to forty minutes, along a haul road with Bulkhaul road trains carrying ore from the mine passing them, their four trailers snaking, drifting across the white line of the road, frightening them awake as they slept uncomfortably in the upright seats, their rolled overalls for pillows. The long journey made for a 510am departure from the camp, and a 650pm return for a day shift.

Where the Bronzewing camp had well-lit concrete pathways, with a considerate planting of native grasses and shrubs along their edges, leading to the hexagons, The Granites had rows of the transportable dongas, facing away from each other, with wide expanses of muddy, red gravel, unlit and undirected, between them. On the way back to his donga, the approach of night brought with it growing paranoia of blindly stepping on a still-lively snake, the long thin shadows of rocks, cast by distant fluorescent lights, mistaking.

But it was the little things, trivialities, those that are noticeable on the microscopic level, the diurnal, which he found the most terrible: where Bronzewing had many varied options to pack for crib, including the dinner for night shift, The Granites had a few platters of cold meats and salad with some loaves of bread. Wilted see-through lettuce, floury pinkish tomato. The only consolation when it came to meals was that they ate on the surface instead of an underground crib room. Even then, they sat, exhausted-looking, on the ground, outside, on the shaded concrete pathways between the transportable offices and the surface crib room, better to savour the openness and the fresh air; and to smoke. Not much talk, each man left to his thoughts; or not thinking at all.

And where Bronzewing had eight or more phones, The Granites had just the four, fitted to a wall in a line—no booths, forced to speak-easy so as not to be overheard. Or loud because who cares. And no one really hid conspicuously like they did at Bronzewing.

The services and look of The Granites camp reflected its unyielding isolation, as if with each kilometre away from a major city or a port meant increasing concessions, like concentric circles, spiralling away from the centre, readjusting their expectations. Anything that was needed or could be brought would need to come from great distances. The closest place to resemble a town was the Rabbit Flat roadhouse, fifty kilometres north-west of The Granites, claimed to be the most isolated roadhouse in Australia. Alice Springs, 500 kilometres away, was the closest city, itself not a true commercial hub, population in the tens of thousands. As was a favourite saying from many of the boys, 'It's not quite hell, but you can see it from here.'

Again a newcomer, he was sent to the Bronx (which also made him realise that he hadn't been elevated from the Bronx the whole time he was at Bronzewing). The donga was exactly the same dimensions and furnishings as Bronzewing, as if they were the identical rooms of a hotel. This time though his door opened onto an uninterrupted Tanami desert. Nothing between them and the bush except the grate doormat. No protection even from an unattended scrub fire that, like cattle, grazed its way past them. No word from the camp as to whether it was deliberate—back burning—or natural. No apparent threat, part of the symbiotic relationship with the bush. Just keep your door unlocked in case you need to run.

It was the stuff of tourism commercials: of flat, distant horizons and big blue skies. Real Aussie outback. But no Paul Hogan and his 'shrimp.' And none of the usual landmarks and natural wonders—no Uluru, which lay to the south, no Karajini waterfalls to the west, Olgas or Kakadu to the north. It was the kind of place where its beauty is most appreciated whilst driving as fast as your vehicle can go in the unrestricted speed limits, and as far as your fuel tanks will take you. The irony was that they were paying him to take this wretched holiday. He would feel differently, of course, if only he had the freedom of a vehicle.

The Onram

He was an Onram driller again, the original old orange rig from Bronzewing and Silver Swan, turning up like a bad orange penny. He was one of the few that knew how to set it up and operate it. The idiosyncrasies of every ancient rig, like an old man and his daily routine, his TV shows, his bowel movements or lack thereof. He seemed to know what he was doing, as good as anyone else.

He had to set up in a cuddy barely off the decline, with trucks grinding past for the whole shift. They had a little 'screamer' fan—about 70cm in diameter—which kept them ventilated. But it was also loud and made any communication with his offsider, Chooky—a poorly spoken Croatian—almost impossible. He was in his mid-forties, grey-haired, average height, and with a visage that looked both lost and knowing, absent but here. The Croats that had been shot in the war were the most taciturn, English or no English. Chooky hardly said a word. Laboured when he did. The dark-pink bullet wounds on his back unmistakable in the showers. They were around his shoulder blade but didn't seem to impede him, or at least he didn't show it. They plodded away, getting a few metres, in silence, with no cross-shift, all the while the screaming screamer fan thankfully filling up the space where language barriers and hard questions could enter.

Aaron

There was some trouble with the rig from the start. It was old, had always been old, bleeding hydraulic fluid, the orange paint peeling. And after it was retired for the new rig at Silver Swan it had been in storage, disassembled, time enough for unused hoses to perish and for metals to rust. The fitter was needed frequently, the boy standing impotent near the fitter as he went about his business. The boy unable to answer his questions, still knowing little about the rig except for the drilling part. Too often, somehow, when the fitter arrived, the problem had fixed itself. Arron, the fitter, already humourless, more so for being dragged down the hole for nothing—the boy crying 'wolf'. He also wasn't happy that he was the drill fitter, which was far less

A Boy Miner

glamorous or vital compared to maintaining the wellbeing of the jumbos and boggers. Arron was in his late twenties, sharp close-cut dirty-blonde hair, the body and flattened nose of an amateur middleweight boxer. He was missing one of his front teeth, the other looking dull-worn and big as an old tombstone. His piercing blue-eyed stare completed the look, and did well to shut the boy up before he had a chance to whine. Like John from the brothel at Hay Street, he was a good-looking man but he'd been wrung out, leaving only yellow smoke stains and anger. He would fix the rig and quickly move on, leaving them to their triviality.

The animosity between them worsened when the boy misplaced Arron's shifting spanner. The rig, leaking more oil than usual, needing constant topping up to save burning out the motor and bearings. Arron lent him the shifter—twelve inch Sidchrome—to undo the cap. Real nice; quality gear; expensive. He was reticent about doing so, loaning out his tools. As he should have been, with the boy losing it within a day, somewhere in the mud under the rig. At the end of the shift, on the surface, the boy confessed it to Arron. Arron didn't say much—just swore once, and stared his discomfiting stare, blaming himself for the error. They didn't speak for the remainder of the stint, awkward at dinner times, on the bus. It was fear and guilt that compelled the boy to buy a replacement on his break. He offered it to him, first day back, and Arron accepted it with a special kind of indifference and aggravation, thinking he might owe the boy a thank you.

Fortunately they didn't need to see much more of each other: the rig had fewer breakdowns and Arron moved to another roster, and eventually he didn't come back. But a few months later he did see Arron again, at home on his break, at the pub in Mandurah.

The boy, on a stool at the bar watching football, waiting for his schoolmates to arrive, turning around at the wrong time. He saw Arron, and turned back to the television, avoiding catching his eye. Because he didn't really like him and because Arron might finally take the opportunity to clip him one now that there was no threat of being booted out of the camp. It was Arron though that spotted him, and eagerly made his way over, smiling widely, a twinkle in his eye, and greeted the boy like an old friend, 'Fancy meeting you here!'

'Arron, hi,' catching the boy off guard, doing his best to mirror Arron's smile, enthusiastic, even as he wanted desperately to flee.

When they went to shake hands, Arron made sure it was with his left, and brought up his right hand in front of the boy's face. There were two fingers missing and it was squashed around the palm.

He was still smiling, with his tooth missing. 'Got it crushed under an engine. Dropped too quick for me,' and chuckled as if it were not too bad a joke.

'Jesus!' the boy replied, in shock, as if there was nothing else to say, before adding an awkward laugh, still mirroring Arron, politely, not wanting to offend, diffusing his horror.

Arron didn't talk much about his hand after, the conversation moving on quickly to his compo and the house he had built with it, as they drank beer. The boy offered guarded conversation, still mistrustful of the 'new' Arron, but also keeping a good humour given the changed circumstances. Then, after some more beer, Arron asked if the boy wouldn't mind coming around tomorrow to help him finish off setting up his new shed. Asked as a favour, again like old mates. Wrote the address down on a beer coaster. He would be the worst prick in the world if he said no; and there was something comforting in having Arron ask him for help instead of the other way around.

They met the following day. And the boy helped with the shed. Some lifting of panels, heavy bits. He watched Arron struggle with threading a nut on a bolt, what seemed the most rudimentary of tasks for a fitter. It was hard, watching him. Unfair, cruel. Arron didn't get frustrated though. Slow and steady. Had made peace with it almost, just part of his new routine. Not usually one for smiling, he almost looked happy, more happiness than he had ever shown at the mine. Blue eyes, afire as if he had discovered true love. Which would have confounded most given his misfortune. But the boy knew why: Arron would never work underground again. No place for the handicapped, the lame and maimed. Which seemed a gift. And he gained himself a house.

He could open a beer still, and at midday they had a few, and talked. He was single. Had a girlfriend once. The boy wondering if she left before or after, and felt bad that Arron was alone, and was in need of a friend. But theirs wasn't a friendship, and it would be too much to ask the boy to placate and feign sympathy for Arron, mangled hand or otherwise.

He made a half-hearted promise to catch him up again soon on one of his breaks. But he was lying, as he couldn't see the point. They were very different people when they were at the mine, even more so away from it. Mining was the only thing they had in common, but it was a commonality that he wanted to keep at the mine. Still wanting to keep himself for himself.

Rash and friendship

'Hey, Shaggy, wait up.'

The boy on his way to the mess, before night shift. Light blue skies, not a cloud for weeks. One cloud, any cloud, would have been a spectacle, a muse for poetry. The boy looked back to see Rash's face alight with his mischievous, goofy, big-toothed smile, his trademark buoyant eyes easy to see even across the twenty metres or so of distance between them as he followed behind. His big strides meant Rash would catch Shaggy whether he waited for him or not. Rash wanted to make it stick—'Shaggy,' from *Scooby Doo*—because of the boy's scrawniness, long hair, sideburns, and stubble. Sounding like 'Sheggy,' because of his Kiwi accent. It caught on quickly, gained traction, like a virus, his name tag no longer signifying a face or character that others knew or remembered. Even blokes he never met before were using it. Neph, the boy from Bronzewing, was nowhere to be found, left down the Bronzewing hole, falling asleep next to the spinning rods of an LM75.

Rash was Rash because of some allergic reaction to the plastic in the gumboots, which was cured by getting hold of some normal steel-cap work boots. He was in drilling too. Big enough to handle the offsider's workload—six-foot-five and fleshy—but he was out of place, clumsy, prone to errors from trying too hard, acting without thinking, on occasion. Like Shaggy. Rash was also kind, friendly, boisterous, witty, laughed, was social, spoke a lot, spoke quickly. Could also, at times, when poked the right way, become hot-headed, crazy-eyed, and intimidating.

They were in the same block, two dongas between them,

sharing the Tanami vista.

Except for Boof, Rash would be the closest friend he would have on a campsite. A friend, not a mate if a difference can be made. A friend because he was older than Shaggy, but younger than most of the blokes out there, because he was earnest, and positive. Certainly he was good for Shaggy, playing the roles of confidante, entertainer, mentor, and older brother. He reminded him that life at the mine was not completely unenjoyable if the right attitude was brought to it. Live each day as it comes. Buddha or similar has probably said something like that before. Life and attitude and positivity, stringing the same words into an affirmation. Rash drank every night at the wet mess. And on the Sunday morning of the fortnight's swing, instead of the robes of the Buddhist, 'Reverend Rash' would don the dog-collar of a priest—a white strip of paper ripped from the border of a newspaper or dirty magazine—and host 'church' at the pub. About as sacrilegious as it could get, but also about as religious as it could get with nowhere to pray that he knew of. A godforsaken place.

Rash lived large when at home, renting an apartment right above a bikini shop in Cottesloe. This was okay for some, but for the boy it lacked direction, didn't fit the boy's story—too sexy, extravagant, and exciting. Short-sighted. Not that he didn't long for it—Rash's wonderfully directionless and consequence-free life. At the same time, Rash was overly thrilled and proud about buying himself a new laptop, whereas Shaggy was steadily accruing his deposit for a house.

They had some things in common. Music in particular. Rash introduced him to some new music, new bands. And he had a lot of new stuff, buying maybe five CDs on each break. Gentler music, convincing the boy that grunge and heavy metal were cool and all but it might be time to shift gears every now and again. Slow it down, find some groove, a different beat.

Rash was gifted in that he could talk to anyone, never one starved of something to say, ready with a joke or a quip, and always an ear for catching a story; but he needed this interaction always, as if his existence was purely a social existence. He didn't seem to dislike his own company but he would rather have that of somebody else. When he did he was confident, one of the boys. Even then, an underlying nervousness seemed to infect him. A tremor of vulnerability. It was his eyes that contradicted him. Darting all around, the glimmer gone, the brown and black of his irises and pupils suddenly dull like mud in winter. Looking heavy and tall and conspicuous. He misinterpreted people, thinking that they were having a go.

Certainly he misinterpreted Shaggy, but everything Shaggy said was misinterpretable, nuances as distinguishable as the fuzz of white noise. After a night shift, back at their dongas from breakfast, the morning well underway with its pressing sunshine and heat, a dingo approached Rash's hut. Rash was excited, holding his hand out for it to sniff: 'Look, Shaggy.' A special moment in the flat dullness.

'Hope he bites ya!' Some sarcasm, but not enough to make it clear.

Rash laughed it off.

Shaggy didn't like that he said it. Sarcasm or otherwise. But he knew why he said it: because he had to say something. He was only now remembering what it was like to be at a camp: he had to be social, show that he was a worthwhile member of their exclusive, isolated community. Platitudinal hellos and goodbyes, repeated, acknowledging the other, essential human contact in the desert.

But he said it also because he was sick of him. Which was not Rash's fault. He was just too much for Shaggy, just as everyone was too much for Shaggy. From being a member of this same exclusive, isolated community. Like his failed relationship with Boof in Kalgoorlie, theirs had quickly become strained by the constant close proximity of existing together, walking to the mess together, being on the bus together, having lunch together. Rash's upbeatness clashed with Shaggy's concerted efforts to maintain the persona, the way of being, he had constructed for himself, that kept the relationships at the mine from intruding on those at home. Just like he had with Arron. If only Rash lived on the other side of the camp, maybe it could have been different. Maybe if there had have been at least one fence separating them, some private space beyond the cell of the donga. Human contact was essential for keeping them from wandering crazed into the desert: ironic that it was human contact that was forcing him to often seek space by wandering into the desert.

Rash forgave him, like you would family. Maybe because he was a Kiwi and his family were over half a continent and the Tasman Sea away. Any port in a storm, any camp in the desert. But more than that. More between them than most in the camp. This was why Rash would invite him to meet on their break. And Shaggy would take him up on the offer, not wanting to let the petty sibling squabbles ruin a good friendship. Taking a chance.

They met a few times: one time they went to a concert together, another they caught up at the Cottesloe pub for the

Sunday session. But other things got in the way and they made fewer plans.

Other times when he made plans with others away from the mine, turned out to be almost exclusively singular excursions. He went four-wheel driving on break with a charge-up guy. One of his best days ever on a break, taking proud photos of their muddied vehicles and blu-tacking them to the wall of his donga. But just the once.

He went jogging with another offsider at camp. They spoke the whole way, which near killed him. Again it was only the once. Always the same, friendships like a singular wave, the ebb, the flow, and returning to the ebb, a lasting ebb. Never the consistency of friendship.

They were conditional, situational, their friendships, founded on an activity or an event. Companionship which is based on doing things together, not just on proximity, of being together, relying on each other emotionally. Togetherness was not the foundation of the activity but was implicit to the activity. Just like the picnic with the Bronzewing crew, or watching the cricket with Boof and Bob. But they were mostly singular, because the situation, their rosters, determined it as such. At The Granites, an ex-army officer now truck driver ran a boot camp after work one night. Getting them fit, maybe even exposing some of the brawny muscle that lay under the love handles. They did it a few times before he changed shifts. On Australia Day, they played a game of indoor cricket. A novelty at best.

Each time, closeness lost some of its strength and meaning once they stepped beyond its fringe of activity. Never able to find a routine outside of the work routine. Besides, everyone was working on different schedules, had other relationships, families that were too full to add another. He felt the same, of course, so careful of who he would let into his life within the camp or beyond it.

Certainly he was stuck in the mindset that his schoolmates were his mates for life and the only mates he would have. He would need to expand his horizons, adapt to new friendships, take what will come. Not just workmates from the mine, but, eventually, other dads from school, nods at school pick ups, maybe a beer after work. All would need to take place away from the mine, in the real world of nine-to-five, consistent, at home, able to commit. He could play sport, join a team if he were at home. He heard that Boof was playing indoor beach volleyball in Kalgoorlie. Boof had made a home, wife and kids, dinner with his family most nights. And indoor beach volleyball.

A house

When he moved back from Kalgoorlie to Mandurah it was to his old room at his parents' house. Everything was left the same, his old single bed that he'd had since he was seven years old, along with bits of arbitrary furniture from another life—his school desk, cupboards for a few trophies and assembled Lego, and a toy-box, unopened from about the time he first began listening to Guns 'N' Roses and Metallica on his dad's old woodgrain speakers, which looked to be the only item in his room that resembled the person he was now. The room remained unpainted from the posters he had ripped from the walls, leaving sticky-tape marks at angles around invisible borders. He had been gone only six months but the independence and freedom that leaving home allows cannot be easily given up. Especially since his younger brother was moving to Perth to study, living on a pittance, whilst his wealthy brother mooched in his old bedroom, returned like a pair of wrong-sized shoes, home for more training in the art of home economics. Nor should he bring his Kalgoorlie lifestyle to his parents' home, staying out most of the night, drunk off his arse, fumbling with keys to let himself in. They were ready to start their new lives, empty nesters, looking to look after themselves.

It was time now for him to start it all up again—his plan—in earnest this time, without the financial burdens imposed on him by the excesses of Kalgoorlie. It was the town he blamed for having too much fun. The bleak atmosphere, the lack of direction, that gave him reason to drink, the life the town job had enabled him to live, which took him away from what was most important—working and making money. He had no other reason to be there. Now, he had security in his job—The Granites was a long contract, lots of gold to be mined—and he had saved a deposit for a loan and so he bought a four-bed, two-bathroom house in Mandurah. The first amongst all his mates. The fruit of labour. The tangibility of bricks and mortar that assuaged all his questions of why, for what, and for whom. Each pay-cheque more an affirmation than what Buddha could tell him. He could open the door of his house, run his hand along the painted walls. He was a homeowner, which seemed absurd considering he didn't have a piece of adult furniture to his name. Nothing except BTATV, the mattress from the back of the Forerunner, and the old family pool table. For those first few days in his new house, it looked more the doss of a heroin addict, like the ones he had been reading about in Irvine Welsh's *Trainspotting*: spent syringes, blackened spoons, and other drug paraphernalia replaced with the refuse of KFC and Hungry Jack's packaging and empty VB cans, until he bought himself a fridge. Or at least a microwave.

He would soon move a few friends in, paying him a bit of rent, and who would bring some furniture with them, giving it the semblance of a proper home.

Hernia
July 1998

The alarm buzzed its psychotic buzz, 4:30 in the afternoon, six months in at The Granites. The thinnest beam of light surrounding the edges of the closed door, the blazing sun outside dying to get in. He sat up and swung his legs over the edge of the bed, and as he adjusted himself he felt something strange, a bulge in his groin—just smaller than half a squash ball, and squishy like it too. It was painless and a mystery, having no idea of when or how it had happened. Possibly from the gym, trying to bench press too much, or just from drilling, lifting something too big for him, reckless with his body, the invincibility of youth, a body that can easily repair itself, as if immortal.

Not wanting to draw attention to it, mostly because it sat less than two inches above his penis, he waited almost a week for his break to see his GP back home, awkwardly covering himself up so that others couldn't see in the open showers. It was a quick and easy diagnosis: hernia. His stomach lining had protruded through a weakening in the muscles of his abdomen. It would need surgery, just to make sure the lining didn't rupture and begin oozing stomach acid all over the place, or something to that effect. The operation was booked for his next break. He told his uncle about the surgery and that the surgeon had said he could be back to work for the next swing but only on light duties.

They cut him open before sewing him up in two places. Walking around like an old man, wincing with every stretch and bend, like an unending punch in the guts with a tiny-knuckled fist. Good to go. Just don't lift anything more than 5kg.

After his op, back at the mine, they told him he would be working on the surface for at least the next two weeks, given menial jobs like those when he crippled the rig in Kalgoorlie. It had the same guilty feel to it, too, like he was on penance for fucking up. It was a mistake he had made—getting injured. Sustaining a hernia was a weakness, like allergies, baldness, or mental illness, a taint that could have easily been avoided if he wasn't such a morose weed of a kid. The belief that illness was a weakness was likely the reason that not one of the miners had ever had a sick day, not in the whole time he had mined. No flu, no strains or pains. Even if they were sick or sore, no one let on. Especially if they were hungover, rat-shit, they still came in. This was evidence of their toughness. Getting on with it. Necessarily so given that the sick pay was about a third of the normal rate, and they had no other financial safety net.

The bosses were lost for ideas on what they were going to do with him, mining being quintessentially heavy duty—nothing of any real use was done lightly or delicately. Leathered hands before kid gloves. The dried fruits of a brainstorm were to get

A Boy Miner

him to wash and detail the mine manager and shift boss's utes, inside and out. He spent the whole shift on them—twelve hours or so—as meticulous as he could be with a mud-caked mining ute, never really clean, even if he had a whole swing to buff out the red-orange stains.

For a few days he was sharpening old jumbo drill bits, using a drill-press-type machine. He had no way of knowing if he had done a good job: the bits looked no different to him when he was done other than looking slightly shinier, which then may have only been the shimmer of the water necessary to dampen the heat from the turning. Sisyphus sharpening his boulder, an absurd task with no end even when ended. But it kept him out of the way and out of sight, better not to remind them of his unserviceableness.

A good part of a week was spent stripping industrial electrical cable of its plastic for the copper, using a Stanley knife. There were hundreds of metres, jumbo cable and 70mm cable with three or more thinner wires inside. He did this in the high sun, for twelve hours, as if it were one of the most crucial tasks at the mine; like he was part of the WWII home guard, gathering steel to refashion into ammunition, all for the next big push into Nazi-occupied Europe. He wasn't sure where the money for it went, nor was he in a position to ask.

He was also tasked with crimping detonators onto detonation cord. They were small detonators, about the size of a cigarette, intended to set off the other explosives. It was a bit of a luxury as he could work in the shift boss's airconditioned transportable office, in his high-backed office chair. The trade-off though was the possible danger of crimping them in the wrong place. 'These little dets could blow your finger off,' they told him. Kind of joking;

or not. They seemed itching to find out. There were blokes with missing fingers still able to work most jobs. Better than a hernia.

The mornings on the surface were cold, starting in the dark. There was no rush, and he would mess around at the start of the shift, trying to look busy, picking things up, inspecting them thoughtfully, before putting them down again, as he waited for the sun to reach over the black horizon. Hidden behind the surface drillers' shed, waiting, wondering how long it would take for the warmth to reach him, like it was a physical wave, the sunlight exciting the air molecules, heating them up, although far slower than the light waves themselves—the ones that allowed him to see, not those that made him feel. Only when it came, finally, the wave of warmth, when the sun was about halfway up on the horizon, a yellowing semi-circle, sitting on the black landscape, like an inverted Aboriginal flag, did he begin his shift proper.

A new fitter for the drills started at the same time that he was on his light duties. Another Mick. This Mick was in his mid-forties, with two teenage daughters at home. He was set to sorting the surface drillers' shed out, including the old rigs and parts, rusted and dusty and outmoded and useless. Shaggy was asked to help out, still to keep him busy and out of the way.

They were both punished for Shaggy's ritual of waiting for the warmth of the morning sun by having it beat down on them for the remainder of the shift. Cloudless blue skies, baking them, worse in the dark breezeless sheds, caplamps on, sweating through their overalls just from standing there—coarse, dry overalls, like oven mitts warmed from pulling a casserole dish out of the oven. The fitter was slim and fit but didn't wear the heat well, his face sunburnt pink, flushed as a marathon runner, stark against his sandy blonde hair.

They took a lot of breaks, out of exhaustion and boredom, sitting together to rest in any shade possible; it was too hot in the little sheds, and the shadows were thinning as the angle of the sun grew more acute. They chatted, getting to know each other a bit, told their stories, bellyached, thrown together as they were.

It was on the third day that Mick made his considered assessment of The Granites. The two of them were sitting outside, on the leeward side of the shed hidden from the offices, half-shaded, on milk crates. Mick had a screwdriver from his tool bag in his hand, wrong-ways round, tapping the handle on the dirt in front of him, kicking up little dust flurries, watching it but thinking elsewhere, for a moment, silence between them. Tapping for a minute or more before finally looking up and away to the horizon: 'No place for a man to work.' He repeated it, sometimes two or three times a day, through dry, flaking lips, stringy bubbles of saliva at the corners of his mouth. Sometimes he added 'Nope' to the beginning of it: 'Nope. No place for a man to work,' as if answering a question that'd been eddying around in his mind.

Each time, Shaggy would respond in agreement—'Yep'— even if Mick's words seemed more an opening statement of a soliloquy than a question directed at him. It was because it was Mick's first FIFO job, or maybe a touch of homesickness, or maybe it was because it was The Granites that made him say it. It was an unusual thing to say—simple, articulate, obvious. Like something a child would say. The emperor has no clothes. The words of some enlightened rebel, speaking aloud what the general population of men at The Granites wouldn't dare think, let alone say. Mick had suddenly understood that they were all part of some elaborate joke, the punchline lost under the humourless weight of each man's self-imposed martyrdom.

Mick stayed for two swings before he pulled the pin; before he snatched it. Came and went without any real hello or goodbye. Not enough time to be missed. Not enough time to be known. From the very first day of his very first swing, Shaggy had been more than ready to quit; more than ready to *snatch* it, and utter it like the harsh-sounding word it was—have to sneer to say it, through clenched teeth, a sizzling hiss and then spit it. Snatch meaningful existence from the jaws of FIFO. Two years on from his start at Bronzewing, the thought of acting on this possibility had been mythologised, a fantasy of wish-fulfilment, full-bore pleasure principle. For others, like Mick, it was an easy decision, were almost blasé about it, like choosing between having either a pie or a sausage roll for lunch. It was not a failure or a loss for them, but necessarily the start of the new, of new possibilities that will reveal themselves sure enough. That's how Mick saw it. Shaggy only saw ends—the black and white of quitting out of weakness, or of not-failing because he was strong and stubborn and was going to ride his story out all the way to the end.

No place for a man to work.

Yep.

When he was near recovered from the hernia, the incision scar between his hip and groin all but healed, they sent him back underground to get drilling again to recoup their losses. Instead of putting him back on the Onram as the driller with an offsider to do the heavy work, they placed him on a one-man drill rig called the Bazooka—a pneumatic rig, run from the compressed air services. It had smaller rods than the Onram and drilled short, ten to twenty-metre holes, with the purpose of fine-tuning the map of the ore seam. Unlike the other rigs, it had no rod-pull function, or control panel, such that the rods had to be pulled by hand using eighteen-inch Stilsons, dragging the rods out. It also didn't have a skid or trailer to move it around; instead, it was disassembled into its various parts and loaded into a ute by hand. If the holes were close enough, it was quicker to simply drag the parts along the drive. Because of this, the Bazooka was more labour intensive than the rig he had reputedly injured himself on.

Within the first few days, when dragging fifteen metres worth of rods out of a hole, he felt a twinge in his groin, right about where the hernia had been. Probably just things still settling down, the new scar getting pulled in different directions, but it was hard to tell. He had waited too long to tell anyone about the original injury, which almost lead to difficulties with determining the liability and compensation for his operation. He got it at work but only went to the doctor when he was at home. He could have got it at the gym—either at camp or at home—which would have raised further questions about whether it was work related. If it wasn't compo then he might have to pay for the operation himself; he would also need to claim sick leave for his recovery. This time, he let them know immediately, just to cover himself.

The reaction was swift and decisive: the following morning, at the start of the shift, he was told that he was going to learn how to drive trucks. He thought it was temporary, part of his light duties, until he was right again. It wasn't—he was now a truck driver. Big, loud, expensive, important pieces of machinery. No more drilling. And it was not up for debate.

In less than twenty-four hours he had been elevated to the higher strata of the mining team, albeit at the bottom rung and with a pay cut of a quarter. It was a strange, sad goodbye to his drilling comrades, some of whom hoped that he would take them with him.

Trucks

When his uncle first proposed to him the idea of working underground, the boy envisioned claustrophobic vertical shafts extending down and vertiginously dark into the ground, tight uncomfortable spaces, squeezing through cracks in rocks. And when Peter told him that trucks also went underground, he was even more confused as to how they would fit or how they could be loaded. It only made sense when he first saw the gaping portal on his first descent with Horse and Peter at Bronzewing. But to say the portal was bigger than he expected did not mean that the trucks had a lot of room to move. The decline and the drives were just wide enough to fit one truck at a time, which meant other traffic needed to give way, pulling off the decline to let the heavy machinery through. The trucks descended at a slow and steady twenty-five kilometres an hour, but the closeness of the walls, services, fans, and vent bags and the clanging of the service hooks made it feel a hundred. They were like trains in a subway, one lane, economically cut to fit, but without the security of the rails keeping them centred. Not even enough space for a light vehicle to squeeze through. He had heard the story from another mine where a truck heading down the hole unexpectedly met a Toyota

Personnel Carrier with six miners coming up. There wasn't room for the two of them and the PC was crushed as if in a vice between the wall and the truck. When the two vehicles were disentangled, the truck was fine, and the six miners were miraculously unharmed, but the PC was half its width, and shaped like a parallelogram.

The first truck he drove was a Toro 40D—dirty, beaten up, the same colour orange as the Onram rig. The already-roughened paintwork meant that his inevitable indiscretions with the wall would be less obvious. It was an articulated vehicle with its turning point behind him, like the tub was a trailer fixed to the cab, but instead of the front wheels turning, the vehicle would pivot around the join. The driver's seat was also on the left hand side, which initially threw out his sense of space between the walls. And along with the brake pedal, there was a retarder—a lever on the steering column—that was used to slow the truck coming down the decline, instead of overheating the other brakes. The trucks didn't have reversing mirrors, or if they did they were removed, given that they would be quickly knocked off on the first run down the hole; and no reversing cameras, so backing out of anywhere took some getting used to. He would stick his head out to see when he needed to back up to the left, but to back up to the right he had to swing the back end from side to side, zigzagging his way up the decline, careful not to squash himself like a cockroach against the unyielding wall.

When he started the Toro up the first time he was awed by the noise and the vibration and the bulk of it. A massive machine, a massive engine, wide and long and roaring, as close to a monster truck as he could get. His flimsy body at the helm of a wrecking ball. He was expected to be in control and responsible as he drove, getting his loads, but just as easily could have rampaged wild across the countryside, unstoppable as a military tank.

It took a while to know how and where to park it so that the bogger had enough room to lift the bucket of dirt and tip it into the tub within the few metres between the edge of the tub and the backs, and away from the services. He had to be precise so that the bogger could take the exact same route as it piled three or four scoops into the tub. It was about getting it done quickly with as little messing around as possible. The bogger operators and truck drivers didn't get a bonus on top of their flat rate for each truck loaded, but the bogger operators did have their deadlines of clearing out the face to let the jumbo back into bore its holes for charge up to load and fire at crib or knock-off.

For each load he had to write on a sheet of paper attached to a clipboard the level from which he got the load, the time of the load, the weight of the load, and the grade of the load. As a driller, he had watched the trucks heading to the surface loaded with grey rock, all looking the same, dull and lifeless as blue metal, with no hint as to what it carried, not like coal and iron ore—black and red. Maybe there was a trace of the white of quartz which indicated that gold was nearby, but even then it was more likely grey-dusted and indistinguishable from mullock, which was the rock from the decline and the drives heading to the ore seams; and there were no big chunks of gold sitting atop the rock in the back of the tub—each tonne had as little as five grams of gold to it, and at most forty. Now on the trucks he learned of the different grades, each assigned a colour: yellow, blue, green, and red. Mullock was white.

The very first load came from Mik, a very recently immigrated Croat and ally of the mine manager. Six-and-a-half-foot tall, a towering figure, late thirties, dark curly hair and thick moustache, intense blue eyes under thick dark eyebrows, quick to anger and reticent to explain both because of language and temperament. The trucks were open cab and with the engines of the bogger and the truck, the vent fans, his earplugs, and Mik's broken English he could hardly understand what was being yelled at him through the radio, this despite being no more than twenty metres away from each other in their respective cabs. He knew he had got it wrong when Mik flung open the door of his bogger and came over to yell at him directly, sometimes going so far as to drag Shaggy out of the truck to park it himself. All the while, Shaggy was sweating from the heat of the engines and diesel fumes, compact in the tight open cab, the paper becoming transparent with the sweat running down his arm onto his hand, down the pen, and onto the page.

The other bogger operator was Flemmo, who was far more relaxed and quickly took a shine to Shaggy, making playful fun of him at the camp, jibes of a friend. Flemmo was also quick-witted, endearing with his big smile, beautiful white teeth, glowing from the frame of his black goatee. Flemmo was closer to Shaggy's age, mid twenties, but had a mature head, and he lived in Mandurah as well. They had gotten close and Flemmo suggested they meet at the pub along with Flemmo's dad—a shift boss at another mine—and Rod, their shift boss from The Granites, who was also his uncle Peter's brother. It was the first time he had had a beer with them, having boycotted all shift changes at The Granites to save his money, to save his health, and to eliminate the possibility of drunken misdemeanours. And having invited some of his schoolmates to the pub as well, it was also the first time that any of his workmates and his schoolmates had met.

Shaggy introduced them to each other, but the atmosphere was already wrong, a tension in the air like it was a face-off between gangs—the hardened miners on one side and the soft-handed civilians on the other. Indeed, the first thing Rod did was criticise one of Shaggy's mates' handshakes, saying he shook hands like a poof. It was a defence mechanism—fight not flight—to show that real men work FIFO. They were hard, harder than any bloke here. Let it be known for those soft white-collar business-types who had the gall to look down on them. Let anyone know who didn't work away. This was the benchmark for a man. If they met that benchmark then they upped the ante by telling that they worked underground—underground was always the trump card. Shaggy's mate explained that he had injured his shoulder at work and couldn't squeeze his hand properly. Rod already wasn't listening; it escalated, his mate not one to back off, bung shoulder or not, and who also worked in mining as a fitter at the nearby ALCOA refinery. And Shaggy the sudden diplomat, an envoy for two warring foreign countries, had to shuffle his workmates to the other side of the bar, all within five minutes of the incommensurable worlds colliding. He chose to spend time with his workmates, knowing that his long-term schoolmates would forgive him. He also didn't want it to get back to camp that he had snubbed the boys from work. Too good for us; rather hang out with his gay mates; that's why he doesn't drink with us at the wet mess: not one of us.

Heavy drinking and they forgot the incident, allowing them to talk and enjoy themselves freely. Shop talk, but they knew each other well enough to leave the prying into their home lives alone.

Hanging shit on each other as if they were still at work. It could have just as easily been The Granites pub for all he knew. Relaxed and drinking in his home pub.

But the good times were soon disrupted. Flemmo senior, one of the more mature members of their party, was suddenly engaged in a brawl at the bar. Flemmo junior and about ten others joined in. A melee of pushing and shoving, hardly a connecting punch thrown, inelegant toing and froing, the idea of the fight more appealing than the harsh reality of the activity. The bouncers broke it up, pulling contestants off what looked like a tug-o-war. Flemmo and his dad were kicked out of the premises, without any sort of a goodbye. By then, his schoolmates had long gone, and Rod was similarly AWOL. So he slipped out of the pub, alone, in a familiar liminal space between home and away.

Truck driving epitomised the Sisyphean repetitiveness of mining, even more so than the tedium of drilling. Which meant he would get it right eventually—the parking, the loading, and the unloading—and through cautious driving, the next few months were incident free. By the third month he had it close to mastered: he knew the best spot to park for loading, how to reverse in one go, and each of his runs to the surface and back were within a minute of each other. No longer was he terrified by the experience of driving in the underground, and now revelled in the exhilaration of the descent, cornering like a go-kart, pushing the limits of the heavy vehicle, knowing its idiosyncrasies, its capabilities. He embraced the power the truck wielded, scattering the frightened utes like a bully of the decline.

He knew he was good when the bogger operators, both Mik and Flemmo, began to ask for him for the first loads. This was not the first show of respect towards him but possibly one of the first that he had merited on the mining side of things. He liked it, them needing him. He was one of the men: he was contributing, making them look good. They knew his name—Shaggy—and asked for him by name. Such small pathetic graces, but the warmth of the esteem he felt was immeasurable. He felt what he had begun to feel on the drill rigs as an offsider with Lee. Of finding that rhythm, that flow, the sweet spot. The synchronisation between man and machine, or man and his own body. This was the crucial moment where even the most mundane tasks become pleasurable, not the task itself, but in the act of doing. Even Sisyphus can be imagined as being happy, as Camus tells us, making the most of his absurd toil.

Nevertheless, the interest and enthusiasm for the trucks soon faded and the work became monotonous and routine. They would drive for six hours straight, up and down the decline, have a thirty-minute break, and then drive for another five hours. The monotony was also possibly the reason why some of the drivers, never named or caught, were putting the trucks in neutral, or 'angel' gear, for the descent, reaching twice the speed on the straight of the decline than if it were in gear. Death-drive, anything to inject even the slightest scintilla of excitement. This was only discovered when the fitters did the computer diagnostics on the trucks, able to identify that it happened but not the driver, even if it was out of only two.

Heading up the decline gave him too much time to think. Mostly about what was for dinner, how much he longed for his

A Boy Miner

bed, but also a good deal of mental arithmetic, dissecting his life into its emotional, logistical, and financial components. Thinking about his relationships, how to find himself a girlfriend. About how he would spend his break, what the highlights could be, his taped TV shows, *Seinfeld* and *The Simpsons*. Thinking about how and at what time he could get to the pub on his first night back, the beer he would drink. Thinking of his money, his house payments, his tax—a favourite subject for many of the blokes up there, as they attempt to squeeze the most out of their pay packets. Thinking about his negative gearing from the rent he was collecting. Adding, subtracting, multiplying, and dividing.

He had no choice but to keep his mind busy, repeating the same internal monologue over and over, like a skipping record, given that they had no radio or music to listen to—just the intermittent call of levels on channel one of the two-way radios, alerting other vehicles to stay out of the way. This left little chance for idle chatter. But they did have a second channel, channel two, where longer conversations could be had, mostly between the shift bosses and jumbo operators, bogger operators, or the service crew. After spending hours listening to nothing other than levels being called and meandering around in their own thoughts, it was a guilty thrill to suddenly hear the call, 'Can we switch to channel two?' Almost all of the truck drivers and bogger operators would also switch to satisfy their thirst for conversation but also for the off-chance that there was some gossip. An ostensibly private conversation could thus have up to ten eavesdroppers hoping to hear the details of some incident or controversy—grown men acting like members of a sewing circle. Of course, whilst they eavesdropped on channel two, the truck drivers were neglecting to call their levels on channel one, making for a harrowing situation for any of the light vehicle traffic, especially those heading up the decline, suddenly coming face to face with the front end of an orange avalanche.

The only fresh excitement was when the old Toro trucks were replaced with more traditional-looking Tonka truck Elphinstone 69D dump trucks—miniature versions of those from open pit mines, like Kalgoorlie's Superpit. They were brand new, the paint barely dry. Unlike the Toros they were closed cabs and air-conditioned, which meant the truck drivers stayed clean and cool and increasingly lazy, no longer wanting to leave the cab unless it was lunch, shift's-end, or on fire. They were also bigger, wider, and taller than the Toros, and seemed to float like a barge over ocean swells. On the first run down he heard the clanging of the tub against the service hooks in the top corners of the backs. Just like everything that went underground, both man and machine, they were worn in quickly, the newness soon rubbing off like the bloom of an overly-handled grape.

Diversity

No one knew what to do with themselves when the two women boarded the plane in Perth. Not as hostesses. Paula and Trudy. Both were starting on the trucks. They hired two thinking it best for them to have at least another woman to talk to, just in case the men snubbed them or were too shy. There had been female geologists at Bronzewing and the camp cleaning staff were mostly women, but none went underground as far as he had seen. This was the second big change to happen there in as many weeks. Their company Eltin was merging with Henry Walker and was now known as Henry Walker Eltin. Suddenly they had to wear new blue overalls with a new logo, but not much else had changed. Until the women arrived. Their appointment was likely a tokenistic gesture—a big new merger company setting a modest gender quota, to show their progressiveness. It seemed the second wave of feminism of the sixties was taking its time to make its way out to the desert, even as third wave feminism was taking hold in the civilised world. Certainly they would have preferred not to have built a new change room to accommodate them.

Some of the blokes were unhappy with the situation, especially the older boys no longer interested in the company of females. Resentful of the fact that they had to tone down the swearing, spitting, and farting; of having to straighten themselves up a little, their dirty stories unfit for fair ears. Even some guts were being sucked in. Paula and Trudy were at once feminine and courageously masculine, and knew what they were stepping into, and were ready to make as little trouble as possible; but still the atmosphere was changed, and not just from the foreign herbal smell of the shampoo cloud that followed the two women around, reminding everyone of home and their lax civility.

It shouldn't have been surprising that they were good at truck driving; the bosses lauded them, telling everyone that questioned their being there about how they took fewer risks than their male counterparts, banging them up far less; they were tidier, keeping the cabs spotless, not putting up with the usual filth; and they were efficient, running laps as quick as anyone. Better truck drivers than half the blokes. Though it was hard to say if they would ever be promoted beyond the trucks—too good on the trucks and hardly suited for much else. Trudy was about five foot nothing and had a soft, round womanly figure, could only just see over the steering wheel, with the man-shaped overalls straining against her big breasts. Paula was only slightly taller, and leaner, but was still soft in her arms and face. The trucks weren't physically demanding; almost every other job was, and, as he knew well, very few concessions are made for the weak, no matter how good it may look for the HR department. Trudy had a partner at home, making it very explicit. Paula was single. Blonde-haired and blue-eyed. Should be on the beach somewhere, bikini, sunscreen. Not here, stirring up the boys. A relationship at the camp could be the best and the worst. Don't shit where you eat.

It had its many shortcomings, The Granites, but it was redeeming itself—politically-speaking—with its attempt at diversity within its ranks. It was almost half comprised of an immigrant labour force, with Croats, Kiwis, Irishmen, and Canadians, and a short, wiry but enthusiastic Chinese engineer, Binh Ngo, or 'Bingo' as he came to be known. The common enemy of inhospitable settings seemed the cornerstone of successful multiculturalism. When the chips are down, colour and creed were about as indiscriminate and arbitrary as their seat number on the plane.

And about the same time that Trudy and Paula made a start they also hired three aboriginal blokes. Again it seemed tokenistic, quotas and such. They deserved tokenism more than anyone, if it can be earned through hardship. This had been their country after all, so let them earn some money out of its pillaging. Billy, the oldest of the trio, in his fifties, was quiet and had worked his life through, and started on the drills. The second, Jack, was early thirties, an ex-professional boxer in his previous life, clearly winning more than he lost because of his clean good-looking face. Together with his height and strong body, his success, he immediately gained respect from the mostly white crew, just as many aboriginals will in a sometimes-racist-but-sports-mad nation. He was on the trucks, as was Jamie, the youngest, about Shaggy's age, who spent much of his spare time in the gym, at the bench press working on his pectorals, following up the session with a string of cigarettes, collapsing his shapely chest from the inside. They were also good truck drivers, but the same questions seemed to loom as to how far up the ladder they could go. Better chance than the women, maybe.

There was some discomfort, he felt, in the disparity between the treatment of the aboriginal workers and the aboriginal people that inhabited the camps scattered around the Tanami, somewhere on the outskirts of the camp. This was most telling with the rules of the wet mess. Unlike Bronzewing, which allowed them to keep beer in their dongas, The Granites banned alcohol from being taken out of the mess. This was because of concerns that it could be moved on beyond the camp to the dry aboriginal settlements. Each can of beer was opened before it was handed over to ensure it got drank there and then, no more than six cans at a time, warming quickly in the heat. The indigenous people it seemed were able to survive the most inhospitable landscape imaginable for forty thousand years or more, and yet had to be saved from drinking themselves to extinction.

He had seen evidence to suggest that it made sense to enforce the ban when driving once from an alternate airstrip because of flooding. They passed a wheelless sedan on the side of the muddied road, five full-blooded aboriginal men sitting on the ground beside it, all floating in a sea of empty VB and Export beer cans. Several smiling, grey hair and beards, thumbs up; the others passed out.

The bus slowed a bit, not to check on their wellbeing but to avoid collecting them, if they were to get up and stumble into the road. The blokes in the bus hooted and laughed, cheering the stranded men on as they drove past, or spoke under their breath at the pathetic state of it all.

But it was Jamie who spoke up the loudest. 'Fuckin abbos!'

The bus roared with fresh laughter. Shaggy laughed too but wasn't sure who Jamie had directed it at: the men on the side of the road, separate from Jamie, or Jamie himself as one of their own, sharing the same blood. The latter made sense. Certainly a bit of Aussie self-deprecation always went a long way. Cut yourself down if you even think of becoming tall; raise yourself up by dragging others down. Or it wasn't about him and his blood at all. Maybe he felt no connection with these people and wanted to make it clear to everyone else there. He was lighter skinned, hardly resembled the men they had passed. Which didn't mean there was no affiliation. Maybe it was just because he was too young to appreciate his history or understand the hardship of the past. Like any young man doesn't, white and black alike.

Daryl and Shit

Driving trucks: twelve hours a day, up and down the decline, for the two-week swings, for over half a year. Thinking on his

A Boy Miner

usual things, but also about how he could stop driving trucks—how he could eventually get promoted onto a bogger, which paid almost twice as much. There had been better odds for promotion on the drills. Each driller had only one offsider, which meant it was possible for an experienced offsider to take his place, with the incumbent offsider needing less orientation to the mine, and no time-wasting inductions. It was easier to show initiative too, owning the rig, like Bob had showed him, and learning the drill rig, like Lee had told him.

On the trucking side, however, there were only two bogger operators for five or six trucks. The odds of promotion to a bogger were far shorter, the competition more fierce and harder to demonstrate being worthy of a promotion, given that they couldn't take work home to get ahead, take extra courses to build the CV. Ambition had to be shown through the dogged enthusiasm for their work. He was quick on the new trucks, getting his loads, was first to get down the hole and water down the piles. That was the best he could do. A good, reliable truck driver, a favourite of the bogger operators, worthy of promotion.

It must have been coincidence then that someone had lent him a copy of Bret Easton Ellis' *American Psycho* around the time its protagonist, Patrick Bateman, the cold-hearted serial killer and Shaggy's biggest competition, stepped off the plane, three months after Shaggy, carrying ambition in his luggage like no one else, Shaggy included. Daryl was older than Shaggy by eight years or so and about his height and build. But where Shaggy had been keeping a low profile, letting his driving do the talking, Daryl made sure everyone knew who he was, engaging bogger operators, shift bosses, schmoozing and gladhanding, and probing, looking for an insight, an edge, ready to exploit any opportunity, smiling with his mouth, but empty in his eyes. He was Patrick Bateman and he was also a pigeon, from his black emotionless eyes, to the sharp, random movements of his head, as if distrustful, paranoid, trying to see everywhere at once, to how he pecked starvingly around his superiors, waiting for some scrap to come his way.

Shaggy didn't hate Daryl, even as he so callously diagnosed and dehumanised him. There was no point hating anyone at camp, too exhausting and inescapable. He said hello in the morning, and they necessarily talked on the radios, letting each other know where they were on the decline, giving way when they met, just as all the truckies were expected to do. But he wouldn't go out of his way to talk to him, or purposefully take a seat next to him in the mess. He would sit next to him if it was the only seat available.

He didn't hate Daryl, but he certainly disliked him because within a week of being on the trucks, Daryl had usurped his established position as the boggers' favourite. This was not because he was a better truck driver (even if he may have been), but because now he was the first down the hole. Front and centre, pole position, on the radio asking where he wanted the bogger ops to meet him before they even knew where they were going. One shift, Shaggy was down the hole first; the next, it was Daryl.

It was a flabbergasting moment: Shaggy making his way to his truck to do his prestart checks—walking just a little faster than the other truck drivers, who seemed less interested in getting there first, caring less about competing with the boy. Shaggy was checking the transmission fluid level and suddenly a rumble of

A Boy Miner

an engine and away, Daryl's truck, leaving them literally eating his dust. Surely Daryl had neglected the duty of filling out his logbook—the newcomer forgetting his routine, Shaggy giving him the benefit of the doubt.

The following shift, Shaggy got dressed as usual, Daryl too, but after grabbing their caplamps he spied Daryl darting towards the trucks just as the rest of the crew went to make a coffee and wait for the safety meeting to begin. Shaggy followed Daryl, stalked him really, like a serial killer himself, at a distance, to keep from being spotted, but also because he was struggling to keep up with Daryl, walking with his long strides, just short of a run; walking as if he were measuring out something by the metre. Shaggy watched him clamber over his truck, checking his oils and fluids, kicking tyres, before returning just in time for the start of the meeting.

He was cheating. An injustice. A traitor. Shaggy would have much preferred a drag race to the portal, pushing and shoving their way down the hole, but not this. Shaggy, filled with loathing, yet awed by its brilliance. Wall Street, business-like, cutthroat. Undercutting competitors. Razor-thin margins. If only Shaggy had thought of it first. He had become too comfortable, taken his position for granted. Worst of all was that Daryl, the interloper, had set a new standard for the rest of the truck drivers and within a week they were no longer sluggish in getting to their trucks but scampering, like sycophantic clones, as if only now infected by the promotion bug, making the long shifts even longer, an unpleasant situation made more so by elevating already high levels of stress.

Daryl would not be assigned any nickname. No Dazza for him. Almost as if he was not to be trusted or embraced by the crew enough to honour him with this sign of familiarity. Not everyone got a name. Sometimes out of respect, or the opposite.

○

Shaggy's work ethic needed to be refocused and redoubled; he reminded himself of his mantra: get the loads to get the promotion, to pay off the house, to get out. Get the loads to get the promotion, to pay off the house, to get out. As monomaniacal as Captain Ahab, his White Whale the mortgage of a suburban brick-and-tile.

But his strong work ethic was a double-edged sword. Something had to give, some sacrifice made. If he was to secure his place as one of best truck drivers to get the promotion then it was essential that, by the end of the shift, his tally of loads taken to the surface was greater than—not equal to—everyone else's. It was imperative that he didn't stop. Keep on truckin'. Except for the lunch break, he drove for over eleven hours. Day shift was not so much a problem; night shift was different. His body had never quite reversed the normal circadian rhythms when he slept through the day, getting no more than five or six hours. When he did sleep, both at night or during the day, he would dream, vividly, that somehow his enormous truck was parked in his donga, looming over him like a yellow monolith. Lights on, engine running, spewing heat, fumes and noise, threatening to crush him under the heavy tire if he didn't climb in. Or he would dream that he was in the midst of driving, up and down the decline, never loading or unloading, just driving. Working as he slept, fighting his way through nightmares, waking hourly to convince himself that it was a dream. Even in the dream, telling his dreaming self

A Boy Miner

that it was a dream. Arguing, remonstrating with himself, waking mentally exhausted.

To their credit, the bosses encouraged them to take breaks if they ever felt tired. Have a coffee on the surface and recharge. Take a short nap even. The trucking crew knew it was an empty suggestion, made only to placate the OHS people's concerns; and no one looking for a promotion would dare give up a run to rest, except for the older truckies who were mining more for the companionship than the money. Like Cowboy, a white-haired, moustachioed and bespectacled Canadian, well into his sixties, sometimes taking to fits of rambling. Cowboy, going about his shift slow and steady; which is to say he was wise and carefree, his job safe because of his past. Cowboy didn't need cash or a promotion, which is what Shaggy was only interested in. Which also made Shaggy fast and unsteady, immature and anxious. He would not take the suggested rest, and at times he became dangerous to himself and others; even more dangerous because he didn't know he was being dangerous: such as when he realised that for periods on some shifts, usually at about 3am, he wasn't calling his levels as he came down the decline—sometimes two or three levels at a time—not because he had forgotten to call them, absent-minded, thinking of something else, but because he had been sleep driving, semi-conscious, on autopilot, from one level to the next, nearly ten seconds at a time. His eyes were open, absorbing data in a pre-cognitive, automatic way, but without processing it. Like reading a sentence, left to right, without attending to the meaning of the words. He was lucky in that he never hit a wall and never hit anyone else. Just as he was lucky when he fell off his parked truck, limply, three metres to the ground, again semi-conscious for the length of the journey, the impact waking him as rudely as his alarm ever had, wondering what had happened. His relaxed legs crumpling underneath him when he hit, like those of a marionette, fabric joints and foam limbs, which was safer than if he were awake.

On another night, he fell asleep at the portal as he waited for another truck to come up. He woke an hour later, still parked up, engine running. The shift boss had been flashing his caplamp in his eyes as he went past, calling him on the radio, the trucks beeping their horns—none would disturb him. Asleep like he was etherised, comatose. And on another night shift he forgot to put his tub down after dumping the truck's load. Half asleep, attentive as a drunk-driver. The truck's alarm that alerted him to the tub being up wasn't working and if it weren't for a final defence, about one hundred metres before the portal, of some cable and drums strung across the decline he would have crashed into the top of the portal, wreaking havoc.

The incident of the tub, and other sundry errors in judgment, chipped away at the esteem he had steadily been accruing. He should have bought a carton of beer each time and drank on it with the boys at the wet mess—laugh about it, ease his conscience and drown the shame. Instead, after shifts like this, he would go to the mess, eat his dinner, head down, fork from plate to face, before heading straight to his room to hurry the new, unblemished day along. In his room to agonise over the details, wonder how long until they fired him. Whether he was pulling his weight, slowing down production. He would try to sleep and bring the new day.

Even then, when he woke (a new sun for day shift, the sun departing on a night shift) there was no real escape from the prestart meeting when the previous shift's dirty laundry was aired.

A Boy Miner

More than this: the bloke who made the biggest mistake the day before was expected to run the meeting and kick it off with an explanation of his incident to the crew, the purpose being to have the miners feel more responsible for their safety, taking ownership, like an estranged couple in therapy working through his affair. In reality, it was a means for scapegoating, intended to reaffirm their shame and self-loathing. This way they could ensure the error wasn't repeated. Don't do what he did. The boy was a regular host.

It was a bizarre and absurd meeting, again straight out of Heller's *Catch-22*. The boy, prompted by the shift boss, would stand up in front of the seated crew, steady his voice, before making his earnest enquiry: 'Were there any incidents of note from yesterday's shift?' A silence followed, given that it was more or less a rhetorical question, like asking whether there are any objections to a couple getting married.

Nothing left except to respond to himself in the affirmative, before narrating the story for those whom may not have heard the gossip about it the day before: 'Well, yes, I had an incident. I accidentally left my tub up because the tub-up alarm wasn't working.'

'What could I have done?

'I should have recognised the issue during my prestart checks and immediately addressed the issue with the fitters.'

'Very good. Any other incidents? No? Thank you, Shaggy.'

The double-edged sword of his redoubled work ethic also lead to a much less dangerous but far more unpleasant and scatological situation. On a dayshift, a bit after lunch, having dumped his load on the surface, he felt something wrong in his stomach. A twinge, a slight upset, but nothing to be overly concerned about, interpreting the stirring merely as a touch of gas, which could easily be solved by ripping off a good solid fart, even if he already wasn't brave enough to try. He could have erred on the safe side and headed to the surface toilets. But he needed the loads and it could wait until the end of shift. So he drove down, each bump a threat to his delicate equilibrium.

His truck was loaded from the very bottom of the decline—a fifteen-minute drive to get to the bottom and a thirty-minute-plus journey to the surface. His tally for the day would be very low because of it and each one was crucial. A few minutes into the ascent and without any warning, his stomach lurched, and began to bubble away like some mean witch's brew. A wicked demon was creating pandemonium within his gut and needed to be exorcised quickly. If it was vomit, he could have easily expelled it from the window of his cab and carried on driving without disruption of his tally. For this situation, though, a toilet was imperative. The surface toilets, he knew, were still some twenty minutes or more away. The only viable option would be the infamous underground toilet, about ten minutes away, up the decline, hidden down a drive. Never having seen it, he imagined a simple, open-air hole in the ground, like an outback long-drop made from an old drill hole, with a few rags and dirty magazines nearby for toilet paper. Even if it was more like a portable toilet used at public events, its condition, like that of portable toilets used at public events, was certainly dubious. And there were no cleaners that he knew of that took a dedicated journey down the mine, Pine 'O Clean in hand, to give it a sprucing.

A Boy Miner

Regardless of its state, this sole underground shitter was his only salvation—a safe refuge in the battle against his innards. And so he sped up the decline towards it, at the eight kilometres an hour that the fully-loaded truck would allow, accelerator foot planted, pedal to the metal, willing the truck forward. Willing the truck and willing himself, alternating between meditation—talking to himself, convincing himself, bargaining with himself—and tensing every muscle in his body in an attempt to master his internal organs. As if his consciousness could somehow intervene in the indifferent material processes of his ailing body.

But the body is no slave to the mind. It was too late. He emptied himself, fully-clothed, seated in his truck, foot still planted. Lee, his long-suffering first driller, would have been proud of his commitment. And at least it was private as such episodes should be.

Though no longer useful to him, he continued his slow meander to the underground toilet, choosing it over the shaming spotlight of the surface. Silent on his whereabouts, he pulled down the drive, which was thankfully dark and unused, and drove until he spotted a port-a-loo hidden at the back. He shut down his truck, and, like a cat burglar, cautiously exited the cab, attempting to leave without a trace. The inside of his overalls, though, had guilt all over them—like a cat burglar that had shit himself.

The only thing for it was to completely strip off—first his belt with his self-rescuer, battery back, hardhat and cap lamp, and set up the cap lamp on a rock, angling it so that it shone some light. He then removed his gumboots and socks (both of which had been soiled when the thick overalls' legs acted like sewerage pipes as he exited the truck), then his overalls, and finally his jocks. Mercifully, the t-shirt he wore underneath his overalls was untainted, and so he very carefully removed it and set it aside in a safe place, as if it were the Shroud of Turin. He then stood, utterly naked, under the water tap that hung from above his head to spray himself and his clothes. Although breathtakingly cold, it had the power of a fire hose, which was most suitable for the job. He hoped only that a ute didn't make its way down the drive and throw its headlights on the depraved scene. Worse if for some reason a rock had fallen on his head. Eventually he would be found, naked, covered in blood and shit, a sex act gone awry. A hard one to explain at the following pre-shift meeting but the message would be clear: 'When underground, don't get naked and don't take your hardhat off, because you could end up like Shaggy.'

First he washed his clothes and gumboots, and then himself from the waist down. He wrung out the overalls and socks as best he could and let the boots drain, before dressing himself. The overalls were still cold and damp, and so he placed the clean and dry t-shirt between himself and the truck seat. As if it had never happened. Never had he been so efficient and methodical in his actions. He thought that maybe this horrific moment might be salvaged by knowing that maybe he had learned something; about how to keep his head, think things through and get a job done in the most efficacious way. He also thought that he should seek out better ways to make himself proud.

It had been nearly half an hour by the time he re-entered the decline to head to the surface. And like some lost plane believed to have been consumed by the Bermuda Triangle, he re-established radio contact and began calling his levels, still as if it had never happened.

Flemmo was first on the radio to enquire about his absence, looking for an explanation or gossip. He told him nothing. Instead Shaggy radioed Bailey, the shift boss. They switched to channel two and Shaggy told the shift boss (and everyone else eavesdropping) that he had shit himself, still wasn't feeling all that flash, and was finished for the day. Bailey had no qualms, not looking for further elaboration of the details, and told him to carry on.

He returned to the surface, dumped his load, parked his truck, showered again, got changed, and threw his overalls in the bin. He wasn't alone: about ten of the crew had become ill and were already on the surface. It was the lunch, most likely spoiled ham or coleslaw dressing. Though it seemed he was the only one who disgraced himself. He had let it slip—the word got around; a few had a laugh, Flemmo particularly, but most let it pass over without further discussion, feeling sympathetic towards him, somewhere between how they would feel if he were cuckholded, or how he had felt about Arron and his crushed hand. Nor was it brought up at the safety meeting on the following shift. Soon it was forgotten, like so many other incidents, true and rumoured alike. One foot after the other, the next day would follow the next.

Love
March 1999

'You're putting on a bit of weight there,' Stumpy, one of his old Mandurah schoolmates, said, pointing at his guts, grinning as if some justice had finally been enacted, what with him being a stockier bloke, lacking the indefatigable metabolism of his ever-scrawny mate. He was grinning because Shaggy was getting fat.

It was a shock, just as much as if he had told him that he was pregnant, or his dick had dropped off. It had crept up, silent, accrued like time spent procrastinating. But he had been driving trucks for about nine months now, sitting on his arse for twelve hours a day, and eating as if he were still working on the drills. He had reached term, not as fecund as old Bob from Bronzewing had been, mesmerising in the geometry of his beer-belly's roundness, but Shaggy had been a low-weight baby himself, as if premature, misshapen fontanels, older than he should be by being born too early.

It was a shock also because, at about this same time, he had met a girl on one of his breaks and was suddenly very self-conscious of his naked body; more so than taking a shower in front of thirty or so blokes at the mine site. Lizzy was pretty, happy, and vibrant. Most importantly, she had a way of making conversation happen; could discourse on her day like all the world had happened, making the mundane interesting not through art but through the act of giving it voice, something that the young and the pretty can get away with when the weight of the world rests on other shoulders. She had a knack of drawing him out of himself, but still he overedited himself, censoring himself of the trivial, even if the textual history of human discourse is flooded with it.

It was necessarily a brief courtship. They were introduced by a mutual friend, a set-up, at the pub, where he was amicable and fun, threw his money around, just as he always did on his break, making himself the centre of attention. He plied them both with drinks, and couldn't help but brag about the house he bought, which he deemed his most impressive quality, assured by the fact of money and wary of depreciating his own value the more he opened his mouth.

And then he was packing to leave. Lizzy in her car on his driveway, him leaning in, a kiss goodbye.

'See you in two weeks.'

'See you in two weeks.'

'I will call Thursday, 730pm, okay?' and confirmed her phone number in his little address book.

Reversing out of the driveway and away.

Back to the mine, calling her at the arranged time, now needing to get to know her over the phone. Again he fell to exaggerating the parts of him he wanted her to know, shaping his personality into extremes, pointed and abstract. Knowing her voice, but, just as it had been with Emma, he had quickly forgotten what she looked like except some parts of her face, a patchy identikit image, torn pages of a collage, resembling parts of other women's faces.

Two weeks and again she was parked on his driveway; and hearing her car arrive from the living room, he ran out to greet her, and immediately said something both cute and stupid: 'You're gorgeous, I had forgotten what you look like.'

'Oh thanks, didn't think I was that forgettable,' sarcastic and good-natured, countering his foot-in-mouth. She was used to talking to idiots.

With that, his place in the world was suddenly at its most uncomplicated and undemanding. At cruising altitude. Giddy on his break. Wanting to share it. He was ready for someone, he thought. He needed someone. Too much.

He told her he loved her too early.

Brett J Jenkins

Service Crew
July 1999

He drove trucks for a year before being offered a promotion to the service crew. Maybe because he was next in line; or maybe because they had recognised his effort, given that he got a lot of trucks out and was also prepared to defecate himself for the good of the company. Rash was happy because he took Shaggy's spot on the trucks, getting himself off the drills. And Shaggy was happy because he got the promotion ahead of Daryl, which was a small victory, and included a pay rise of over thirty percent. Not as much as a promotion to the bogger operators and the service crew would be more labour intensive, but at this stage, he wasn't picky; and by the time Daryl got his pigeon-headed goal of being promoted to the bogger, Shaggy was finalising his end game.

The service crew was a two-man team with the role of handymen of the mine, essential in keeping the machines going and the mine extending. A three-man team would have made it easier, but two could do it. Their machine was the IT—the frontend loader with a basket attached, like the one he had briefly familiarised himself with in Kalgoorlie when he and Boof were expected to run their own services.

Poetically, the service crew were responsible for the veins, lungs, bowels, and nervous system of the mine; more prosaically, they were responsible for the compressed air and water services, ventilation, pumps, and electrical cables. Amongst other things, the water was needed for the machines to drill, clearing out the grit of the hole, and to water down the freshly exploded pile of dirt. The ventilation needed to be extended down the decline and into the drives to keep fresh air moving and to blow out the exhaust fumes. The pumps stopped the mine from flooding from the water from the machines, the groundwater, and the rainfall coming down the hole. They were attached to return pipes sending the muddied water up through intermittent sumps and pump-stations to the surface. And the electrical cables kept power to the fans and machines, including the jumbos and the drill rigs. The service crew were also responsible for repairing torn vent bags, changing pumps, and installing the fans, power boxes, sprinkler systems, and communication cables.

The cushy year he spent on the trucks left him unprepared for his initiation into the service crew. Like his transfer to the trucks, there was almost no warning—he was now on the service crew. He would be working with the outgoing service crew—Brendon, who was moving on to charge-up, and Tezza, who was moving to a different roster. His first task was to assist Brendon in the basket with concreting cable bolts. This involved pumping concrete into six- and nine-metre cable bolt holes, 60mm in diameter, drilled into the ceiling by the jumbo. There was a second basket that had a built-in cement mixer trough and they mixed the bags of concrete with water. The cable bolts themselves were inserted by hand with a foot or so remaining outside of the hole. Each had two tubes taped to the length of them: one for pumping concrete; and one as a breathing tube to let you know when the hole was full. They would jam rags and foam at the entrance of the hole to seal it so that the concrete didn't drain. Then they pumped the concrete up the first tube. The seal was always poor, and the only way you knew the hole was full was when the concrete poured out of the second breathing tube. They then pinched the tube and tied it in a knot. Concrete would be flicked over him, or run down his arm. They worked for twenty minutes at a time, close to the ceiling of the drives, where the heat and fumes would steadily build. Within ten minutes he was soaked with sweat and beginning to feel dizzy.

'We shouldn't be working in these conditions.' He told Brendon this, the lead for the crew, which was both brazen and naïve. Sounding soft.

Brendon reacted hotly. 'You haven't even done anything yet! Why the fuck do you have a t-shirt under your overalls?!'

He had always worn a t-shirt under his overalls—the thick, coarse hessian-like material never felt good on his back, especially when he sweated.

'It's still too hot, Brendon; and there's too many fumes,' Shaggy said, raising his voice to what he hoped was a reasonable level, like talking down a suicide jumper.

But Brendon had heard enough of reasonable talk and as good as jumped, signalling to Tezza in the IT cab for the basket to be lowered. Unceremoniously, he kicked the boy out, before heading back up to finish the job alone.

Shaggy walked away, got some air, slowed his pulse and the throb in his head, and when Brendon came back down to get another bag of cement, the boy asked to be let back in and help finish the job with him. Brendon was reluctant but he conceded, given that he was assigned the role of training up the boy.

There was a lesson in all this, or a warning that was unspoken, loose thinking that needed to be fastened tight in the mind: health comes second to the job, not because they didn't believe in looking after themselves, but because there was always someone else who believed in it less; someone else willing to do the job unflinchingly, ready to take his place if he didn't. There was no union to step in and fight for better working conditions. No one was handing out the literature of Marx and Engels, banding together to scream the communist catchcry 'Workers of the world, unite!' This was the job. Unwritten but nevertheless bold-faced as a WANTED poster.

Even the bosses had begun circulating the propaganda-like three-word slogan 'Have a go,' which was a suggestion that, even if a task seems difficult or hard, make an attempt. Test yourself, see what you are made of, be the best you can be. How most of them understood it, through the subterfuge, was that even if it seems that a task was too dangerous or detrimental to your health, have a crack at it anyway—have a go—because we need to keep things moving and you need to get paid.

Again he would need to adjust his attitude: get on with it, take the risk. Before someone else did.

Dave P

Pointing with an indifferent finger, half-curled, indefinite, Dave P ordered, 'Grab that bag.' No handshake or a 'How do you do?' He just turned and walked, ambulatory, towards the service crew ute across the red dirt gravel patch of a carpark. He walked with a strange lilt, a saunter, hips swaying almost effeminately, completely out of place amongst the thickened atmosphere of hyper-masculinity. And yet absolutely confident in his place, uncaring of the opinions of others. It was the tool bag Shaggy had inherited from Brendon, which included some C-spanners for poly-pipe joins, a pair of side-cutting pliers, a hacksaw, shifting spanner, and a gimpy. An array of tools that seemed to cover almost every aspect of the job. They used wire to bind things. Or mining safety clips. Nothing overly complex or finicky. Twist it, cut it, or hit it. And if you are going to hit it, hit it hard, fuck ya.

He grabbed the tool bag and followed Dave P to the ute and they both drove around to where the IT was parked. 'We're hanging vent bag. You're in the IT. Meet me at the face of 1120.' He left the boy and drove off in the ute to find what he needed. It wasn't much of an introduction, but Dave P's reputation was such that the boy shouldn't have expected any different. Dave P had come over from the cross-shift service crew, and he was a 'fuckin' prick,' or so he had been told, words floating on the shift crossover. A misanthrope to the core—the type that didn't appear to belong in mining or FIFO or living in a camp, and yet didn't belong away from it either, having done it most of his life.

The cold shoulder because he didn't like being assigned a skinny kid—worse, an ex-driller—who had very little common sense or knowledge about the mine except where to park a truck. Give him the boy, that'll show that fuckin' prick.

He was married, some kids. Maybe—he wasn't forthcoming. Tall, early forties, a large, clean oval face, weak chin, with a slight overbite. Sensible hair, straight, parted keenly. He was educated, academically minded. His opinions, if he offered them, were considered and lacked prejudice. An intellectual—even shared his last name with a famous second-century astronomer and mathematician, which may have given him his elevated sense of importance. Aristocratic, entitled. Seemed he could have taken up any number of white-collar careers. Business, law, politics. Something must have gone wrong for him to end up here, cheek to jowl with the great unwashed.

A Boy Miner

At the close of the first shift, at dinner in the mess, the boy thought he would be torn as to who he would sit with—the truck drivers and bogger operators that he had worked with and knew well, or with Dave P, his newest and closest workmate, to better forge their relationship. But it wasn't up to him. Dave P was ahead of Shaggy in the line, and after filling his plate made his way over to a far corner of the mess, choosing to sit alone, his back to the rest of the crew—his new crew. It hadn't been the best shift: from the underwhelming introductions, the rest of the shift was equally fractious, with Dave P barking instructions from the basket, and the boy operating the IT poorly, jerking the basket around, driving too slow or too fast, not having used one in almost two years. But at the end of the following shift, and the next, and the next, good or otherwise, Dave P chose every time to sit apart from the crew. This was how Dave P liked it, content with his own company, finding the time alone that Shaggy had often longed for, but which now looked miserable if he were ever to get it.

Dave P finished his dinner, left, avoiding the wet mess on his way home, just as Shaggy did. He did see Dave P there once or twice, usually when one of the big bosses had flown in, whom Dave P considered his equals, especially the 'seagulls,' those that flew in, shit on everything, and flew out. He had previously been a shift boss and manager himself at other mines and they were old acquaintances, which entitled him to a level of arrogance and also explained the bitter chip on his shoulder—no longer in charge but knew it in himself that he could do the shift boss or managerial jobs better than most. He seemed accepting of his position on the service crew, though, not begrudging it, as if resigned to contradict his apparent blue-blooded lineage; about as much as the boy was rallying against his own red-dirt-blooded heredity. Dave P did as he was told and whether he believed it was right or wrong would do it anyway, deferring to his bosses, without question, taking no responsibility. Preferred it for the freedom that the service crew gave him, having the run of the mine, maintaining its enduring force. And doing so in his own time: he worked methodically, slowly, canny enough to know that, if he was destined to spend most of his life working as a labourer, then it wasn't a sprint but a marathon; that he should save just enough of his strength to fall over the line.

They alternated between having a dirty, tough, sweaty shift of labouring in the basket, and a clean, easy shift in the air-conditioned cab. Dave P explained the jobs to him; but he didn't really speak to Shaggy: he spoke disinterestedly like a bored tour guide, a disillusioned lecturer, looking everywhere except at the boy, looking over his head, as if for a much larger audience behind him. The rest, Shaggy learned from the basket, on his own, with Dave P barking orders at him from the IT. No matter how prepared they were on the ground, installing fans and cable-bolting holes took some coaching to get right. Dave P was patient in the sense that he was happy to let Shaggy struggle away until he solved it, in no rush to complete every task expected of them. Only when the boy was absolutely spent or if a more urgent job had arisen would Dave P begrudgingly exit the IT cab, climb up its arms into the basket, to offer his sagacious advice.

A Boy Miner

Each day brought new problems for solving. In this, the job was better than most as it was varied, less repetitive, even if it was one of the most hot and dirty. On his days in the basket he would return to the surface, soaked from sweat, face covered in dust, as if he'd participated in some inappropriate blackface routine, like he had seen in the other service crews when they surfaced, never knowing how it happened. He felt like a hard man, one of the last to get to the surface, walking from the ute to the change rooms, covered head to toe in shit, the incoming shift still nice and clean as they exited the bus. It was mostly the vent bags, the dust settling on them from blasting, loosed when they moved them around from drive to drive. At the end of every shift, he would wash his hair and scrub himself with the gritted cleaning soap, leaving raw pink flesh. Even then, the deep pores in his nose remained black-clogged, as if dotted with cracked pepper.

Suddenly, he had the weathered appearance of a proper miner—overalls faded and torn, salty sweat-stains, and dust. Truck drivers and bogger operators hardly needed to labour—just drive and operate—with almost no need to even leave the cab, especially with the air-conditioning of the newer machines. He knew some bogger operators who wore the same overalls for almost the whole swing, whereas he was going through a pair a day, sometimes two, a load of washing after every shift.

At the end of the fortnight, when they flew back home, he

watched Dave P leave the terminal as if they were all strangers exiting a regular commercial domestic flight, without a wave or obligatory 'Enjoy your break'. No doubt there were louts and drunks on the plane, and the stink continued to be unbearable, but his level of antipathy towards the crew suggested that each carried with them a crying, spewing, shitting baby. Dave P walked his sauntering walk towards the nearest bus stop to wait for the next. No family member to come pick him up. Was it frugality that kept him from hiring a taxi, or a stubbornness that kept him from calling his wife or a friend? Or resignation that the break was no different to any other; not an event to be celebrated, to be made the most of. It was to be ambled through, like he was grocery shopping, indifferent and bored. It certainly wasn't Christmas: Shaggy at his most joyful blasting down the freeway to Mandurah, stereo at full noise, the freedom of the road, having penetrated the imagined perimeter of the camp, risking speeding tickets as he made his way home. If he had a hat, he would have held it out the window and yee-hawed like a cowboy herding strewn cattle.

The mine, charge up, and stopes

There wasn't much to see when he was on the drills, stuck down empty drives as they were, dead ends, away from the action. Even on the trucks he didn't see much of the mine except the decline and the drives where they were loaded. And he never really got to see the jumbo or charge-up crew working, both of which were necessarily elsewhere when the bogger moved in. Now on the service crew, he had a legitimate reason to be anywhere, with a role to play in almost every facet of the mine. This also meant that he was expected to work with the explosives, restocking the surface explosives magazine and transferring them underground. There was no training and he had no licence or clearance to work with explosives. It was before the September 11 attacks: before the two planes rudely penetrated the Twin Towers and changed everything. Different times. And he could easily have taken detonators and explosives home—enough to destroy a house or a shed. Maybe blow up a lake for the fish. All for a bit of a laugh—a larrikin kind of thing. He didn't, though. But he could have.

Sometimes he was called upon to help the charge-up guy load the jumbo-drilled wall with explosives—help stick the detonators into the dynamite sticks, which were two feet long and an inch or two in diameter, soft and wrapped like polony. They would then push the dynamite stick to the end of the hole and fill the rest of the hole with anfo (ammonium nitrate/fuel oil)—harmless pink beads, ironically looking like popping candy, which could only explode when ignited by a much larger blast. They pumped the anfo into the holes, under high pressure, from a compressed air tank. When the hole was filled, the anfo would spray out onto the skin, the chemicals burning in any cuts on his hands or arms. The mass of detonation cord hanging from the wall looked like a multi-colourful spider web, or the tangle of wires at the back of an old supercomputer, all running to the hub of bell wire, which was rolled out down the drive and far enough around the corner to the detonation switch for firing.

There was a very real tension all the while, working at the face of something that would be blown up by the explosives, enough rock to fill the fleet of dump trucks. And they worked with more haste than he was comfortable with. They had to work fast because there was only a small window to charge up the face. Once the jumbo was pulled out, it was a mad scramble to get it charged for blasting at crib or the end of shift. This would give enough time for the smoke and dust to settle at the respective lunch break and the shift crossovers before the bogger came and loaded it into the trucks, clearing it out for the jumbo to begin boring holes again.

Charging up was safe in the loose sense of the word; but if it went wrong, it went really wrong with no chance of survival. Like standing in front of a firing squad armed not only with bullets, but cannon balls and car engines. What kind of body to recover? Tense and frantic as they charged.

Working on the service crew also meant he could see the stopes, which was where the bulk of the ore was found, leaving huge cavernous openings, the size of an apartment block once the ore was blown up and bogged out. The stopes were created by drilling from the first level before blasting it so that it dropped down to the ground floor, and continuing to do so right up to the penthouse. Each level that was taken away created an increasingly deeper chasm underneath, which also meant that each time they went up a level they were drilling right above it. As he stepped around the level, there was a matrix of holes filled or being filled with anfo and the larger diameter polony sticks, like landmines, more disconcerting because of their conspicuousness. The stope blasts of a level were many times more powerful than the blasts at the faces and the vibrations could be felt even from the surface. To retrieve the blasted dirt from the ground floor, they used a

A Boy Miner

remote-controlled bogger operated from a little office, placed at a safe distance. The operator would watch a screen, fed by video cameras attached to the bogger, and bog out the pile of dirt at the base of the stope. This was because the walls were too high for scaling, leaving huge slabs of rock weighing several tonnes hanging several storeys up, ready to drop at any time. If he waited around long enough he would hear the echoing boom when they fell. Even a five-kilo rock could be fatal. Only a few years earlier, in Kambalda, two men had died from a rockfall, which was why the opening of the stope had more warning signs than anywhere else in the mine.

    He got to walk past the warning signs and see it up close one night shift when a rock was blocking the opening at the base of the stope. It was as big as a car and too big for the bogger's bucket, which meant they would need to get in there and break it up using a small amount of explosives. He and Dave P were called to help the bogger operator, Buck Rogers, and the shift boss, Proccy. Buck was an enigmatic Kiwi—non-smoker, late twenties, ex-army, weedy, shaved head, enjoyed the job, smiling a huge smile most the time. In contrast, Proccy, a Canadian miner, smoker, well into his fifties, belonged nowhere else, looking and walking as if he were made of rock—had become the thing he was mining. Not carved from marble like Michelangelo's David, aloof and naked, but more an animated boulder, dressed in weathered, blue overalls and gumboots. Resting on his rounded shoulders was a head like a square lump of mottled clay, a pocked meteorite, which housed small eyes hidden deep under his brow. Across his forehead were deep raked lines, except for an oval-shaped clearing to his left, where the fissures would part, drift around, before meeting again;

a smooth rock outcrop in the middle of a running stream.

Proccy, Buck and Dave P discussed how to break the rock up, Shaggy hanging back as the men spoke. Considering the best and safest way of fixing the problem before Proccy decided it, in his curious Canadian way of stating things in the form of rhetorical questions: 'I want a 10-metre length of 70mm poly, and we're gonna fasten a couple of sticks of explosives to the end with duct tape, eh? Run the det cord back through the poly, eh? And put it just there,' as he shook his head side to side to indicate the spot just beneath the rock with the beam of his cap lamp. 'Get behind the ute for the firing, eh?'

The four of them fed the pipe up to the rock, carefully, steadily. But it was awkward and wasn't finding the mark until Proccy, without any hesitation or pause, caution be damned, took it upon himself to climb up the pile, each knowing there was no good reason for taking such as risk. But this was night shift where the rules were suddenly vague and open to interpretation, riddled with imagined loopholes. 'Safety before production' on day shift, the inverse when the sun went down, and Proccy wasn't letting one little rock slow the movement of dirt. Proccy may also have been deliberately flouting rules that had become increasingly conservative, not like the old days, and needed to justify the 'danger' money they were earning. Working underground wasn't enough—they needed to demonstrate, to themselves at least, that they deserved their pay, even if no one would ever know about it. Still no one thought to stop him: not Dave P who took no responsibility for anything; not Buck who wanted to get his loads out; and not Shaggy who learned from Brendon to keep his mouth shut. And maybe also because of the glint of his excitement that betrayed the gravity of the situation.

Proccy, amazingly lithe for someone his age and wear, scrambled his way up, beyond the rim of the wall into the open stope, and placed the explosives where he wanted it; each second he was out in no man's land was like firing an empty round in a game of Russian Roulette, his fate inevitable if he played long enough, waiting for a rock to drop, sure to kill him instantly. With the explosive secure, he scuttled back down the pile, seemingly driven by adrenaline more than fear. They waited in makeshift safety, fifty metres away, around a corner, behind Proccy's ute, fingers holding their earplugs in tight as an unofficial and undocumented firing took place. The boom shuddered through them, a tremble in the ground, a sudden gust of wind, carrying with it smoke and dust. It worked, cracking the rock into manageable pieces for the bogger, and they carried on as usual. The only evidence of the firing was a broken window on Proccy's ute, parked too close—shattered from the shock wave. There were plenty of plausible alternate explanations for a broken ute window, and Proccy had a few up his sleeve just in case.

Courage

It felt good when the bogger operators asked for him as a truck driver, and the pride and sense of worth gave him some pleasure in the work. But it felt even better when he had jumbo operators asking for him. They knew his name and sought him out at the beginning of the shift to make sure he was available to extend their services or vent bag. Even Jim 'Bulldog' Honey, the grumpy truck driver from Bronzewing that had once inauspiciously ordered him to let go of his truck, now at The Granites, back on a jumbo, came looking for him, needing a vent bag extended—fresh, cool air being a most valuable commodity underground. Rewarded with a thumbs up or a tempered but sincere, 'Thanks, Shaggy,' if they were willing to shut off the machine for a moment and chat. Nothing more, but enough to give him a sense of satisfaction that made him want to do better and work harder.

They always preferred to talk to Shaggy. Maybe because he was younger and more malleable and he wouldn't say no. Most likely it was because Dave P was indeed a prick and they didn't want to be in debt to him, even if this was his job. This was because Dave P's manner of speaking was condescension and patronisation. He devoured the earnest as lack-lustre prey, but appreciated sarcasm, a measure of intelligence, as good as any IQ test. Following most conversations with Dave P, the bogger operator, jumbo operator, fitter, or driller would come up to Shaggy, within or without Dave P's earshot, and say with unconcealed venom, 'What a fucking prick/cunt/dickhead/fuckwit,' and squeeze the boy's shoulder in a show of consolation.

There was also evidence of a new kind of courage in his work. He *would* try things; he *would* have a go. The jingle had taken hold. Have a go. Coke is it. No more nukes. Wheedled its way into his sub-conscious. Fortune favours the brave. He who hesitates is lost.

When he was expected to wade waist-deep in his overalls into the sump at the bottom of the decline to rescue, replace or move a Flygt pump, by hooking it to the arm of the IT, he took his socks off, left them in a safe spot, and kept his gumboots on and took the plunge into the cold grey muddied water, mixed with oil, diesel, and at least some parts urine, everyone pissing wherever they liked, with some running down the decline.

He would also work until he was soaked through with sweat, until he felt dizzy in the heat, when cable-bolting, extending vent bags. Like Brendon had on his first shift on the service crew. This was the job.

And he proudly wore the polo shirts and jackets given to the crew for making metreage targets, or LTI (lost time injuries) milestones, revered the coffee mugs, the torch, and any other company-logoed items rewarding them for their and his work. Courage. Positivity. Pride. New strings to his bow. Feathers in his cap. Now, if he poured custard onto his silverside, he would be more likely to embrace the gaffe, laugh it off, rather than shrink in embarrassment. Dave P was also warming up to him in his cold way and Shaggy was doing anything to get a genuine smile out of him, which sadly meant all the world.

This is not to say that his old self wouldn't protest against this new self—fighting against his place within the mine. The boy in him, the lazy kid looking for the easy way out, reappearing on occasion—a neglected self looking for validation, like the ungrateful boy that had been given the job by his uncle Peter. As if he still didn't understand that he had chosen his lot from his own free will. He was not being held here or forced in any way. He was free to choose, condemned to be free, condemned to choose, so says the great French existentialist Jean-Paul Sartre. Sartre maintained that, even when imprisoned by the Germans in 1940, he was free to choose, to act. He could sit quietly in his cell, or he could dash his head against the wall. Even if they tied his arms and legs to keep him from dashing his head against the wall, he was free to struggle against his fetters. Freedom is a state of mind. To find any meaning in life, we must convince ourselves of this—free will must surely triumph over fate, if only in appearance.

Shaggy hadn't the luxury of a prison to hold him to his commitment, nor were his arms and legs bound. He had committed himself. To be considered a man, he would need to have made peace with it, and cease blaming others for his path. He chose to buy a house and had set the goal of owning it outright. He chose this goal for his future family. Nor could he say that this spectral family had taken his freedom, just as so many men at the mine would have him believe, having forgone their own sense of freedom. And yet he would forget all this and become petulant—the antagonist in his own story, revealing his old self.

It was the end of a night shift when Dave P insisted they pick up some empty pallets from the underground magazine and take them to the surface. Except for the shift boss and the charge-up guy, they would be the last to surface, would miss the big bus, and need to wait some twenty minutes for one of the bosses to take them home in a ute, a bit after 7am if they were lucky. The boy whined all the way to the magazine and was still complaining as they were loading the pallets. Dave P was his usual plateau of indifference, until he angrily threw the heavy, mud-soaked ropes across the pallets to the other side of the ute, hitting the boy across the face, cold and wet, stinging nylon thread, his eyes saved by his safety glasses. The boy saw Dave P's usually ambivalent face flash a twisted meanness, before settling on a scowl. The throw of the ropes was more symbolic than set to inflict pain, as if intended to slap the boy out of his hysterics, telling him to grow up. It was a rare show of emotion, which made it more telling. Like when Shaggy's well-mannered mum swore at him for the first time, as if for a moment the devil had her tongue.

They drove up the decline in silence until almost at the portal, when the boy relented: 'I'm sorry…It's just that time of the swing.' Like he had some special miners' PMS that always came over him about four shifts out from break, when time began to slow, when they started thinking about the break, almost done but not quite; false starts to the celebration, don't pack your bags just yet. Dave P didn't respond, looking straight ahead. But the boy, searching for any sort of a reaction, spotted a grin distorting the blank oval of his chinless face. Maybe not wholly as a victory over the boy, but also out of recognition. Dave P felt the same, even if it was never visible on the surface. The silence continued until the following afternoon, when they woke up to do it all again, one more shift closer to their break.

Two fires

It was RJ who lit it. No doubt about it and that was the story Shaggy was sticking to. A few shifts in, back from break. The start of the shift, before the prestart meeting had begun, and they were messing around on the surface over near the dump. Him, RJ, Rash. It was a cold morning, their earplugs like little stones as they fitted them in their ears. RJ thought it would be a bit of a lark to light up some of the rubbish in the bucket of the IT to warm them up. They laughed, feigned warming their hands, rubbing them together theatrically. In their minds there was heat. They put it out, the tiny fire, kind of. RJ drove it over to the rubbish tip.

The boy and Rash walked back to the offices.

The prestart meeting was underway by the time they got there. It was outside, bigger than usual—a special address from the management team. There had been a serious emergency the day before—a bogger had caught fire underground. It was at the end of the drive and out of the way but high enough in the mine to cut the top half of the decline off. No one was hurt, which was the good news. But a bogger half killed and a week or more to clear up the mess had tempers flaring at the surface. Wringing of hands, or on hips, shaking of heads. Mumbling, murmurs. Rumours like dying reverberations of a long-extinguished blast. Think of the share price. Are we heading home early? For good? This was why they were on the surface, with not much else to do, idle hands the devil's playthings.

It was ten minutes into the meeting when Shaggy saw the smoke coming from the tip, right from where RJ had been just moments ago. He stood in such a place, on the outskirts of the meeting, that he could easily see the fire through a gap between several transportables—a hundred metres away, just for him to see, accusing him across the way. He watched it billow, setting in, black smoke from plastic, waiting to see what might happen. Wanting to step out of the line of sight so that he could stop looking at it—stop bearing witness; wanting to not only feign ignorance but be properly ignorant. He knew it was RJ's lighter. Somehow, that little flame had stayed alight. Plastic melting in the IT bucket without visible flame. Not burning like wood, but still burning. And not black like it was now.

He wasn't saying anything; there was no way he was going to be connected to it. Besides, he didn't want to interrupt the meeting that was being hosted by some of the higher-ups, flown in to oversee the aftermath of the emergency. Sure as hell, if he didn't keep his mouth shut he would be hosting tomorrow's. They weren't blaming the bogger operator or anyone in particular for the underground fire but they would be looking to make an example of the poor fool that fucked up next.

Also wondering, if he were to raise the alarm, should he shout just the one word—'fire' or 'help'—or should he add an adjective—'huge fire'—or an instruction—'quick, a huge fire'—all the while pointing with a trembling guilty finger. He wondered how his voice would sound if he yelled 'fire.' Would it be loud enough: his voice was deep but didn't always carry when he shouted. Would it sound urgent enough to be thought authentic, genuinely panicked and concerned, or would it be hesitant, an afterthought, giving him away? Even if he wasn't involved, he was unsure as to how urgent he should sound, drawing attention to himself as much as the fire, jarring the quiet, even with the voice of a mouse. An imposition on fifty or so men and a few women in the crowd. Not one to make waves.

He was only dragged from this unbecoming mire of thought when someone else saw it 'first'. 'Fire,' the man yelled, loud, urgent, and panicked, pointing to the fire with an accusing finger sharp and hard as flint, arm straight as an arrow. The prestart meeting scattered, bogger operators were ordered to fill their buckets with mullock and blanket it out. Everyone else watched as the fire grew and grew. Huge truck and bogger tyres on fire; hundreds of metres of odd-lengthened poly pipe, plastic wrapping from explosives, plastic coating of cables. Enough to burn for days.

But it was out after half an hour and the enquiry started not long after. He was called in by Brooksey, the mine manager. He was a suspect. Rash and RJ too. Called in separate. No time to get their stories straight.

'Know anything about how the fire started, Shaggy?'

He and Brooksey didn't speak all that much before the fire, Brooksey speaking to Dave P for the most part, so Shaggy was already nervous. And he was never a good liar, his mother's honesty leaving him hamstrung.

'No, Brooksey. No idea, eh,' he said unconvincingly, hesitant. The way he said it was wanting to give him RJ but also knowing that he would be ostracised if he did. RJ was well beloved by all. Endearing like Boof, and harmless. But he would give him up if his hand were forced. He didn't smoke. He had no lighter on him. He was no boy scout. Did he rub two sticks together? No chance.

They let him go; could have pushed him harder and he would eventually crack. Knew he was in on it somehow. Wanting him to confess to stupidity.

Rash was a good liar or at least a better liar than him.

Interrogation over: an accident. Cause unknown. Back to sorting the less mysterious incident in the underground.

RJ didn't thank him for not ratting him out. Didn't say anything. As far as he was concerned, they were all in on it—all guilty, sharing in a dark secret like they had murdered someone, tell-tale heart of the victim beating the same rhythm in the ears of the three of them. RJ may have pulled the trigger but they told him to do it.

From that day on, RJ looked at him cautiously, sideways, wondering how much he had spilled to Brooksey; and both lost a bit of their sense of humour around each other, knowing how close they were to getting fired—getting each other fired. And he knew Shaggy would give him up, sing like a canary 'cause sure as shit Shaggy wasn't getting fired for someone else's stupidity. He had plenty of his own, thank you very much.

Compensation and Shadows

Home for his twenty-first birthday, a party at his house, with forty or so friends and family. His brother, now almost eighteen, and his band playing his favourites. It was smiles and drinks and music and dancing. And the past few months had still felt as if everything was working. More so at this point in his life, this moment, everything was in its right place. He and Lizzy, together now for two months, were getting to know each other more, growing closer. He was at ease, comfortable, loved. Fortune was smiling on him.

Indeed, only a few weeks later he came into some money, compensation from the less-than-routine recovery of his broken leg, fought for by his usually un-litigious parents, both of whom had suffered emotionally and financially from the ordeal. Seems that the doctors and the hospital had erred.

It was enough to go close to paying his house off. Which meant this could have been the end of it, his mining career. Pull up stumps. Paroled. Instead, he bought a second house, a cheap half of a duplex unit just down the road—an investment property—thinking that it was too early to finish what he had begun. That it was somehow cheating to get out this easy. That he could *really* set himself up—the words spoken by almost every money-addicted FIFO worker that has chosen to sacrifice their life, to say goodbye to their friends and families and live most of their lives amongst strangers.

Lizzy said it wasn't a good idea, maybe thinking that he wouldn't be able to quit for a bit longer yet. She needed him home if she were to mould him, make him a proper boyfriend. Smooth the rough edges, panel beat the dents, manipulate some uniformity. She had already begun to recognise inconsistencies in who he was, if there was any possibility of consistency to begin with. He was becoming increasingly moody on his breaks—despite the compo, the joy of his twenty-first, both of which distracted for a while. And she was also young and was not the type to wait around for an unknown. He was also stingy and scrooge-like—most unbecoming of any boyfriend, more so for a so-called cashed-up bogan (an epithet that would also find its way into the FIFO vernacular), tight with his money except for when it came to drinking or any other self-indulgent whim that took his fancy. Or for the two houses, neither of which she was invited to live in. She stayed with him on his break in his house but was never an occupant, bringing with her toiletries and a change of clothes, and not given a key, reaffirming her status as a guest only, kicked out each time he left for the airport.

She put up with him and his moods and his selfishness. Conceded to the force that was him on his break. The week off was his to celebrate; and she was happy to come for the ride, but only as a spectator to the show, a bystander to the parade, waving to no one in particular. This was the *compromise* of every partner left at home waiting for the return.

Still very naïve in how to treat women. That was his problem. Women a mystery as they have always been for men. Men are from Mars (the outback), women are from Venus (everywhere else). They were a puzzle he wanted to solve, figure out, a Rubik's Cube, interested him, challenged him, but he became frustrated when the colours didn't line up, bullish twisting, a slight to his ego. When they were together he expected lots of sex, his libido building the whole time he was away, and wanting to make up for the two weeks' absence. The rest of the time he wanted to spend with his mates at the pub, leaving her for the most part emotionally unattended. He spoke to her as he would a man, expected her to be emotionally tough, driven, and above all independent. She wasn't getting his best self, which for him was the bloke at the pub, having a laugh, playing pool, feeding the jukebox, half-cut and no thought of quitting for home, even as his mates bailed on him to sober up and get some much-needed sleep before work the next day.

At first they had exchanged letters, loving and silly and only occasionally straying into the deeper questions of life; and he rang her every second day, planning the break together, maybe out somewhere nice for a dinner. What food do you like? Somewhere nice, maybe? As the months slipped by, he rang her every three. Less time waiting at the phones, and more time to think of stuff to talk about. And he could save money on phone cards. She was upset. Upset because quantitative discussion, the numbers and frequency, seemed to trump any sense of qualitative discussion. This was despite his increasingly short responses to her perfectly reasonable questions. By six months he was running low on small-talk.

Not that she had a choice in all this, numbers and frequencies. Only he could initiate it, picking up the phone and dialling. She had no way of calling him: not out of the blue, not just because she was thinking of him, wanted to hear his voice, or because today she had had a difficult day and needed someone, that closest someone, to talk to. All control was his, wielding power over her from thousands of kilometres away, just as he did when he was home.

From the end of his last relationship with Emma, fleeting as it was, and the beginning of the new, he hadn't learned much and hadn't changed much; was possibly worse than before. Repeating himself, like a romantically-arrested Sisyphus, forgetting that he had done this all wrong before, once again leading to nowhere. And it was him that sped along the honeymoon period, his honeymoon self, exhausting it also, as if it were better to establish a routine and keep the focus than nurture the fresh tendrils of love. But they were close and in love for his twenty-first birthday in May and the months beyond that; and theirs resembled as good as any FIFO relationship, as good as any relationship that he had come to understand from the blokes at work. Whether a nineteen-year-old girl wanted to stick around for the longer haul was no guarantee, though. There were plenty of good reasons not to. He could list them for her if she had the courage to ask.

◎

He had his reasons for keeping her at a distance and taking her for granted, which had nothing really to do with her personally, or at least nothing that was unusual to any relationship this new and between still-young people. His reasons were that he could see no future for the relationship as, even if she was willing to stick around, he felt that she wasn't really sharing in his common goal.

The decision to buy the duplex was his and only his. He spoke to her and about her as if they had no *shared* desires or *shared* plans, even for the near future. This is not to say that he didn't have clear designs about what would come: to make money, buy a house, pay it off and leave. It's just that these plans didn't include anyone else, especially if they weren't contributing, or worse hindering its fruition. It was all for *his future*. More importantly, it was also for the future of his *future* partner and his *future* children—the shadowy figures of his nuclear-family dream. Shadowy figures without form, actors, in the wings, waiting for their cue to be summoned to the stage, to play their crucial part in his make-believe theatre. As beings, they were like the imaginings of faces and bodies of characters from a novel, built up from scant details, before the film adaptation sweeps the shadows away. These figures, these beings, served an essential purpose in his story, but lay on its other side—the other side of the conclusion. In the midst of the current story, the present relationship, immediate and living, it was not her *and* his dream—not *their* dream; it was not *their* house, nor *their* children that he envisioned. She was not *the* shadowy figure that lay at a distance in front of him. It wasn't personal. Her only mistake was that she was present, and was particular, had a face, colour to her eyes, a voice, which was too soon for his plan. She was no more than a financial impediment to his objective—an impediment to the life he would give the special ones he would meet in time, when the shadowy figures are realised, given flesh and form.

It was a cold and selfish way of seeing things. For him, though, this attitude was crucial for both his prospective family, and more importantly, for his own well-being: he would need to be selfish to achieve his goals; he would need to be selfish so that he could leave mining before he lost himself.

Explosives

There was far more pressure as a service crewman than what he had ever felt as a truck driver striving for a promotion. And for truckies, the outcomes, good or bad, were spread over the whole truck driving crew. Being a load shorter than others did not lead to demotion—truck drivers were already at the bottom and had nowhere to go—and they wouldn't be fired as long as they were consistent and didn't smash up the trucks. The service crew, however, had to get its job done—they needed to keep the machines going, otherwise everyone lost.

He was far more stressed at the beginning. Pressure from doing a new job, with so many other tasks, new tasks. Learning how to get the vent bag up quicker, learning how to drive the IT, keep from killing Dave P in the basket, his sudden involvement with explosives. And learning how to do it all in the heat.

This pressure came to a head about four months in as a service crewman, on the first shift of a swing. He had been awake since two in the morning and flown for six hours to site to start his half day shift. He was tired, and out of sorts, just as he always was on the first shift, the difficulty of trying to shift gears from relaxing in suburbia to working underground. His first task was to use the IT and the forks to move pallets of twenty-five kilo bags of anfo from the underground magazine further down to the second underground magazine. Bags stacked two metres high and wrapped around with plastic. The first pallet had been knocked around and was leaning precariously, ready to spill, and Shaggy was trying to straighten them out by hand before attempting to move it again, all the while cursing out his cross-shift who was responsible for leaving them in this state, knowing that charge-up was waiting on him. No time to linger, must always keep moving, keep the focus, even if it is the first day back.

Sure enough, the orange flashing light of the shift boss's ute came around the corner. It was Proccy, the unflinching hero of the stope firing. Proccy didn't normally need to speak to Shaggy directly or interact with him one on one, not even at the stope firing. He would speak to Dave P, looking past the boy, part of the background, like muted wallpaper at an art gallery. They had only spoken once before, back when Shaggy was drilling on the Bazooka for the two days because of his hernia before being sent to the trucks. Proccy had come by to check on him, part of his rounds, the boy having been left at his rig without a vehicle. Proccy parked his ute some 100 metres or more back and around the corner, and was on foot, cruising the drive, inspecting the rock wall. Intermittently, he would pause a moment, taking a closer look at some feature of the wall. Looking like he was long homeless, shuffling from bin to bin, not expecting to find much of anything, and not wholly disinterested in what was found, but emotionless about what he did.

He carried with him a small pick hammer. Prospecting the drive, the Bazooka always closest to the ore body. Every now and then he would chip a shard of rock from the wall before spitting on it to rub it clean, looking for flecks of gold, smaller than salt flakes, duller than jewellery, but unmistakable by its colour.

He walked over to Shaggy, holding out the rock in his saucer-size palm that sat at the end of a forearm the size of the kid's thighs: 'Look at that, eh. There's the gold,' as if to remind them both of just what it was they were doing there, in the dark, hundreds of metres underground, and thousands of kilometres away from those that loved them.

Shaggy nodded, responded politely, 'Oh yeah,' which sounded both like a revelation and a question. Convinced the kid understood, Proccy let the rock fall from his hand, suddenly indifferent to the object, despite having only a moment ago revealed its hidden value. It was illegal to keep and remove from site; and, anyway, it was still worth next to nothing. The rock landed dully at Proccy's feet, and quickly disappeared amongst other identical rocks—grey and worthless. Not looking to where it landed or leaving it in a place that he would remember to come back for later, Proccy continued his fruitless shuffle.

Their meeting in the underground magazine was different, and Proccy far from indifferent. Slamming shut the door of the ute, Proccy stormed his way over to the antithetical boy, still struggling with the unbalanced stack of anfo. Each of Proccy's steps was laboured, struggling against invisible mud, the ground beneath clawing at his gumboots, wanting him to return to whence he was made.

'What the fuck are you doing down here Shaggy, eh? We need that fucking anfo, eh?' The eyes beneath his brow bulging, his granite voice, deep and bellowing. A tongue of spitting lava.

The boy, though, was himself blowing up, he was TNT, and responded immediately, unleashing his own violent spray: 'I'm moving it as fast as I *fucking* can but it's a *fucking* mess!' The sentence trailing off, as he was already returning to his task, not interested in Proccy's rebuttal, which the boy seemed to expect to be physical more than verbal.

This was out of character for the usually meek and unseen kid. As if a body of flesh had suddenly materialised from a shadow, a doll becoming animated. Proccy stood and paused, his hands on his hips, concentrating on a spot on the ground a few feet in front of him, as if figuring how to move a fallen tree blocking the path of his ute. When he worked it out, he lit himself a cigarette and stepped over to where the boy was toiling away and took a turn himself at stumbling out of character.

'How was your break anyways, Shaggy, eh?' Suddenly earnest and humble, conceding that the boy was indeed a human being with human emotions, offering the boy a cigarette.

'Good,' he responded stubbornly, like a spoiled sulky child, before politely refusing the smoke, his mood softening. 'Yeah, pretty good, actually.'

For the next fifteen minutes they discussed their breaks, running through the headlines and highlights, laughing a bit, momentarily stepping out of the perennial flow of the mine. It was an initiation of acceptance, of breaking bread together, even if it began by smashing a loaf over each other's mulish heads. He learned that hard men appreciated straight talk. They liked to see backbone, conviction. And he learned that hard men could be otherwise.

A few months later, night shift, Shaggy saw Proccy's other side for a second time. It was when Shaggy had done his best to accidentally cut two of his fingers off. A backlog of mullock meant that he was needed on the trucks for a shift. A stray rock had landed on the engine covers of his truck near the cabin when he was being loaded. If it wasn't moved it could either damage the cab or roll off the truck onto the decline. It was fifty kilograms maybe, and flat and awkward. He felt strong; would move it by flipping it end over end. But it caught on a latch, listed sideways, and squashed his fingers between it and the steel engine covers. It hurt, but he was in a hurry, holding up the line, and had a second successful attempt at clearing it. Only when he returned to the cabin did he pause to inspect the throbbing in his fingers. There was a lot of blood or at least more than he would have expected. Rock, when shattered by explosives, creates shears of scalpel-like edges; and without his gloves it had cut deep into the index and middle fingers of his left hand. On cue, just as he did every time he injured his fingers and saw the darkness of his own blood, he fainted; not immediately, but in a prolonged way, a steady shutdown, conscious that he was slipping into semi-unconsciousness. The window of his vision blurred and then darkened at the edges, slowly reducing, as if he were heading down into the dark of a long tunnel, the long straight of the decline, facing backwards, moving away from the portal, watching its light slowly closing to a pinpoint. He didn't mind pain, needles, and he had on separate occasions broken his nose, wrist, and leg. But anything to do with his fingers, he always went to jelly.

Somewhere in the background, Flemmo in the bogger was on the two-way asking him if he was okay, wondering why he hadn't moved his truck. But by now Shaggy was a passenger in his body, aware of what was happening, yet unable to move, or see. He could only respond in hushed mumbling tones, more to himself than anyone. 'Just leave me alone for a moment. Be patient. Just got to wait it out.' Like him waiting to discover the meaning of life.

Within a few minutes, the dark in front of his eyes began to clear, reversing up the decline, exiting the portal to the surface, returning to himself. Flemmo had by now come to his cab to check on him, big smile across his face, thinking it was hilarious seeing him lolling around as he found his bearings.

Just to be sure, Proccy was alerted to come check on him. Whether it was the blood or the fainting, Proccy thought it best to whisk the boy to the surface for some repairing, if only to cover his own arse. No-one was going to bleed to death on his shift, no matter how pathetic the wound.

Shaggy sat in the little shift boss office, hands still shaky from the experience, as Proccy applied several Band-Aids to the two cut fingers, doing so with a tender and steadfast dexterity that contradicted his thick, gnarled lumps of hands. The cuts weren't deep, not enough to need to fetch the nurse to maybe sew some stitches; or Proccy felt that the kid's hands were in need of a few unkempt scars to give them some character. Relative to Proccy's own, the boy's hands were those of a woman, delicate and thin, or an unmanly man, white-collar, good only for pen-pushing. So he stemmed the blood, but kept a clear gap between the recently-parted flaps of skin, as if to delay the healing process, maybe a bit of bacteria in it, and accentuate the new feature to the boy's hand.

When it was done, the boy stood, itching to get back down the hole and bring his truck to the surface. But Proccy told him to take a seat and relax for a bit.

A pause and a silence. A breath. Once again stepping aside from the torrent of the mine.

Then Proccy said, 'How about you make us a coffee, eh.'

'Sure,' the boy replied, happy to have some small way to repay Proccy's tenderness. 'How do you have it?'

'Make it black and spit in it twice.'

Millennium and a break-up
December 1999

The approach of the new millennium and the excitement of turning the clock over into its third thousand common-era years was lost to the outback. The cynic in him knew it was merely a number, numerology a false art. Meant very little in the grand scheme of things, even if it felt like some significant change was nevertheless afoot. Certainly there was a global fear of chaos descending, Y2K bugs about to cast them all back to the dark ages. None of this was much of a concern at the mine: they were not entirely off grid, but they didn't have much to do with the so-called internet and its digital trappings. Just as they were ignorant of most things. The boy at least didn't see any news or read a newspaper for the two weeks he was away and hardly cared for it when he was back. The world was carrying on without him.

He would be home for it, midnight, 1999 ticking over to 2000, but had missed the build up. And, anyway, he had his own little bit of hysteria and chaos that would do well to shadow it all.

He didn't have much of an idea when he found out, just before Christmas when he was away, that Lizzy was ready to break it off. Out of the blue. It was a surprise because everything seemed to be going well enough: not perfect, but well enough. He had bought her Christmas presents before he left, really made an effort, his way of compensating for his absence, his apology for having to work. That he had to do this was the same for all the partners, husbands, and dads, the unshakeable guilt of being a FIFO worker. It was all on them to say sorry for being away; it was them who were letting everyone down by working over Christmas. She said she would give him his presents when he got back in time for New Year's. Which suddenly made a lot more sense: no point wasting money on a dead man walking.

It was the day before Christmas Eve when he called her. He was unusually chipper; and she was unusually quiet. When he was quiet on the phone, which was often, it was because of his long-term malaise: there was nothing too desperate needed to get him down. Which is why he asked her what was wrong. She said, 'Nothing. Nothing's wrong.' Again he asked and again the same response. Three times he asked, willing her to spill it, knowing that she had waited by the phone prepared, well-rehearsed on what she had to say, even if she was reluctant to execute. Worn down, Lizzy told him that it was over; that they should break up. She had made up her mind. For the life of their relationship, it had always been him making decisions for the two of them; now it was Lizzy's turn, even if she had to wait for him to call before she could tell. She had finally worked out what he had been implicitly telling her along: that he wasn't putting her first, and maybe never would.

Lizzy had been away in the UK for his last break, partying with cousins for the most part, relatives of her English-born parents. Enjoyed herself so much that she came home with a touch of a British accent. There was no denying the coincidence of her trip and her breaking up with him. Maybe a bit of distance and a long plane ride home had given her time and objectivity to help work out the pros and cons of waiting for him—waiting for him to return from the mine; waiting for him to quit the mines; waiting for him to make up his mind about where she fit into his life. After adding it all up she finally made up *her* mind about what he imagined, he hoped, was still a hard decision for her. He wasn't that bad after all.

They had been together for about nine months, during which he was physically at home with her for only a third of the time—three months of the nine. They were together, a couple, in that they were connected by the formal nature of a relationship, by the concept of a partnership, looked good on paper, but with the majority of their togetherness spent apart.

He was shocked and lost when he hung up the phone, and over the next few days he broke out in sobs, in the moments when he was on his own between jobs, when his mind would unfocus from the task in front of him, his thoughts flitting from being present in-the-moment and agonising over the details of how it went wrong. He cried not so much from the ended relationship, not because he necessarily loved her, even though in a way he did, but because he needed that bond of companionship to get him through each stint, to give him a reason to come home, to help bear life in the camp. This is what many of the men there must have felt. All of this shit meant nothing if it wasn't for them at home. It was for her and for the two of them that he was doing all of this, even if he knew that this was not true at all.

He was also angry at himself because he had let his guard down by letting her in, relying on her companionship, and now he was weakened for it. Once again, he would need to learn how to fortify himself against loneliness; embrace it to keep from going under.

He had learned something else when she was in the UK—something that not many at the mine experienced or could understand: being home alone whilst their partner was away. He flew in and got home late in the afternoon. His housemates were out, playing indoor beach volleyball, reminding him of Boof and his choice of the town life. He waited on his own, drinking, listening to Radiohead, feeling sorry for himself until nearly 830pm when they got home. By then he looked broken, as if psychologically tortured, a combination of forced sleep deprivation and solitary confinement. The rest of the break he was cursed with the freedom of the single man. He could do as he pleased, but at the same time was aimless and empty. Even with friends, he felt out of place, everyone in their relationships, being comforted by each other, the closeness, the intertwining of lives. This is what Lizzy must have felt for the past nine months, every time he flew out. Watching her friends being loved and held. Her on her own, telling everyone about the boyfriend she had working up north. The mythical boyfriend that strangers never saw—as ever, romanticised by absence.

There was no form of consolation in the camp—no counsellors or psychologists to help get him through. No one to say, 'There, there, it will be all right,' and pat him on the back. No doctors there to offer him a pill to make the pain go away.

And an underground mine was no place for him to lose his shit—no place to be unstable and dangerous. Not that it was uncommon. A few months earlier, he had heard rumour of an air-leg miner that had tried to take his life in the underground. Bluey, one of the hardest-looking guys there, with one of the toughest jobs—rise mining, working in a confined space, boring holes with the old-school air-leg drill, louder than a Harley or a drag car or a machine gun, covered in grit and water, raining down from the upholes, and hot all shift. A Kiwi, bikie-type, black eyes, short as a jockey, with number-two shaved red hair—fiery as a solar flare and seething with small-man syndrome. His wife had ended it with him, also over the phone. Was nothing Bluey could say to fix it. Nothing he could do either, flightless as an emu, with near four thousand kilometres of desert to cover.

Something in him must have given way and he straight up tried to kill himself. Not in the usual way, hanging or cutting himself: his method was passive. He walked past the DANGER signs and the chain fencing into the cavern of an open stope, and climbed his way to the top of the scree pile, where he stood, arms spread (Shaggy imagined), hardhat tossed aside (Shaggy imagined), waiting for a rock to fall on him and crush him to death. It was for the mine to decide his fate—to take the direction of his life out of his hands. Shaggy also imagined the breezy winds that get sucked through the stopes, and the faint, ceaseless reverberations of the cavernous space—the loneliness of a place that no one should dare enter. He also imagined the darkness. Did he turn his lamp off like Shaggy had done that time, take his earplugs out, as he waited? For how long would he wait? And how would they retrieve his body? Bog him out like mullock?

Nothing happened—he wasn't killed. He didn't kill himself. Shaggy didn't hear if he walked himself out or was dragged out. And like Shaggy's trouble with the spoiled food, the incident faded away from truth, to rumour, and finally a whisper trailing on the wind. Nothing had happened. Even for an attempted suicide, there was no counsel, no special meeting with all of the crew, no psychologist flown in specially to talk about mental health, or of coping with living away from home, how to deal with the lives from which they were mostly absent.

Shaggy wasn't ready to attempt anything this drastic, even when there was no retrieval of his own relationship. Christmas came and nothing could have been less cheerful and he hurried it along as fast as he could. The following day, Boxing Day, he called her, imploring her to reconsider, take him back—he could change. But, no, he wasn't quitting his job for her. No. This was the line she had drawn but she likely already knew that he wouldn't cross it. Indeed, before he had even returned it seemed that she might have moved on, maybe even found someone else. And when he did come home, New Year's Eve of the new millennium, he didn't bother to call her, not wanting to further spoil what was supposed to be one of the biggest celebrations in Mandurah, let alone the world. At the pub, midnight, he stood around as if dumbfounded. The pub erupted; people kissed and embraced and loved each other. He seemed to be standing outside of it, as if watching from the moon.

When she told him she wanted to meet a few days later, she didn't understand why he hadn't called. This seemed to be a problem for his relationships generally. He was expected to talk, reveal himself, get what was in his head out so that they knew more of him. He thought too much though, thought too darkly, too seriously. He didn't know it, didn't have a name for it, but for too long he had been playing the brooding Byronic figure: 'The Byronic hero, incapable of love, or capable only of an impossible love, suffers endlessly. He is solitary, languid, his condition exhausts him. If he wants to feel alive, it must be in the terrible exaltation of a brief and destructive action' (Albert Camus, *The Stranger*). He was invoking Byron and Camus themselves, but also Rochester, Mr Darcy, Heathcliff, furled brow, aloof, attempting to understand the world purely through thought, but without the same sex appeal, and he was too good to be a bad boy. He expressed his suffering authentically, without affectation, which may have been attractive to some—Mary Shelley, Jane Eyre, Elizabeth Bennet, Catherine Earnshaw—but now had become both annoying and exhausting.

They did eventually talk, a post-mortem for their deceased relationship. She told him that she was tired of his inattention, his depressive moods, tired of him not trying to do something about his mood swings. She told him to do more on his break. He needed a routine, something to keep him busy. He should go surfing, get himself a hobby. As if the hurdles of depression were so easily overcome.

He listened, content to listen, and agreed with much of what she was saying, not seeing the point in arguing. But it was clear that she didn't understand what his breaks at home were like, just as he hadn't understood what it was like for her when he was away at the mine. She didn't understand the loneliness of the break. At home, in his empty house for most of the day, waiting for her to finish work, for his mates to finish work, trying not to spend money on anything. He didn't have Boof flying home with him, like he did at Bronzewing. There was Rash, but he was in Perth. And Flemmo had a wife and kids, not to mention the brawl he got into the last time they met at home. Whatever fun he was supposed to be having on his break would need to be had by himself. But left to himself, he was unmotivated, directionless, and sedentary, as if he were unemployed again, and all he could think about was how he wasting his time at home instead of making money. She also didn't understand what it was like to be isolated from the fabric of ordinary life, the everydayness, knowing nothing of popular culture, the music, TV shows and movies that everyone was talking about. What it was like to miss whole seasons of football; how he felt when he was away for her birthday, his parents' birthdays, his brother's eighteenth birthday. A phone call to make up for his absence was never good enough.

But he didn't tell her this.

When he returned to the mine that next swing, the heartbreak lingered, but had also begun to break apart, dissolve, reforming as resentment and anger; he could feel it in the elevated beat of his heart the more he thought about it. It was good, embracing the emotions that would best harden him against the hurt. But the anger particularly was also a coping mechanism, a method of self-care, and clarity. He would need to think of himself not only as a selfish provider for his future but also to think of keeping himself together, such that he would have any future at all. And he also knew in himself that, sooner rather than later, he would need to get out. And he decided that the year 2000 would be his last—one more year. He would cross the line that Lizzy had drawn but, as always, he would do it on his own terms.

He told Buck Rogers, the remote bogger operator, who had become one of his more trusted confidantes, that he was snatching it—said it like he really meant it, hissing and spitting. He had made up his mind and needed to tell someone, someone who would understand. They were pretty similar, him and Buck: Buck hardly drank, and knew how to save his money. And knew what Shaggy meant when he gave his reasons for wanting out. Shaggy would be home for next Christmas, free from the mines. No more apologising for being away; no more apologising for doing his job. He hadn't achieved his goal of owning his now two houses, but it had come to him that he could no longer keep on like this. It wasn't for him. He didn't fit. He knew this from day one. The breakup was a gadfly stinging him out of his slumber. It was Socrates asking him to examine his desires, his prejudices; asking him 'why, for what purpose, and for whom?' reminding him of what it all meant. It used to be his pay that provided an answer to any and all of these questions. Now, he wasn't quite sure, knowing only that he didn't know.

He didn't see his quitting date necessarily as the beginning of a new future he was creating. It was merely the negation of the future he was currently lumbering towards. Like his first decision as a driller's offsider where he told himself he would not not be a driller's offsider. It was not 'start something new' that drove him. It was 'stop mining' that determined him.

It was a conversation with another John—Johnboy—a few swings later that helped him better understand his revelation. Johnboy was a trainee mining engineer and had a foot both in the underground and on the surface. As an engineer, he had to know everything about the mine, which also meant spending time

A Boy Miner

working in every job for a period. He had been to university and was too smart for the underground but revelled in getting his hands dirty all the same and took on every new challenge with energy and enthusiasm. They were close to the same age and were as good a mates as anyone he had met at the mine. And they would have caught up on their breaks, except Johnboy lived in Adelaide, flying there instead of Perth.

It was the end of the day shift. Johnboy had spent the day in one of the old orange Toro trucks, with no air-con, sweating and full of fumes for a whole shift. Exhausting even if it was just driving. Shaggy had come out of the changerooms and spotted Johnboy on his own, sitting on the concrete curb, waiting for the bus to arrive, his face still flushed, right up to his red crew-cut hair. He looked as if entranced, staring out to the horizon, the line separating red and blue.

'You okay, Johnboy?'

He heard him, but took his time, still trawling through his thoughts, before turning to Shaggy and stating outright: 'I think I got jaded today.'

Shaggy paused, thinking on it, thinking on possibly one of the most profound statements ever uttered on a mine site.

'Nah, I don't think you can get jaded in a day. Couldn't happen as sudden as that.' This was his rapid-fire attempt to make Johnboy feel better, but also to put it to bed quickly, denying him his feeling.

They both went quiet, wondering, before John reluctantly agreed, slowly nodding his head before turning back to the horizon. It was always towards the horizon that they looked, searching for answers and consolation. The outback offered nothing but horizons; in every direction, lines of sight that gave a false sense of ending. If you could flatten it out you would end up looking at your own back. Horizons empty of markers for mapping and orientating, and navigating. Empty of answers. Just shimmering mirages, like the kaleidoscopic auras of a nascent migraine, scrambling consciousness.

They both left it at that, with not much more to say. As always, better to not talk too much on these things just in case an unwanted truth were suddenly revealed, undermining all their hard work to suppress it. But Shaggy should have been more concerned; not just for Johnboy, but for the fact that Johnboy was the least jaded bloke out there, the last canary of hope in the mine. Everywhere around him there were blokes who were jaded. Divorcees, alcoholics, smokers. Families that they no longer loved—that no longer loved them. Drifting apart from loved ones. No end to working away, goals becoming lost. To be jaded was to prefer to be there, in the outback. Why go on break when everything you need is right here. They had found the perfect work-life balance. Cooking, cleaning all done for you. Drink piss with your mates. No dressing up. No commitments. No parties. No food shopping. Making money was all they were compelled to do, fulfilling the only social role they knew. Knowing also that this is reality, with no room for romance. That this is as good as it gets.

You can't get jaded in a day. He said this and felt right about it. But maybe you could. That day in which he had lost her, maybe that was the day he became jaded. He saw it for what it was: the killing of enthusiasm for what he had been endeavouring to achieve. That was what being jaded meant. There had been an apotheosis—a highpoint—with her, in life, with his house, his friends. But it had to come to an end before he was ready. Like closing at the pub, the good times shutting down, wanting to hold the moment for as long as he could, tipsy and still not stumbling too much. It *could* happen in an instant but mostly goes unrecognised; others saw it in him. Not in a day. And not on a day, but already happening before the day. She saw it coming before he ever did, before she had broken it off. When he did, it was too late.

He had become jaded; and he had aged, in his thoughts and his looks. He was losing his hair, which he had kept long to his shoulders, determined to keep alive the grunge of the nineties, so pivotal to his formative years. A receding hairline, less and less to gather in a ponytail, more forehead in the mirror. Barely twenty-one years old and going bald. Could he now be called a man, now that he was balding? If he was now a man, because of how he looked, it too hadn't happened in a day: his youth was being taken away from him, by increments, recessions and concessions, in both time and appearance.

He had aged in other ways. Like those old men who, also by increments, recessions, and concessions, steadily withdraw from society as they age, freezing themselves in a particularly comfortable time, unyielding to changing norms and trends. Clutching at fashion, music, old ways of thinking. Jaded like the old young men here. Maybe this was also what being a man was: becoming jaded, leaving youthfulness, enthusiasm, and aspiration behind. Leaving themselves behind for the good of others. This is why he had to quit.

He told Buck his plans, and later let Rash, Flemmo and Johnboy know. But mostly he kept it to himself until there were a few months to go. He had it in his head that if the bosses knew he wanted to quit, then they might move him on earlier, either because he would become lazy, no head for it anymore, or just to spite him for thinking he could leave when he wanted to. Before then, it was going to be a slog—a whole year of knowing he was quitting. Setting a date was setting a countdown that could be measured in many ways: in days, swings, months. And as each measure ticked away, he would make a coil of himself, tightening the screws of his asceticism, denying himself, readying himself for the final push to the end. He spent little on supplies from the wet mess and kept his phone calls brief, stretching the credit on the phone card for as long as he could. He called less often and fewer people until he was left with no-one to call except for his brother who was bringing the Forerunner to pick him up from the airport.

His breaks at home had also become unpleasant affairs for himself and friends and family around him. His first few days home still shared the semblance of joy that he had always felt. And the first night was celebratory, surrounded by friends, fewer than a few years ago, but the best friends, fonder for his absence.

But to channel Hunter S Thompson, it had all hit the high-water mark, the wave had broken, and rolled back, revealing the low tide, the refuse below the surface. On the last day of each break he resembled a dark spectre, in purgatory. An embalmed corpse slouching around, ticking off items on a list that he needed to do—his incidentals as he called them—paying bills, packing his bag, keeping himself distracted from the inevitable drive to the airport. He went to see his parents and other important friends to say goodbye for the two weeks. As if he weren't coming back. It had the solemnity of a wake, but instead of his corpse being mourned by those left behind, he imagined they were secretly rejoicing his departure, taking his dark mood with him.

◉

At the airport, 3.30 in the morning, waiting to board, watching infomercials on the lounge TVs. Teflon frypans. Abdominal crunching machines. Somehow capable of sucking the life out of a husk. And then boarding, a file of melancholy. Miserable, the lot of them, such a lonely hour, departing their families and friends, none of whom were waiting around to wave them off. The routine of FIFO wearing away any sense of novelty or romance that an airport terminal might once have held.

On more than one occasion, when sitting in his seat on the plane, in the air, flying back to the mine, watching the landscape degenerate into a raw patch of mange, he would entertain wild, morbid fantasies of the plane crashing, somewhere in the flat of the desert, away from buildings and powerlines and trees—away from anything that could make for a messier collision with the ground. A soft crash, if it were possible. Like ditching into the ocean. They—the miners, the pilots, the hostesses—would all survive, of course. Dazed from shock, but alive, walking away from the crash like any other landing, just a little bumpier. They would call it 'miraculous' on the news. A miracle. He couldn't die either, even if the idea of it sounded clean and simple—alive with problems and then dead with no problems. But he wouldn't have the guts if the plane did start a nosedive. Alarm bells, oxygen masks, whistles attached to life jackets, emergency exits, and white-knuckle panic.

Suddenly, life would be worth living. A life flashing before his eyes, a life not yet worth dying for. The bravado of theory would most certainly succumb to the cowardice of praxis. He couldn't do it to his mother either. Couldn't break her heart.

And he meant no harm to others—not his mother, nor the airline crew, and not his mining crew. They would all live to mine another day. Not him though. He wanted to temporarily disappear, 'poof!' like a magic trick, magicked out of existence. Not dead, just absent for a while, forgotten about. Time enough to work it all out. Or he would be in a coma, which he saw as the best, most realistic way of having a timeout from life—a pause in existence, where he didn't have to worry about things and others needn't rely on him. Time off from what he understood to be the burden of his social existence—being with others, in relationships, wanted and needed, or just there, part of the routine in others' lives.

In his mind—the story he would tell himself—he would be injured from the plane crash, just enough to need an extended hospital stay, enough to miss a fortnight's swing or two. But 'it'—his vague, non-fatal injury—in his fantasy, wouldn't be improving. Something wasn't right. A sorry-looking doctor, the embodiment of an empathetic bedside manner, face grim but strong, would be hesitant to break the terrible news that the boy would never mine again. At first, Shaggy would be conflicted, but then relieved, knowing that his burden had been lifted. He would be pardoned, absolved of his duty. Like Arron with his maimed hand. Like the air-leg miner walking into the stope, waiting for something to fall, the choice would no longer be his. Instead of a stope, though, a higher authority—a trained physician—will have decided for him.

His self-imposed martyrdom would end, and he could feel at ease with the outcome, knowing that there was nothing more he could do. Choice is freedom, freedom is choice, but he would gladly shackle himself to this singular scenario, a prisoner of the fates, just like Paul the truck driver, gambling on his uninsured Porsche. Having fate decide his exit from mining may mean that he had gotten what his weaker self had always wanted, the sooky kid that wanted to quit; but his stronger, martyred side—his falsehood—could finally yield, content, knowing it wasn't his decision to make. This was his fantasy.

He flew almost 240 times, which included the stopovers at Kalgoorlie for refuelling. It seemed only a matter of time.

Three deaths and six months to go
June 2000

Mostly the service crew's jobs were running vent bags and water and air services, or carting explosives. But occasionally they were needed for more bespoke jobs, like erecting temporary vent walls for blocking off unused drives, redirecting the airflow to others. They also built more permanent bund walls, which were like retaining walls. This involved sealing up a drive at the base of the stope by building a sandbag wall and spraying it with concrete. The stope could then be backfilled from above with unused mud, slurry, and rock, putting the piles of mullocky dirt on the surface back into the hole, all part of the rehabilitation process once the mine is spent. It took a few days to complete building it. They made good walls, sturdy and straight.

He was working on one with Dave P when he heard about

it, that at Bronzewing, his first mine, now run by a different company, a similar type of wall had just collapsed, and 18,000 cubic metres of backfill had broken through the base of the stope. It killed three men, buried them like a mud slide or avalanche, with no chance of survival. One of the three men was someone he knew from primary and high school. Tim had lived just around the corner, less than five hundred metres from where he grew up. He had been to Tim's house for a Christmas party when they were kids; had played indoor cricket together. The dead boy was one year younger than him—twenty-one years old or thereabouts. In essence, they were the same age, from the same home town, had been at the same mine, doing the same job.

    He didn't pay it much attention when the news came through; nor did he really pause for a moment to give his respects, as if what had happened was all part of the job—a possibility that was never really given much thought by anyone but shouldn't have been a shock when it did. He was cold in this, callous. Calloused as his hands, impervious to the hardships of others. Almost like the dead men deserved it; knew the bargain they had entered in to. Getting rich quick meant risk. They were aware of this; they knew they were taking danger money just as much as they were taking living-away-from-home money. People will die. They chose it. Condemned to choose.

    He knew that they—the dead—would have families and real lives outside of mining. People that would be grieving for the unexpected but very possible misfortune. But for him the dead men were like the strippers he met in Kalgoorlie: one-dimensional, ghosts, without shape, or lives beyond their chosen occupation. Expendable as anyone. Don't be shocked when the mirror is held up. Don't be upset when reality kicks in.

He carried this attitude for the duration of his mining career. And it had intensified the longer he was away. The unfeeling nihilist. He was Albert Camus' other existential hero, Meursault, from *The Stranger*, reacting or not reacting in a way that society would deem fit. Not mourning the proper way.

When a rise miner—a bloke that he had worked with and knew well—had fallen five metres from a platform, injuring himself badly enough to need a month at home to recover, he hardly gave it a thought, indifferent to it as if the injured man were an ethereal member of the faceless public.

Others were more affected, Rash particularly, who brought it up at breakfast with him and Flemmo. 'Poor guy. Hope he's okay.'

Shaggy's response was swift and incontrovertible: 'He didn't *die*,' as if to make a point of Rash's overreaction, alive or dead being the only two modes of existence, hoping to think less on it and end the conversation. And the rise miner *didn't* die. Not like those others from Bronzewing. Not that he mourned them appropriately either.

Rash was aghast—a pall brushed his face, as if he only now recognised that for over a year he had been in the company of a psychotic serial killer, the heads of retired jumbo operators in his freezer, poetry written in shit on his donga walls. Shaggy was Patrick Bateman, not Daryl. 'Fuckin' hell, Shaggy.' Said with a nervous half-laugh, but not doing enough to wholly contradict the genuine disdain in his big honest eyes.

Flemmo laughed too, both at what Shaggy had said and at Rash's reaction. Not at all nervously, nor to ease the tension—just because he knew them well enough and knew they were being exactly who they were. Empathy and apathy sitting across from each other with nowhere else to go and no other option except continue to sit and eat their end-of-shift breakfast/dinner, a bowl of Coco Pops for dessert.

Shaggy didn't chip in a shift's pay to help out the family, which is what they did when someone was killed or injured bad enough. Each was expected to do so—a mining code of sorts, of which there were only a few. He didn't then and he didn't for anyone else. This was him at his most selfish, the plight of others no longer his business. And it was selfish, but in his mind, this selfishness was more than easy to justify: a day's pay meant an extra day he would need to work to make up for it; an extra day in which he himself could be killed. And they all earned more than him and had worked for longer; they should have saved their money for death or injury—the rainiest of days.

When he and Dave P worked on their next bund wall, similar to the one that killed the three men, they built it just the same as their last one, sturdy and straight, comfortable in knowing that it was good enough and that they had done what they were asked to do. As before, it wasn't engineered in any way. There was no employment of the principles of physics, torque or tension, or mathematical equations worked out to ensure its reliability. Not even a plumbline or the bubble on a level to make it exact; nothing other than their eye. They just built something from bags of concrete that went hard when they dried. It wasn't their responsibility if it failed. That would be for someone else to decide.

The new boy
October 2000

Time passed. Three months to go. Four swings. He could finally announce it the shift bosses and the mine managers. He assumed they would be devastated, given that he had taken the bullet by working with Dave P for one-and-a-half years. Turned out they already knew and were closer to indifferent than despondent. He even asked Brooksey, the mine manager, if he could have a reference. Brooksey said no because he didn't do them, which was fair enough. There were many valid reasons not to. Most likely because Shaggy, despite his diligence and sacrifice, and the good work he had done, had nevertheless fucked up more times than anyone else there. And Brooksey probably also felt that Shaggy was due to be the cause of something really horrific and costly. It was only a matter of time, which Shaggy believed as well. Shaggy had no idea what he wanted a reference for anyway. Another mining job? A fresh start in iron ore, coal, some new resource to be clawed out of the Earth? Really it was just to say that he had worked there. He had worked. Here is the evidence of someone who witnessed it, without Pete keeping an eye on him: three years at The Granites without being sacked.

When he began telling the crew he was leaving, he seemed to relax a little, to pull his head from the mire. He looked like a new man, grown a foot taller. But his fresh perspective was torn: looking towards home, and at the same time realising that maybe, possibly, despite his remonstration and concerted efforts to the contrary, he actually could have belonged there. Not because of his nature—not because of his red-dirt blood, which had been at odds with his identity from the start, from when he first stepped off the plane at Bronzewing. Instead, he had been cultivated, nurtured into his place. He had come to fit the mould: he had grown into his overalls, his belt with his self-rescuer and cap lamp battery was snug on his hips; he was known by most of the crew, the fitters, his cross-shifts. Hadn't said much but enough for them to accept him. He had fucked up a number of times, and he had no way of forgetting this himself; but he was useful, needed. He told himself this over and over, and although he may not have cared for it much, he had become a bona fide member of The Granites crew—an old timer, part of the furniture. Banged up and barnacled as one of the old Toro trucks. Three years was no short stint at The Granites and he had seen many come and go. Seen them out like they were fads, flashes in the pan, one-hit-wonders. He stuck it out which meant a lot.

It was the arrival of a new boy—not much younger than him—that seemed the catalyst for this unexpected revelation. The new boy was given the position of nipper—the jumbo's offsider—which was a high-pressure job, working with the jumbo, right up at the face, one of the most crucial, immediate elements in the mine's development, and left no room for idleness or complacency. Because of this he would have it harder than Neph—the boy from Bronzewing—had ever had it in those first few swings, where being lazy on the drills and losing a few metres was really only an issue for the drillers, some of whom weren't so money-hungry as others.

A Boy Miner

By the end of his first week, the new boy was being called Tired Cunt—TC for short so as not to offend the few there that might take offence. And also so it could be said over the radio: 'You got a copy, TC?' It was a punishment—not an endearment—nor was it ironic. This was the case for many of the nippers who were often young and inexperienced. The previous nipper was called 'Fucknose' for the duration of his first stint because he cut his nose on some mesh. It must have been a hard fortnight for him because he didn't come back.

Shaggy didn't know TC's real name, but knew him well enough in that he could have been Neph's mirror, dumb and dull-eyed, except that the new boy was slightly taller and had layers of baby fat on him. He had a big arse and thighs that rubbed together, hindering how he walked, waddling instead of striding. His hands were always on his hips, too tired to let them hang, and his movements were slow and tired, just as his name suggested.

They had greeted each other every day with the typical indifferent civility that a camp requires, but they met properly when the shift boss asked Shaggy to give TC a lift to the surface. TC had fucked up the nipper's ute the day before by pouring too much oil into the head, filling it right to the top instead of checking the level on the dipstick. Full to the dipstick, not full to the top. Shaggy would have made the same mistake given the opportunity.

Except for the echoing drone of the ute, windows down, they drove in silence, Shaggy loathing TC for disrupting what he was doing, having to chauffeur him around, fucking with his schedules, making it unlikely for him to get the list of jobs he wanted done by the end of the shift. What was he meant to write in his notes when he didn't get it all done: '230–330am: Took TC to surface to help TC do TC's job because TC is a stupid tired cunt'? Shaggy belonged in FIFO, belonged to the underground, because he worked hard and detested TC's laziness; but he belonged more because he loathed those that didn't. It was a strange way to feel; strange because the resentment he felt felt good. Warm like a cuddle. TC a scapegoat for all the things he had hated about himself when he began—the boy he was then; how he was once viewed by the other miners. He had no sympathy for TC, and wasn't going to talk to him as a passive-aggressive punishment. The new recruit in the jungle, kept at a distance and anonymous, soon to be fired. Shaggy the one shaking his head, having evolved beyond this useless prick. All he saw was someone that was holding up the mine; Shaggy interested only in the bigger picture. Shaggy was the company man, the salaryman—and TC was stalling the operation with his fat and blank face. When you get the chance, pass the shit down the line. Shaggy'd earned the right.

    Once on the surface they began loading split sets and plates for the jumbo. Shaggy throwing them in furiously, quickly, four or five at a time; TC doing the same, just as angry, but only two at a time, using one arm, the other arm limp as if he had suffered a stroke, incensing Shaggy even more.

    For five minutes they did this, still in silence, except for the brutal gun-shot-crashing of the metal bits thrown indelicately on the metal tray. Until Shaggy rediscovered a trace of his mother's empathy. Until he realised he was again plagiarising the narratives of others—taking on someone else's story, their attitudes, prejudices. He held his palm up, signalled for TC to stop a minute, took their earplugs out. And he heard Proccy's softened voice echoed in his own: 'So how's it going, TC?'

A Boy Miner

'Okay.' A gun-shy response—TC wary, knowing that if he spoke he could leave himself vulnerable and possibly open to ridicule. Shaggy must have appeared ready to pounce on anything stupid he might say. Or he didn't want to disturb the image he was making for himself, whatever that may be. But it was enough to get the ball rolling, the opening of a dialogue, the initial salvos of peace talks. Shaggy told him stories about Jim—TC's jumbo operator; the same Jim that had left him on the decline; the Jim who also needed Shaggy to run his vent bag. Jim, the 'grumpy old cunt,' Shaggy called him. Speaking like an old man to a young boy even though there was barely a year or two's difference between them.

TC smiled, gave a tempered laugh, allowing himself, that is, the boy from home, to come to the surface. Like gold panned from river dirt. He then spoke a few words, called Jim a cunt, following Shaggy's lead, finding common ground. This was Shaggy's atonement, his salvation, making amends for who he had become. At the same time feeling older, and that he had cleaved some distance between the man he was becoming and the boy he recognised less and less. He also understood the patience of Lee, Dave, his uncle Peter, and many others who knew that kids, young men, were much the same, resembling themselves in their past lives, where they had expectations that something else, maybe something better, was still possible. It was these expectations that made them lazy, careless, thoughts elsewhere, giving imagined form to shadows that belong only to their future selves. Not here though.

At the time, TC was young and therefore useless, but as a miner, he would come to fit. A few months passed and TC worked harder, earned scraps of respect, and was accepted because he hung around long enough to steel himself and know his place. Long enough to be worked into the fold. He kept his initials, even when they no longer signified any relation to their original meaning or the person he once was. Not being who you were at first was belonging.

The last shift

He was finishing with two other long-time Granites miners, Sunshine and Macca, both bogger operators. Sunshine got his name because he spent too much time on the surface, wrecking his gear, or some other reason from the past, true or otherwise. A sunshine miner. There was probably a Sunshine at every underground mine. He was about Shaggy's height, but thinner and more muscular, like a greyhound, more from a lack of eating instead of exercise. More smoking and drinking than push-ups and jogging. The top of his head was shaved almost to the scalp, but he had kept long blonde mullet tendrils hanging from the back. His earlobes hung low with heavy rings and he was tattooed on most of his body with green-blue ink. His voice was buoyant but harder, louder, and deeper than his size suggested; he couldn't whisper to save his life. He was there when Shaggy arrived.

Macca started not long after Shaggy. He was taller and looked like an accountant with a sensible haircut, soft voice, and black-rimmed glasses. Macca was divorced, paying child support for two kids, plus some alimony. He said he was sharing a rental no better than a halfway house. He said he was living on nothing, giving all his money away. Which was the case for a few blokes there. He said this not in his usual measured voice, but biting and raised, his accountant's face twisted with hate. He was going to stop earning so that he could stop paying.

No one would suspect that the three of them had worked the same job—a rough bikie-type, an accountant, and a boy, who at the age of twenty-two was retiring from mining. Each of them had their reasons for leaving, but the future was unsure. Some vague promise of a city job, mining or otherwise. It all sounded very hopeful but was most likely temporary. Until they got sick of home life, the lower wages. FIFO would lure them back.

The three of them blew the last shift, which was expected of them—a tradition for celebration—but it could have also been so that they didn't get themselves killed from going underground one last time, believing they were jinxed for having snatched it. Instead, they went drinking that morning with the crew from their shift, shouting drinks for everyone there: Sunshine, Macca, Rash, Flemmo, Johnboy, Buck, Trudy, Paula, Proccy and Rod, his shift bosses, Micko the fitter, and other crew members that he had come to know. Shaggy smiling, speaking, caught up in the emotion, ecstatic, almost a stranger by the time they all left the mess, resembling little of the boy some of them had known three years—not exactly the stale bottle of piss from Bronzewing, but that second-last morning, again, he poured like champagne.

He stayed to the last, before heading to bed, slept magnificently, woke in the afternoon, five hours later, drunkenly stumbled to the mess, ate some dinner, before joining Sunshine and Macca and their cross-shift's after-work drinks, again shouting beer and staying to the last. The following morning he woke up, again stumbled to the mess, ate breakfast, and for a third time shouted more drinks for his crew, ready for the flight home. He was pissed for some twenty-four hours, which almost made up for him not having a single drink in the three years he was there, not even at a shift change. There was no chance of him not being ready to go when that last plane arrived, considering he had packed his room the best part of a week ago.

They showed him a heartfelt respect at each drinking session, his crew and the cross-shift whom he had occasionally worked with. Respect for doing his job well. Not making life harder than it needed to be. One of the fitters even came over and gave him a strong handshake, praising him for putting up with Dave P for so long. Suddenly overwhelmed with emotion and drink, Shaggy almost kissed him on the cheek, like friends from the Old World, greeting each other after a long absence, refugees shipped across oceans on different boats.

He had also been good listener: there were many out there that needed to have their voices heard, and Shaggy seemed to have a look about him that invited them to. They were crowded in together at the camp and each needed their space, but also desired someone to be there every now and then, just as he had desired it. Sharing the burden, bearing witness. This was a final reminder that he could have enjoyed himself more at the camp, if only he had let his guard down. Instead of being elsewhere in his mind, he should have been present and taken it for what it was and needled out the pleasure any way he could. They had given him chance after chance. He wished he had done it differently. He wanted to have another go. Maybe, do it right this time.

They presented each of the three of them with a long-sleeve Callie shirt, signed by all the crew. Trudy and Paula seemed the instigators. Paula had a thing for Sunshine, which possibly explained why there was so much effort, which he hadn't recalled seeing before when others had left. It may have been just for Sunshine but they didn't want to play favourites. Or just that the three of them were considered old-timers at the mine, having served their sentence, and seen so many others come and go, cycling through those that could only hack it for a short term.

The boy said his goodbye to Dave P three times, with each becoming increasingly incomprehensible and ineloquent. There was no hate towards Dave P. Instead, there was a fondness, given that they were very much alike in that they didn't really belong, but had persisted. Dave P was too old now to change, whereas the boy believed that he had done enough. When he told Dave P about how he was thinking of applying for university, Dave P had laughed derisively, as if it were a vain, pointless goal. Or Dave P was jealous of the boy, not of the boy going to university, but of the boy still having possibilities before him. Maybe jealous of the boy's innocence, the boy's belief that a positive change will come, that the future will necessarily reveal something more than what he already has; that life is more open than closed.

Dave P had taught him some things: about who he was now as he departed FIFO, and more importantly, who he could be if he stayed in FIFO. And Shaggy was thankful for what he had learned, albeit in a veiled way. Dave P maintained his indifference, keeping the boy at an emotional distance. No need for feigned intimacy even if they had worked with each other, just the two of them, for a year and a half, for twelve hours a shift, for two weeks at a time. He wasn't getting close to anyone, not even if the best offsider, the most malleable and complicit offsider he could ever ask for was abandoning him. He seemed disappointed in the boy and wouldn't look him in the eye. As if Shaggy were his teenage son stubbornly turning his back on the family business, choosing pleasure over duty, freedom over blood, existence over essence.

At touchdown, exiting the terminal, they parted ways, as good as strangers.

Endings

When his father quit mining and Kalgoorlie, prompted in part by almost being crushed in a front-end loader rollover, prompted also in part by his mother missing her own mother and sisters in Perth, he moved his family to Mandurah, bought a boat and a block of land as close to the Mary Street jetty as he could afford, to fish, prawn, and crab as he pleased. A proper sea-change. Seagulls and salt air.

Shaggy's exit from the mining game was just as decisive but far less spectacular. As he flew into Perth, National Jet flight NC715, 19 December 2000, landing, exiting the plane, collecting his bag, which weighed only slightly more than the one he carried with him on his very first flight, he finished—it was ended. He had achieved his goal, and resolved the plot. For him the absurd Sisyphean cycle was broken: he was leaving the rock behind, having come to rest at the bottom of the mountain. For this, he felt no trepidation or guilt. Instead, he was comfortable knowing that many others were waiting in line for the same opportunity, willing to begin the same push.

He saw himself not as someone completing a chapter in his life, ready to begin a new one. He wanted it to resemble the conclusion of a small book, a novella—the back cover was closed, the thin leaves of the book and the thicker covers pressed firmly together. If it could be fastened it would. A static object. The book signifies existence and presence. Outside the book there is an absence. For some, it is an absence and a space that opens up for a sequel. As if it were a volume in a much larger series. But his was a book that had properly come to an end, the protagonist as dead as dead. The story had been determined, was meaningful, whole and complete. He would be starting a new book, with a new author and new protagonist, with only fleeting semblances and distant filiation to his mining self. Even if they shared the same name their identities were already drifting apart, like flotsam from a shipwreck. The younger self was static as the book, inert as a photograph, and his future later self dynamic, amorphous, unwritten, in the mode of becoming anew.

Very quickly, maybe within weeks, he could not recognise this boy from the mine, the boy in the picture, overalls and gumboots and hair to his shoulders. The boy who was physically stronger and mentally tougher than the man he was now. His older self could not go back and do what his younger self did. Nor had he necessarily grown stronger for the experience—the strength gained by the boy was temporary and contextual, like fitness without consistent exercise, and as time passed he weakened, returning not quite to his pre-mining self but to a more innocent self. One that had new expectations but was also naïve, uncertain. Discovering the world, suddenly concerned with it.

He had achieved his goal of paying for his house, which was the only part of his plan that had been given boundaries and rendered into a definite object. Again it was the physicality of labour that had made it something tangible. The rest remained in shadows, at a distance, waiting.

◉

Boys become men, eventually, inevitably. But how to define it. In a moment or by subtle changes, imperceptible increments that accumulate over a lifetime. Easier in the distant past, with rituals, hunting, killing and eating wild animals, stamping manhood in blood. Part of the becoming is physical: he was stronger and more than capable of growing a thick beard. The other part is psychological, social, attitudinal. The boy was thrust into the role of a man before he was ready. He had to assume the role of a man, like an actor, reading lines given by previous actors. Others seemed to instinctively know their lines, their costuming, their stage directions: profanity, tattoos, the affectation of a cigarette.

The anthropologists, sociologists, psychologists, philosophers would contend that the sign of becoming a man is the acquisition of a matured state of mind, an ability to reason. It is when you enter into the realm of society, participate with the running of the world, transcending the individual. A more aware sense of responsibility. Practical as men should be, there were key, tangible indicators: getting your first job, getting married, starting a family (he had his first child at thirty-five, which was seemingly too late).

It could be all or none of these. Yet most would agree that the day one dons a hardhat, cap lamp, and self-rescuer, and begins drilling into a rock wall a few hundred metres or so below the dirt of the Earth's surface in an underground mine, then you are probably as close as you are going to get to experiencing being a man or at least doing one's best to resemble one. Acting the part, costumed as a miner, vent bag dust for makeup. Not even then: Trudy and Paula, right there to contradict him.

    He had finished his duty as a Kalgoorlie-born boy. Bled the red dirt in his veins. Not all, and not as much as some—but enough. His penance for Western Australia, the mining state. Made a man. Through his triumphs and failures. The feathers in his cap and the black eyes. Made a man—a quavering man, a shadowy man, stepping in and out of the darkness, showing himself when necessary. Being himself and not. Remembering and forgetting. Hypocritical, contradictory, flickering.

Acknowledgments

I would like to thank my beautiful partner Melanie and my darling son Hunter for their patience and support for my writing, Dr Brooke Dunnel for her editorial support, my Uncle Peter for giving me my start, and my family and friends for bearing with me through the tumult.

www.ingramcontent.com/pod-product-compliance
Ingram Content Group UK Ltd.
Pitfield, Milton Keynes, MK11 3LW, UK
UKHW041302180426
11947UKWH00009B/624